La Raza: Forgotten Americans

La Raza: Forgotten Americans

edited by
Julian Samora

UNIVERSITY OF NOTRE DAME PRESS
NOTRE DAME   LONDON

Foreword

This publication, resulting from prior collaboration among scholars, was initiated by the Rosenberg Foundation as a memorial to Charles de Young Elkus. Mr. Elkus was the architect and pioneer of the Foundation and for a quarter of a century helped shape it in the forceful and adventuresome direction he believed Max L. Rosenberg wanted. The qualities of Charles Elkus left their stamp on the Foundation: willingness to explore, to experiment, to encourage creative people, to take risks, to try new ways. For many decades he maintained wide interests and activities in fields of special concern to the Foundation, ranging from child welfare and juvenile justice to Indian affairs, Spanish-speaking Americans, and the arts.

Following Mr. Elkus's death in 1963 the Foundation Trustees decided to undertake a memorial which would contribute to the future of one or more of the social movements in which he had a life interest. The Trustees sought to do what they believed he would have wished: to stake out issues and directions, to enrich those who participated, and to increase knowledge as a basis for action.

After considering various fields and possible ways to proceed, the Foundation commissioned Dr. Julian Samora to select eminent authorities on Spanish-Speaking Americans to meet, plan, and write papers which might be especially timely and influential now.

In keeping with Mr. Elkus's and the Foundation's inviolate policy of providing freedom for grantees, the opinions expressed and the issues implied in the volume are those of the writers and not necessarily those of Mr. Elkus or of the Foundation. He would want the publication bold and honest from the writers' viewpoint even though some of it might be controversial.

The Trustees lovingly dedicate to the memory of Charles de Young Elkus this contribution to the current scene as one appropriate way of honoring him consistent with his character and spirit.

Roy Sorenson

Acknowledgments

The idea for the present volume was first suggested by Mrs. Jackson Chance, Executive Director of the Rosenberg Foundation, in the fall of 1964. Since then Mrs. Chance has devoted much time and effort, at crucial stages, in the development of this publication.

Mr. Herman Gallegos was most helpful in the selection of topics and has given encouragement as well as critical advice.

Most cooperative and generous with their assistance were the board of directors and officers of the Rosenberg Foundation, Frederic B. Whitman, president; Judge Ben C. Duniway, vice president; Fred H. Merrill, treasurer; Mrs. Eleanor Anderson, Mrs. Allan Charles, Richard E. Guggenheim, Frank H. Sloss, Roy Sorenson, and Dr. Malcolm S. M. Watts.

The following persons, together with the authors, attended an editorial conference at which the papers were reviewed and many helpful suggestions were made: Dr. Ernesto Galarza, Mr. Martin Ortiz, Mr. Paul Ylvisaker, Mr. Leandro P. Soto, Mr. Eduardo Quevedo, Mr. Eugene Gonzales, Mr. Bernard Valdez, and Mr. Albert Peña, Jr.

Florence R. Lawrence typed several revisions of all the manuscripts and attended to all of the details of this project.

It would not have been possible to produce this volume without the excellent assistance of Mr. Grant Lee of the University of Notre Dame Press.

My wife Betty and my family were most understanding of the amount of time and work that this project required, even at times when they were inconvenienced.

I am indebted to all of the persons mentioned above, and I am grateful to them.

For many years I have admired the patience, tenacity, and

courage of the Spanish-speaking people, the subject of this
report. This population, exploited at times, living mostly on
the fringes of society, misunderstood by public and private
agencies, and largely ignored by the federal government and
its programs, has managed to survive with dignity, composure,
and pride. No other population has contributed more to American society and received so little in return. It is at this late
date that *La Raza* is coming into its own, and I am hopeful
that this volume will contribute in a small way to their quest
for justice and equal opportunity.

Notre Dame, Indiana   Julian Samora
June, 1966

Contents

Introduction

JULIAN SAMORA

The Setting

This collection of papers attempts an assessment of the status of a minority population of the southwestern United States concentrated in California, Texas, New Mexico, Arizona, and Colorado. This is the largest ethnic group in the Southwest and among the largest minorities in the United States. Its political potential is so great that politicians have called this group the "sleeping giant." The term suggests that the group has seldom exercised its potential influence, but when it does, it will be considerable.

The heterogeneity of the population is a striking phenomenon, related to a peculiar set of historical circumstances, which began with the early exploring and colonizing efforts in North and South America by Spain. Among the first colonizing efforts following the great exploring expedition of Coronado in 1540, was that led by Juan de Oñate in 1598, which established a colony, San Juan, in what is now northern New Mexico; from this settlement twenty-five missions were established in New Mexico by 1630. The Spaniards were driven out by the Indians in 1680, and it was not until some twelve years later that Diego de Vargas reconquered the province and established foundations for the settlements that exist to this day. In these New Mexican villages and their extensions in southern Colorado the heritage of sixteenth-century Spain was established and has existed to the present time. The villages remained isolated and relatively undisturbed, with few significant changes, before the 1940's.

Shortly after the initial colonies in New Mexico, the Spaniards colonized in Texas (1640), and at a later date settlements were established in California and Arizona. For more that two hundred years the Spanish-speaking people in the Southwest led a rather precarious existence, being in a relatively hostile environment and very much isolated from their native land—isolated, too, from the great center in the New World from which they had sprung, and even isolated from each other. These settlements were removed from the mainstream of European historical developments between the 1600's and the 1800's; nor were they involved in the great political revolutionary movements of the early 1800's, although one of these, the revolt of New Spain from Spain, affected them directly, in that they became Mexicans for a brief time. Even the great westward movement of Americans did not immediately affect the village people to a very great extent because of their geographical isolation. The war with Mexico, through which the United States acquired a substantial portion of Mexican territory, brought United States citizenship to those Spanish-speaking people who remained in this country. Thus, the Spanish-speaking people in this country were by nationality first Spanish (1598–1823), then Mexican (1823–1849), and then American, following the Treaty of Guadalupe-Hidalgo. It has been estimated that by 1850 there were 100,000 Spanish-Americans in the United States. In spite of the changes in nationality and the encroachment of Americans, up to the turn of the century the Spanish settlements in the United States remained essentially Spanish folk societies with a variety of admixtures from the indigenous populations.

It is of interest that even today, after more than a hundred years of American citizenship, the descendants of those early colonists have not accepted completely the life-ways of the dominant society and are in many instances highly resistant to complete acculturation.

The Mexican-American population in the United States was numerically insignificant until the turn of the century. Between 1910 and 1930 there was a very large immigration from Mexico. The immigrants were primarily laborers who came to work in the agricultural expansion of the Southwest. Some came to work on the railroads in both the South and Middle West. Others traveled as far north and east as Chicago and

Detroit, attracted by industrial expansion in the Great Lakes area, as well as the defense industries during World War I. Many were fleeing the Mexican Revolution of 1910 and its bloody aftermath. Since 1920 there has been a continuing, yearly immigration of Mexicans to the United States, with the exception of the depression years when many Mexicans were repatriated. Most of these people and their descendants, who call themselves Mexican-Americans, are American citizens by naturalization or birth.

A Word About Numbers

It is impossible to determine accurately the number of Mexican citizens who have migrated to the United States. Nor has it been possible to get an accurate count of the Spanish-speaking people in the United States. In 1930 the Bureau of the Census attempted to enumerate the Spanish-speaking under the heading "Mexican." The instructions to the enumerators were "All persons born in Mexico or having parents born in Mexico who are not definitely white, Negro, Indian, Chinese, or Japanese."

The difficulty with this definition [Saunders, 1949], aside from the confusion of racial and cultural concepts that it contained, was that it excluded persons whose grandparents, great grandparents, or even more remote ancestors had come to the Southwest by way of Mexico. In New Mexico, for example, only 61,916 "Mexicans" were enumerated in 1930 when it was a matter of common knowledge that the Spanish-speaking made up half the population of the state, or something over 200,000 persons.

In 1940 the Bureau of the Census dropped the classification "Mexican"; instead, to enumerate the Spanish-speaking and other foreign language groups they asked the question, "What was the principal language other than English spoken in your home during your childhood?" This question excluded a large number who identified themselves with the Spanish-speaking group but whose principal language during their childhood was English. In 1950 and 1960 the Census attempted an enumeration by Spanish surname. This criterion makes for greater accuracy, but it excludes a number of persons who identify with this population but whose surname is not Spanish, and, of course, it includes a number of people who through inter-marriage have a Spanish surname but do not necessarily iden-tify with the population.

Yet another reason for the undercount is the large number of Mexicans who have entered the United States illegally and have become "lost." As late as 1954 it was estimated that more than one million such persons entered the United States dur-ing that year. Although this "wetback movement" is very much on the decline, it still may be a significant population move-ment into the United States.

Another type of immigrant is the *visero* or the passport Mexi-cans. These come to the United States legally, primarily for work, under a passport program. What percentage of them get "lost" in the United States is unknown. Still another type is the commuter, who crosses the border every day or once a week for temporary or permanent employment in the United States. Although few of these actually become legal residents of the United States, they are residents without responsibilities for all intents and purposes.

Since the Census makes a special enumeration of the Span-ish-surname population for only the five southwestern states, we have no accurate knowledge of the number of Spanish-speaking persons in other parts of the United States. We have no way of knowing with sufficient accuracy how many of this population have moved to other parts of the country. We do know by observation, however, that thousands live in the urban areas of such states as Kansas, Illinois, Indiana, Michi-gan, and Ohio, to mention only a few. We also know that this population makes up a large portion of the agricultural migrant work force and that large numbers of these laborers are drop-ping off the migrant stream and settling down in almost every state in the country. Other large groups of Spanish-speaking people in the United States are the Puerto Ricans, other Latin Americans (perhaps the most significant number at the pres-ent time being the Cuban refugees), and the Filipinos concen-trated primarily on the West Coast.

A Word About Labels

Although our concern in this volume is with the Spanish-speaking people of the Southwest rather than the United States, it is still difficult to find a descriptive term acceptable to all of the people within the scope of this study. The terms Spanish-American and Hispano are perhaps most acceptable to the populations in northern New Mexico and southern Colorado who have had a minimum of Mexican cultural influence. The people who came to this country at the turn of the century and their descendants find those terms totally unacceptable and prefer the term Mexican-American. Those who have arrived most recently prefer the label Mexican. In certain parts of the Southwest the innocuous term Latin American has often been used, probably because the term Mexican as used by Anglos has so often carried derogatory connotations. Yet the Spanish word Mexicano when used by Spanish-speaking is perfectly acceptable to most of the population. Puerto Ricans, Cubans, and others, however, prefer their own nationalistic labels. The Bureau of the Census' definition "White persons of Spanish-surname" is hardly satisfactory to anyone. For our purposes we are using the most descriptive, inclusive, and least offensive term, Spanish-speaking, throughout the volume although some of the other terms also appear interchangeably.

The Presentation

In Chapter 1 Professor George I. Sánchez presents the historical background of the population. It is within this historical setting that the remaining chapters can best be appreciated. This discussion focuses on the conservation and persistence of the native language and the encounter of the population with the American public school system. The analysis is interspersed with constructive criticism.

The great majority of the Spanish-speaking people in the United States profess affiliation with the Catholic Church. This population, with few exceptions, has been taken for granted by the parishes in which they have lived in the Southwest. Twenty years ago Churchmen became aware of the true situation and proposed positive programs which are now beginning to bear fruit. Many years ago some Protestant denominations recognized the plight of this population and began ministering to them through a variety of welfare programs. The influence of these denominations has been significant and has resulted in a substantial number of conversions. In Chapter 2

Reverend John A. Wagner presents both an assessment and a critique of the role that the Christian Church has played in ministering to this population.

In Chapter 3 Professor John R. Martinez presents the very difficult problems a minority group encounters when it attempts to participate effectively in the political arena of the dominant society. His analysis points to the ambiguity of roles leaders and organizations must accept, adjust to, and perhaps overcome in order to increase political activity and achieve a voice and a vote that are respected.

Chapter 4 summarizes the conditions and problems of seasonal farm laborers, the majority of whom are Spanish-speaking. Reverend William E. Scholes' brief history of this labor movement includes a description of the types of laborers and their living and working conditions. The chapter concludes with a discussion of current legislation and prospects for the future.

Mr. Lawrence B. Glick surveys the civil rights status of the Spanish-speaking in the Southwest, in particular the deprivation of civil rights in education, employment, housing, law enforcement, and jury service. Although the situation of this minority differs from that of the Negro, there are sufficient data to suggest that the Spanish-speaking have less than equal opportunity in many areas.

In Chapter 6 Professor Paul M. Sheldon discusses community participation and the emerging middle class. These data are drawn from a larger research program that was conducted in Los Angeles. Membership in organizations and general participation in the community of a middle- and a lower-class sample are contrasted. Aspects of the process of adjustment to the urban society by the socially mobile individuals are suggested by a profile of the successful "average" person.

Professor Donald N. Barrett has prepared a detailed analysis of the demographic characteristics of the Spanish surname population in the five southwestern states. Particular attention is given to age, sex, and family structures, to educational, employment, income, housing, and fertility characteristics. The data, taken from The United States Census Reports, offer comparisons of the population in 1950 and 1960, the only years for which comparable data are available.

The last chapter, by Herman Gallegos, Lyle Saunders, and Julian Samora, addresses itself to questions and issues concerning action programs, policy decisions, and research. Most of these are raised throughout the volume; others were proposed and discussed in an editorial conference after the papers were completed.

i: *History, Culture, and Education*

GEORGE I. SÁNCHEZ

There are nearly four million persons with Spanish-Mexican antecedents in five southwestern states: Arizona, California, Colorado, New Mexico, and Texas. Most of them speak Spanish and, considering the circumstances, remarkably good Spanish. Although most of them speak English also, it is quite surprising that there are many present-day Spanish-Americans whose families have been exposed to the English language since the American occupation about one hundred thirty years ago, and yet they speak only Spanish. When one compares this situation with that of European immigrants who came to this country much later—Italians, Germans, Poles, and so on—many of whom have lost their original vernaculars, it would seem to indicate an unprecedented cultural tenacity (except for some Indian tribes, the Eskimos, and the Aleuts).

Why have these Americans of Spanish-Mexican backgrounds been so stubborn in relinquishing *their* vernacular? What institutions and forces made this possible? One would expect to find some concerted effort of these people to retain their language, some source of cultural pride. Or, one would expect that the English-speaking dominant group had recognized the values inherent in preserving the Spanish language and had instituted programs to that end. That is, one would expect some positive reason—some wise head, institution, or policy that has conserved this cultural resource. Sad to say, the major factor is none of these but a complex of factors that are much more negative than positive. The conservation of the heritage of the Spanish language is an eloquent illustration that it is, indeed, an ill wind that does not blow someone some good! But let us approach the matter with circumspection.

We must understand both the positive factors in the development of the Spanish language, its introduction and perpetuation in this area, and the negative forces that have resulted in the failure to make this population monolingual and English-speaking. The former is, essentially, a matter of tracing historical antecedents; the latter is one of evaluating the failure of the schools in their obstinate persistence to make English the only language of this group. This failure, more than anything else, has preserved Spanish in a bilingualism of a wide qualitative range, although among the disadvantaged classes the Spanish is superior to the English, and there is also a large group of persons of Spanish-Mexican descent whose English is excellent and whose Spanish is very limited or nonexistent.

This dualism suggests that the paper be presented in three parts: first, a historical perspective of the positive features of the process; second, an attempt to evaluate, with historical and other evidence, why the schools have not succeeded in obliterating Spanish as the mother tongue of most Americans of Mexican descent in the Southwest; and third, a brief attempt to blend these two, seemingly disparate parts into a constructive summary. Each part will have a separate bibliography, and except where specific data from a source are quoted or paraphased, there will be no footnotes.

I Spanish in Spain, New Spain, and the American Southwest

The Spanish language heritage of Americans of Spanish-Mexican descent has many historical, geographic, and ethnic facets, which we will try to present in logical separation in this part of the paper.

Spain and Spanish

We usually think of Spanish as a Latin language, *romance*. It is that, of course, but in some important ways it is not Latin, not even European. Spain has been a cultural crossroads from the earliest days of recorded history. Prehistoric man, Phoenician, early Greek, Carthaginian, and other early peoples blended their genes and cultures to form the Spaniard that later the Romans and then their conquerors ruled. The languages of the people of Spain received infusions from all of these cultural contacts, especially from the Latin of the Romans. Then came the greatest invasion of all, that of the Arabic-speaking Moslems in 711 A.D.

The "Moors" were in Spain for almost eight hundred years, ruling virtually all of the Iberian Peninsula for a time, until they were slowly pushed southward by the Christian armies. During this long period a remarkable process of acculturation took place. Although at times the conflict was bitter and bloody, there were long periods when Christians, Sephardic Jews, and Moslems lived in comparative peace and tolerance. Cities controlled by the Moslems tolerated the subordinate Christian people; those controlled by the Christians, in turn, tolerated the subordinate Arabic-speaking minority. In both, the Jews played a leading role as businessmen, brokers, financial counselors. The effect of this strange coexistence on the Spaniard—and on the Spanish language—is incalculable. The Sephardic Jews and the Moslems brought to Europe the wisdom of the Middle East, of Egypt, of North Africa. They brought institutions, technologies, value systems, instruments, and formal learning that, blended with what they found on the peninsula, produced the Golden Age of Spain in the fifteenth and sixteenth centuries.

Although the effects of this acculturation are evident in many fields—architecture, religion, agriculture, educational institutions, political science, folklore, value systems, and so on—nowhere is it so clearly revealed as in the Spanish language. Today there are at least 4000 words in Spanish that are not Latin but Arabic. Many of the words for luxuries little known to the Iberian Christians before the coming of the Moslems are Arabic. The finest jewels are *alajas,* pillows are *almohadas,* fine carpets are *alfombras.* Although the Christian could say "Que Dios nos . . ." when he expressed a devout hope, he quickly adopted the Moslem prayer to Allah to the same effect that has become the Spanish word *ojalá* ("would that . . ."); this expressing condition contrary to fact, necessarily requires the subjunctive mode. Then there are the words that refer to a process, such as *adobar* ("to conserve"). The word adobe, now a good English word, comes from this verb; and one may have, in Spanish, an *adobe* of meat or of vegetables just as one may have an *adobe* of clay and straw!

There are many other Spanish words that are written and pronounced virtually the same way in Arabic and in Spanish.

The words for shoes, for trousers, for neckties, for socks, for shirts, and for many other articles are essentially the same in Arabic as in Spanish. It is not within the scope of this paper to point out the contributions of Visigoths and Greeks, and others, in the formulation of Spanish. Suffice it to note that although the foundations of Spanish are Latin, *romance,* the structure is a variegated one to which many tongues contributed.

Spanish and New Spain

When Spain, in the phenomenally expansive mood of its Golden Age, came to what today is Mexico, it did not come to a wilderness nor to a cultural vacuum. There were millions of people in the area that came to be known as New Spain, people who presented a kaleidoscope of cultures, of languages, and of degrees of civilization. Conservative estimates place their number at ten million, although there are authoritative sources that go far beyond this estimate. The bibliography to this paper lists sources that elaborate upon the indigenous peoples of New Spain at the time of the Conquest. Those reveal the wide scope of the cultural attributes of these peoples. More particularly, they reveal the great linguistic variety. The Maya language, the language of the Aztecs, the languages of the Pueblos, the language of the Otomíes—these and many others differed from each other as much as Chinese differs from English! Peoples living in close proximity spoke vastly different languages. Some, like the Navajos, had linguistic relatives only far away—the closest relatives of the Navajos (and their cousins, the Apaches) were in the interior of Alaska! These variegated tongues have had a tremendous influence in the development of Spanish in this part of the New World. In the three colonial centuries, less than one million Spaniards came to New Spain—one million Spanish-speaking people among ten or more million native peoples who spoke diverse languages.

Also, in New Spain the Spaniard came upon flora and fauna, processes, and customs, for which he had no terminology and so had to accept native designations. Although that strange, wonderful new bird, the turkey, could be described as *gallina de la tierra* (as people in New Mexico still call it), or the Spanish word *pavo* could be used (as it is in some places), it was very easy to fall into calling it a *guajolote,* or a *cócono,* or

some other Indian name. In many instances there were alternatives, but what to call a "ring-tail cat"? It had to be *cacomistle*
(which now is the proper English word for that beautiful crea-
ture). In the nomenclature of birds and animals, regionalism
and a great deal of confusion prevail because of the variety of
native languages and the application of Spanish names to crea-
tures that were unknown in Spain. So the raccoon is a *tejón*
(Spanish for badger) to some, *mapache* to many others,
whereas *tejón* is still a badger in places like New Mexico! In
many instances, however, alternatives were virtually impossible. A *quetzal* could hardly be called by any other name, nor
could a mocking bird (*sinsontle*), although one can stretch
things a little and call him a *burlón* (which really means
"mocker" and has an unkindly connotation). The names of
plants (*mesquite*, for a simple illustration), the names of foods
(*nixtamal, tamales, chile, et cetera*), and the names of many
objects in Mexican Spanish are Indian. The centuries of contact between the invaders from the Iberian peninsula and the
peoples they conquered gave a wondrous flavor to the language of New Spain. It is this well-seasoned Spanish that is
the heritage of the Americans of Mexican descent in the
Southwest.

The Spanish-Speaking in the Southwest

Spanish-speaking people have been settled in the Southwest
for more than 350 years. The villages north of Santa Fe, New
Mexico, founded in 1598, are second only to St. Augustine,
Florida, settled in 1565, as the oldest settlements of Europeans
on the mainland of the United States. The New Mexico settlements, followed a century later by those in Texas and later by
those in California, represent a Spanish colonial effort that left
an indelible imprint upon the history and culture of the Southwest and the United States. More important, that colonial
endeavor left people from California to Texas whose descendants constitute a part of the group we now refer to, very
loosely, as Spanish-speaking.

The colonial Hispanos were not culturally homogeneous.
The Nuevo Mexicanos, settled in the region as early as 1598,
were different from their cousins, the Californios and the
Texanos, who arrived much later. The date of migration and
settlement, the attendant cultural concomitants, geographic

isolation, natural resources, the number and kind of Indians among whom they settled, and many other factors resulted in not one Spanish-speaking people but several, each with distinctive cultures. The outlook on life and the values, the allegiances, the biology, the very speech of these colonial settlers varied greatly; and though all were Spanish-speaking, they can be thought of as different peoples.

Until about the mid-nineteenth century, the Californios, the Nuevo Mexicanos, and the Texanos went their separate cultural ways, held together only lightly by, first, the slender threads of Spain and, later, for a brief time, the uncertain bonds of independent Mexico. The annexation of Texas and the occupation of the rest of the Southwest by the United States changed the course of human affairs in the region, but the change was a slow one, unplanned and haphazard. The United States had not developed the social and cultural institutions to carry out an effective program of acculturation among her new citizens. The new states and territories were left to shift for themselves, with an understandable lack of success. The Spanish-speaking peoples of the Southwest remained Spanish-speaking and culturally isolated—unassimilated citizens, subject to the ever increasing dominance of a foreign culture.

Other things being equal, time alone would have had its influence, and the Hispanos would have become full-fledged English-speaking Americans. However, not only were the social institutions inadequate, but also changing conditions made it impossible for time alone to bring about their assimilation. After 1870 the southwestern scene changed rapidly. The coming of the railroad brought new economic opportunities and made old ones more attractive. The region ceased to be the "Wild West." It became instead a land where minerals and lumber, cotton and corn, cattle and sheep, fruits and vegetables gave rise to new economic empires.

These developments in themselves were not hindrances to acculturation. On the contrary, they should have done much to aid it, just as economic expansion in the East accelerated the Americanization of the heterogeneous masses from Europe. However, in addition to the fact that southwestern developments were based largely in rural life and on the production of raw materials, in contrast to the urban-industrial situation in the East, this area was sparsely populated and, insofar as the "American Way" was concerned, culturally immature and insecure. Worse still, since labor for the new enterprises was not available from the East, the Southwest had to turn to Mexico and the Orient. As a consequence, the region, already suffering from cultural indigestion, added to its troubles by importing thousands of Mexican families, again postponing the day for the incorporation of its Spanish-speaking population.

Even thus enlarged by immigrants from Mexico, the Indo-Hispanic group could have been assimilated had the United States taken time to assess the cultural issues and the increasingly complex socioeconomic problems—particularly those of this ethnic minority. But before 1910 almost no one seemed aware that there were far-reaching issues and problems. Virtually no thought was given to the educational, health, economic, or political rehabilitation of the Hispanos. And after 1910 the opportunity had passed. Until then the issues and problems were still of manageable proportions. They were soon to grow beyond all hope of quick solution.

The Mexican Revolution of 1910–1920 and World War I combined to bring many thousands of Mexicans to the Southwest. Large numbers came as displaced persons, driven across the border by a chaotic civil war. Even larger numbers came as contract laborers, recruited by the trainload to work the beet fields of Colorado, the gardens and groves of California, the railroads of the entire West, the copper mines of Arizona, the cotton fields of Texas, even the iron works of Chicago and the coal mines of West Virginia.

The consequences of this free and easy dipping into the cheap labor reservoir of Mexico are not difficult to observe. What for brevity I choose to call "cultural indigestion" can be documented by health and educational statistics, by pictures of the slums of San Antonio, and by depressing socioeconomic data from all over the Southwest. Suffice it to say that once again the Southwest pyramided problem upon problem, burdening itself with a situation for which sooner or later there would be a costly reckoning.

In a way, World War I served a good purpose. Full employment, good wages, and the educative results of military service stimulated acculturation in the Southwest. However, the issues were much too large and complex to be met adequately by the by-products of war. More research, more planning, and more well thought-out action programs were needed.

The "boom and bust" days of the twenties and the slow recovery during the thirties saw a little alleviation of the socioeconomic difficulties confronting the Southwest. Thousands of Mexican nationals were repatriated through the joint efforts of the United States and Mexico. However, natural increase soon more than made up for their loss. Then the depression years bred more misery, more problems. During these critical times there was a growing interest in the plight of the unemployed, of out-of-school youth, and of common people in general. This interest was first expressed by state and national surveys: President Hoover's Committee on Social Trends, California Governor Young's Committee on Labor, and the Texas Educational Survey are examples. The "New Deal" reforms helped to relieve some of the most acute problems and stimulated the nation to a greater consciousness of its socioeconomic defects. In particular, more attention was given to studies of underprivileged groups and of cultural and "racial" minorities.

The condition of the Spanish-speaking people in the Southwest was not completely overlooked. Taylor's studies in California and Texas called attention to the plight of the agricultural worker, particularly the migrant Mexican. Manuel, at the University of Texas, was inaugurating educational studies of the Spanish-speaking group. Sánchez was working in the fields of bilingualism and of school finance and administration in New Mexico. Tireman, also in New Mexico, was addressing himself to the teaching problems presented by the bicultural situation. Other researchers concerned themselves with a variety of spot studies.

Some reform measures looking toward the effective acculturation of its population (50 per cent Spanish-speaking) were undertaken by New Mexico in the thirties. These involved far-reaching changes in the sources and distribution of school funds, improvement of public health services, more scientific land use, increased and more effective political action by Spanish-speaking voters. As a result, by 1940 the Spanish-speaking people of New Mexico were more nearly assimilated than those of any other southwestern state.

There were similar improvements during the same period in parts of Colorado, Arizona, and California. Texas, on the other hand, lagged far behind. The educational and health levels of the Texas-Mexican were the worst in the region. There fundamental civil rights were most flagrantly violated. Effective Spanish-speaking leadership was lacking. Conditions of employment and standards of living were woefully low. In a manner of speaking, Texas had become the "horrible example" in the acculturation of Spanish-speaking people. However, there was a growing realization there as elsewhere that none of these states could attain its potential cultural stature until the maladjustments were overcome, and in the last few years Texas has begun to buckle down to the long-postponed task of incorporating the Spanish-speaking one-sixth of its population.

World War II had its good effects also. As in World War I, military service and improved economic conditions gave a great boost to the assimilation of Spanish-speaking people. In addition, largely in response to pressure from Spanish-speaking groups, the federal government began to sponsor programs designed to improve the bicultural situation in the Southwest. More important, Mexico and the United States agreed to regulate the flow of Mexican labor northward across the border.

Whether the two governments realized it or not, this struck at one of the roots of the overall problem. As noted, time and again, just as we have been on the verge of cutting our bicultural problems to manageable proportions, uncontrolled mass migrations from Mexico have erased the gains and accentuated the cultural indigestion. Now, when the entire Southwest is inaugurating large-scale programs of acculturation, the control of Mexican immigration is most necessary. It would be shortsighted and tragic indeed if the two governments were to deviate from this sound path toward acculturation.

The most serious threats to an effective program of acculturation in the Southwest have been the population movements from Mexico: first, by illegal aliens, the so-called "wetbacks," then by the *bracero* program, and finally by the commuters. [These are discussed in detail in a succeeding chapter.] Unless we can end the legal or illegal entry of large numbers of Mexican aliens, much of the good work that state and federal agencies are doing will go for naught; much more time and effort and many more millions of dollars will be required to bring Texas and her sister states to a desirable cultural level.

II Bilingualism in the Southwest: A Tragi-Comedy

In trying to assess both the teaching of English in the Southwest to children whose mother tongue is Spanish, and the persistence of Spanish, we are torn between two ways of getting across a basic point: current practice doesn't make sense. One could use the "academic" approach, muster an unassailable array of evidence—historical, experimental, comparative, and the like—and, by prolific footnoting of authoritative sources, make a case for the thesis implied in the heading above. This thesis, that we have been foolish in dealing with the English-Spanish dichotomy of the southwestern cultural reality, can be documented easily. One could with equal confidence appeal to common sense and simple logic, and in plain English, to puncture the balloon that has been blown up with the hot air of "language handicap," the perils of bilingualism and all the other clichés with which educators cover their lack of preparation and understanding. I will use both approaches, emphasizing the former at first and the latter subsequently.

Historical Perspective

The place of vernacular languages in education has been a concern for many centuries. The influence of language development upon personality, the function of language in our thinking process and the implications of bilingualism have occupied thinking men profoundly. The subject is a vast one in which distinguished contributions have been made over a long time.

It is not the shrinking world that justifies the study of foreign languages and demands the conservation of the foreign home-language resources of our peoples; the wisdom of the ages dictates it. The recorded history of foreign home-language in education goes back four thousand years to the time when the Semitic Akkadians conquered Sumer and gradually imposed their tongue, Hebrew, upon the Sumerians.[1] In turn, Aramaic supplanted the old Hebrew language, and just as Sumerian had become a "sacred language" when Hebrew became the vernacular, so Hebrew became the "sacred language" and Aramaic the vernacular. Time after time through the ages a foreign home-language has become the medium of religious instruction as a new language became the vernacular—for Hebrew, Greek, Latin, Arabic; in India, China, Europe, Russia, in our hemisphere; in the spread of Buddhism, Christianity, Judaism; in the Hellenization of Rome, the Latinization of Europe, the Westernization of the Americas; in the rise and fall of imperialistic colonialism—in each of these we find bilingualism in education.

These examples point to the unquestionable value of the vernacular in education, particularly when the mother tongue is not the language of instruction. For further support for our conclusion we can turn to the great thinkers of modern history who have expressed their views on this topic—Juan Luis Vives, Pedro de Gante, John Amos Comenius, John Locke, Johan Heinrich Herbart, John Dewey—and to contemporary psychologists, linguists, and philosophers such as Frank Laubach, who have concerned themselves with the place of foreign languages in education. It is a shock, then, to observe in the schools of the Southwest how violence has been done to the lessons of history and the views of great thinkers.

These make it very clear that in teaching native and foreign languages, we are dealing with more than a twenty-minute period in the daily schedule, with more than superficial sophistication, with more than vocational advantage and financial profit. The works of Vives, Herbart, and Dewey (particularly *How We Think*) show the vital role of language in intellectual development, the overwhelming significance of a child's mother tongue in the process of education in a second language. These factors have been completely ignored in the teaching of Spanish-speaking children in the schools of the Southwest. Herein lies part of the explanation why many of these schools, particularly those of Texas, find teaching English to Spanish-speaking an almost overwhelming task and why their failure is excused by assigning to the child's home-language a deleterious influence upon his educational development.

A quotation from the careful historical study of vernacular languages in education mentioned earlier applies here.

> From time to time in education the question has arisen whether a child should be taught in some language other than his native language. In those cases where some language other than the native language has been used as the vehicle of instruction, usually the results, if objectively viewed, were convincing enough from an empirical basis to bring about a change in policy.

The effectiveness of using the native language is tied in with the interpenetration of emotion and language. For the preponderent group of children, emotional satisfaction and release accompany the use of the vernacular; while frustration accompanies the use of some other language. Neglect of the native language or, worse still, its suppression is damaging to the morale of the student, and results in rebellion against, or apathy toward the educational process. Especially in the beginning years of school, but later as well, facility in using verbal symbols is essential for facility of thinking. The processes of thought seem to be blocked by the awkward use of the language.

This in no way means that the introduction of a second language, with the goal of developing bilingualism, blocks the processes of thought. Where a second language is introduced at the proper time with sufficient motivation for the student, it might be considered distinctly a potential aid to thinking. The Iliolo experiment has given objectively derived information on the use of the vernacular and the introduction of a second language. The vernacular was shown clearly to have advantages as the language of instruction, and the students, with whom it had been so used, were able in six months of studying a second language, to catch up with a matched control group which had been studying the second language for two years, and using it as the language of learning for all school subjects.[2]

There is much evidence to support the conclusions reached in this historical research. Of telling significance also are the experiments and conclusions of modern psychologists and sociologists.[3] For instance, Maier relates an experiment in which a rat was rewarded with food when it jumped for a certain card and was not rewarded when it jumped for another card.[4] Then the cards and consequences were interchanged, with a resulting sense of failure and frustration for the rat. Maier says, "He soon restrains his tendency to jump, holding himself in a crouching position on the platform in a hopeless or defiant attitude." How many times have I seen this repeated by children with a foreign home-language! How many times have I seen a child cringe and crouch, physically and emotionally, because the language of the home was taboo at school and the language of the school was nonfunctional at home. Here is the genesis of the *pachuco*, the delinquent.

Social psychologists recognize the fundamental importance of esteem in personality formation and motivation. For example, Maslow, in a report on "A Theory of Human Motivation," emphasizes that "Satisfaction of the self-esteem need leads to feelings of self-confidence, worth, strength, capacity and adequacy of being useful and necessary in the world."[5] What can contribute more to self-esteem than the recognition and appreciation of one's vernacular? We all love to be addressed, even if brokenly, *en la lengua que mamamos* ("in the language we suckled," in our mother tongue). So in filling the esteem need, as well as in avoiding psychological confusion, the home-language of the child is a highly potent educational instrument. Cheavens, again summarizing, says:

> Use of the vernacular languages of minority groups living among people of another language has usually sped up the process of acculturation and made easier the learning of a second language for communication with the majority group. Where this policy has not been followed and the vernacular language has been neglected or suppressed, the result has been a continued cleavage between the minority group and the majority group.[6]

A recent study at McGill University also supported the idea that bilingualism is highly desirable.[7]

The Southwestern Reality

As stated earlier, this matter of a foreign mother tongue can be approached in various ways. For us in the Southwest it is a matter for simple language and simple logic. Instead of operating in the abstract, we can use our everyday circumstances as a basis for our convictions about the place of a foreign home-language in our culture and the value of that language in learning English. We do not have to defend the merits of acculturation and bilingualism. We derive much of our cultural substance from Spanish, a native "foreign" language, a language bequeathed by Cabeza de Vaca, de Niza, Serra, Zavala, and a host of others. It takes only very elementary research to see how the Spanish-Mexican contribution undergirds the culture of the Southwest.

Limiting our remarks to Texas, one cannot help seeing how Texans identify with Spanish-speaking people. The terminology of the cattle country (rodeo, lariat, ranch, remuda), the place names, the names of people, the every day words (adobe, amigo, patio), and the customs of daily living all evidence this acculturation. And all of this is capped by the satisfaction of those Anglos who are bilingual and those Latins who know English as well as they know Spanish. The Alamo is as much a symbol of biculturalism as it is of political freedom. After all, it was a Mexican flag flying at the staff that the heroes of the Alamo defended. So we in Texas do not consider the problem of foreign home-language as remote, or of narrow significance in educational psychology, in curriculum, and in the teaching process. Foreign home-language is real to us, and the prospects are just as real.

Contradictorily, because of unfortunate incidents in our past, a tradition of disparagement developed here toward "that Mexican" and all that the term stood for, including language. Along with that, the immature psychology of "speak American" and the defensive provincialism of "despise that furriner" have led to the downgrading of the Spanish language and of those who speak it. Otherwise competent scholars speak of the language of the people of the Southwest as "border Spanish," as a dialect to be avoided. Some, in their ignorance, even refer to it as "Mexican," distinguishing it from Spanish to avoid dignifying it (and ignoring the fact that the Mexican language is *Náhuatl!*).

We extoll the virtues of foreign languages in the development and the achievements of the educated man; we decry their decline in public education; we view with alarm our backwardness when we compare ourselves with the Russians and others; we subsidize the teaching of foreign languages. Yet in the Southwest, one of the world's great languages is suppressed. It does not make sense!

In Texas there are about 300,000 Spanish-speaking children in the public elementary schools, and more than 35,000 in the secondary schools. For only a negligible few of them is Spanish being used as an educational device; and, if they succeed (and many do not) in retaining and developing their home-language, it is not because the public schools have planned it so. What a waste of the assets of the vernacular in education.

Education and Reality

An annotated bibliography on the education of Spanish-speaking people in the United States,[8] although not all-inclusive, lists almost nine hundred items: books, articles, bulletins, and theses. I have been working professionally in this field for more than forty years, and I have been highly critical of our schools' efforts for at least three-fourths of those years; still I was amazed at the persistence of the assertion that bilingualism is bad, that a foreign home-language is a handicap, that, somehow, children with Spanish as a mother tongue were doomed to failure—in fact, that they were *ipso facto* less than normally intelligent.

This sounds like an exaggeration, but these views can easily be documented. For example, in the first draft of a recent handbook for teachers of preschool-age, non-English-speaking children, the Texas Education Agency says, in the second sentence of the introduction, "Solely because of the language barrier, approximately 80 per cent of the non-English-speaking children have had to spend two years in the first grade before advancing to the second."[9] The devastating fact is that Spanish-speaking children in Texas schools *do* spend two or more years in the first grade and then, frequently, more than one year in succeeding grades until in sheer frustration they drop out of school. But to attribute this educational tragedy to the fact that they begin school speaking only Spanish is a gratuitous conclusion not borne out by the history of education in this country or elsewhere. One of the most important facets of the genius of the American school has been that—without distinction as to caste, class, home-language, national origin, and the like—it has been able to process children from all over the world in its normal operations as they become, usually averagely well-educated English-speaking citizens. To excuse the failure of the Texas schools to do the usual job by accusing the Spanish-speaking children of virtually inherent fault reveals a professional blindspot so elementary that it is difficult not to question the professional competence and integrity of the educators responsible. As a result of my protest, the draft of the handbook was changed to read in the published version, "Through no fault of their own, many non-English-speaking children have had to spend two years in the first grade before advancing to the second."[10] I protested that too, of course, for the implication is that the fault lies in the fact that they were born into Spanish-speaking families; this is certainly not admission that the fault lies in the schools! This is pathetically demonstrated when (on page 3) the bulletin suggests that one way of determining who is eligible for the preschool instruction can be discovered by "Noting all eligible children whose names indicate that they are of foreign extraction."

In Texas, much more than in the rest of the Southwest (though the rest is not entirely blameless), Jim Crowism has extended into the educational system.[11] As late as the 1940's, some school systems segregated "Mexican" children throughout the twelve grades of the public school. This extension has served to blind school people, from those in highest authority to those at the classroom level, to the fact that they have used "language handicap" and "bilingualism" to justify "racial" discrimination and their failure to do the kind of teaching job with these children that the American school has done with hundreds of thousands of other children who were similarly situated. Somehow, too, the political effectiveness of the Mexican-American has been spotty, so that the educational policy in New Mexico (where the Spanish-American has carried political weight for generations) and that in Texas (where political awakening of the Latin-American is just now taking place) have stood out as contrasts. The other southwestern states fall between these extremes, with educational effort reflecting the Mexican-Americans' political effectiveness.

What should be emphasized is that factors other than professional considerations have determined what should be done in the education of Spanish-speaking children. In the process, language and language-teaching have been so distorted that only a resort to common sense and the fundamental principles of the teaching profession can shock us back to the conclusions that the pages of history and the research literature underline.

Much is being made in Texas of the efficacy of summer sessions for non-English-speaking children who will enroll in the first grade in September.[12] It is widely implied that these summer sessions constitute the solution to the perennial and frustrating problem of the child with a "language handicap," and statistics are offered to prove that the majority of the children who attend these summer programs do not have to spend two or more years in the first grade but make the grade in one year (many do not!). It is abundantly self-evident that the extension of good education downward is good for all children and that one should expect children who are fortunate enough to get a preschool preparation for the first grade to make better progress, at least during the first few years, than their less fortunate fellows. It stretches credulity, however, when it is alleged that a few weeks of vocabulary building during the summer can substitute for the extra one, two, or more years that (by implication) a Spanish-speaking child otherwise would have to spend in the first grade!

What is being argued is, in effect, that a forty to sixty day summer session program for Spanish-speaking children is the equivalent of the extra nine months (or more) that the children would have to spend in the regular school in the first grade if they did not have the summer program. There must be something radically wrong with the regular first grade operation if the schools can do in eight weeks (summer) plus nine months (regular year) what, otherwise, takes eighteen or more months of regular school instruction! Why not do the equivalent of the eight-week summer program at the beginning of the regular year? Then, even at worst, one could expect logically that at the end of the first grade the children would be no less than eight weeks short of competence for second grade work—and, of course, hardly proper subjects for the repetition (one, two, or more times) of the entire first grade work.

This illogic is repeated in the "Texas Project for Migrant Children."[13] So-called pilot schools have been established, in South Texas, where children of agricultural migrants are arbitrarily segregated from the other children. All of the migrants there are of Mexican descent. There is great pride that the migrant children achieve as much in vocabulary and reading comprehension tests as the children in the regular schools. The fact is that the regular children, on the average, made only .58 of a grade progress per school year in comprehension.[14] Also, in the migrant schools 38 to 45 per cent (or more) of the time is allotted to "English, Language Arts," a much higher percentage than in the regular schools.[15] This kind of statistical legerdemain by a state education agency is wondrous to behold.

Although Texas is probably the "horrible example," the other states are not thereby exonerated. One more illustration from the "migrant bulletin": on page 1 the statement is made that "Most of the migrant children are educationally retarded from one to three years." Maybe this is true, but no proof is offered. However, Table V on page 11 shows that, on the average, on the comprehension pretest, the migrants were only .10 of a grade behind the regulars in the second grade; only .05 of a grade in the third grade; .17 of a grade in the fourth; .16 in the fifth; and .43 of a grade in the sixth. Adding the statement above and these figures gives a resounding condemnation of the regular program.

In the only official statistical report of its kind for that state, the Texas Education Agency in 1957 revealed that there were 61,584 Spanish-surname children in the first grade in the public schools of the state, that only 15,490 reached the eighth grade, and that there were only 5,261 in the twelfth grade.[16] Add to this the previously quoted (under-) statement that "Solely because of the language barrier, approximately 80 per cent of the non-English-speaking children have had to spend two years in the first grade before advancing to the second." The statistical evidence is an eloquent indictment of the educational program, which goes far beyond the condemnation of errors that a 40-60 day summer session program in vocabulary building will eliminate or even make much of a dent. No complacency is warranted, and little satisfaction can be derived from the unquestionable good that the summer schools do. Unless drastic reforms are instituted in the programs of the regular schools, the pupil statistics of a few years hence will not be much different from those of 1957—even though, in the meantime, every child were to go to a summer school. The 1960 U. S. Census of Population bears this out.

As has been implied, indictments such as these are not as applicable to the schools for the rest of the Southwest as they are in Texas, but it is not difficult to find illustrations of the same faults in other states. Numerous practices would be funny if they were not so tragic. One school system, by regulation of its school board, required that all children with a Spanish surname spend three years in the first grade. A federal court changed that. A doctoral dissertation proved that Spanish-speaking children who had preschool instruction in English did better in school than those who did not have that advantage. There have been various "experiments" wherein the intelligence of Spanish-speaking children has been "measured" by partially or completely translated tests. One test publisher reports that the company's intelligence test (standardized in

English) was administered in Spanish to Spanish-speaking children—without even token recognition of the fact that translation does irreparable damage to the test norms and that the Spanish of the children was untutored (unlike the situation of the English-speaking norm children). Other investigators, proud of their recognition of the "language handicap" of Spanish-speaking children, have chosen to test the intelligence of these children with "nonverbal" tests, overlooking completely that the nonverbal tests are as culturally based as the verbal tests and that neither can test what is not there.

Then there are the teachers who are so impressed with the "inherent" talent of the "Mexicans" in music and art that they believe this supposed talent explains (and justifies) inferior achievement in less exotic fields—an inferior achievement that is a product not of the "artistic temperament" of the child but of the inadequacy of the educational program. One could mention the remarkably consistent positive correlation between "racial" prejudice and discriminatory practices that have used the excuse that the children had a "language handicap." Again, the federal court cases reveal some of the tragi-comedy of the situation. In one case, the parents of a Spanish-name child were very happy that the little girl had to be sent to the segregated "Mexican" school because there she could learn Spanish.

One could go into a lengthy recital of the varied irrationalities that have characterized the "teaching of English" to Spanish-speaking children in the Southwest, irrationalities that have vitiated the thinking of both top-level experts and less "authoritative" workers. Such a recital would serve only a negative purpose. One can do better (with the negative features in mind) by trying to find out ways of doing a better job.

The Ways Out

The lessons of history, the experience of other countries, the dictates of ordinary judgment suggest various ways for the school to approach the education of children with a mother tongue other than that which is the language of the school. A number of these approaches will be summarized.

1. It is virtually impossible to avoid the conclusion that children should be started off in their formal education in the mother tongue. There can be argument as to when the second language should be introduced and to what extent it should

supplant the mother tongue, but the evidence is overwhelming that the home-language should be the springboard for the proper development of the second language. This procedure, followed in some countries now and in the past, has demonstrated its merit. However, it has some serious disadvantages in our society. For instance, it would involve the "segregation" of the foreign home-language child, a practice with many features that are not only objectionable but intolerable under our philosophy of the "unitary" school and our denial of the "separate but equal" doctrine. This incompatibility of our way of life with what might be pedagogically ideal leads us to the contemplation of possible compromises or alternatives.

2. The first compromise would be that the mother tongue be used partially in the instruction program. This partial use of the child's vernacular could vary from the teaching of one or more subjects of the curriculum to an occasional and informal use in the everyday relationships between the teacher and the pupil. The advantages to the child with English as a mother tongue are obvious. This would call for teachers who are bilingual and so is not feasible, at the moment, in many schools of the Southwest. However, the talent potential for large numbers of bilingual teachers is here, and it would require no great effort to recruit Spanish-speaking high school graduates to enter teacher education programs if there were reasonable assurance of employment.

With notable exceptions (New Mexico is probably tops in this regard), the teacher of Spanish-Mexican descent is seldom found in schools where the enrollment is predominantly of the dominant (Anglo) group. Further, that teacher (who is woefully in the minority even in schools where most of the children are Latins) usually is admonished that she must not use Spanish in dealing with Spanish-speaking children. Incidentally, Spanish-speaking children generally are forbidden to use their mother tongue, and it is not unusual for severe punishment to be meted out, even in high schools, if pupils resort to Spanish in their conversation. In a climate of this sort, language teaching and language development go out the window, and the teaching of English becomes bewildering, frustrating, and oppressive to the child, who sometimes rebels violently.

3. There is, as a natural consequence of the above rationale, the possibility that the schools, even without bilingual teach-

ers, could give status to the vernacular of the Spanish-speaking child and employ teachers who would give him a sense of satisfaction and belonging in his accomplishment in the Spanish language and the culture it represents. In a recent publication I offer rules that will help non-Spanish-speaking persons to pronounce Spanish names, words, and phrases correctly.[17] This compromise fits in with everything the authorities in intercultural education advocate. Under this plan, the dominant group child benefits as much or more as does the child in the subordinate group. The procedure would involve only more professional sophistication and could be attained easily if the educators would concede that the schools are dismal failures in the education of Spanish-speaking children.

I am reminded here of the findings of Ginzberg and Bray.[18] They have shown that southern Texas, where the Spanish-speaking people are concentrated, had an almost unbelievable rejection rate for "educational reasons" during the draft of World War II—a rejection rate that was, in terms of area and population, the worst in the nation, not counting the statistics on Negroes but including those on Indians. If these schools are doing such a poor job for the Spanish-speaking child, they cannot be doing justice even to the English-speaking youngster.

4. There can be no argument that, speaking generally, the Spanish-speaking child in the Southwest is socially and economically disadvantaged. In health, wealth, and welfare he is at or near the bottom of the scale when compared with his fellow Americans.[19] This offers special challenges to the school, in the teaching of English as in all parts of the curriculum, for any child, regardless of mother tongue. The fact that his state of socioeconomic disadvantage is usually accompanied by a lack of knowledge of the English language is nearly always interpreted as "language handicap," or "bilingualism." As a consequence of this confusion, the school addresses itself to a fruitless hunt into the mysteries of the deleterious effects of being unable to speak English, instead of adapting its program to the requirements of children who are disadvantaged socioeconomically. An ordinarily good school, confronted with the challenge of handicapped children, would give special care to the selection of teaching personnel, would keep class size to a minimum, and would channel more of its special aids and services to them than elsewhere.

There are various legitimate questions that can be asked about teaching English to Spanish-speaking children. To qualify, should the teacher know Spanish? The answer is, "To qualify, the teacher of Spanish-speaking children should be an unquestionably good teacher." It would help for such a good teacher to know Spanish (to have casual conversation with the child, to talk with the parents, to appreciate the problems and virtues of bilingualism), but the important thing is that she be a good teacher and that she be given an opportunity to do her job (reasonable class size, at least average help from her superiors, and the like). If the teacher does not know Spanish, she should at least understand why some of her Spanish-speaking pupils have particular difficulties.

5. The importance of a reading readiness program for children in the first grade is hardly a subject of debate, though one might debate the duration of such a program. For English-speaking children such programs should extend beyond the middle of the first year; this may be a radical position, but let us agree that the English-speaking child should undergo a reading readiness program of six weeks at the beginning of the first grade.

If the English-speaking child, who has been acquiring facility in oral English for six years before enrollment in school, needs a six-week readiness program before starting to read, shouldn't the readiness program of the non-English-speaking child take longer? Should the Spanish-speaking child be expected to be as ready to read with six weeks of "readiness" as the child with six years and six weeks? This is not an argument for having the Spanish-speaking child spend more than one year in the first grade, for his language development is essentially the same as that of his English-speaking fellow student. But he does need extra time, before beginning to read, to acquire facility in the recognition and use of the new linguistic labels. This is not an argument, either, for separating the two groups of children in the first grade. It will not hurt the English-speaking child to extend his readiness program to eight or twelve weeks or more. In the process, the Spanish-speaking child will have a chance to get a good start in the catching up process that should be virtually complete by the end of the third grade. Criteria for judging progress and grade placement should be modified accordingly; for it is with the development and progress of the child that the school is concerned, not with seeing to it that predetermined standards are rigorously met. The assumptions upon which those standards are based are usually grossly inapplicable. Failure to take such matters into account is behind the failure of many schools to do an adequate job for the non-English-speaking child.

The "Teaching of English"

Stated or implied throughout this paper is the conviction that the schools of the Southwest are not faced really with a problem of language handicap, in the fact that large numbers of the pupils come to school speaking little or no English. The issues are not truly linguistic, but rather lie in the areas of social policy, of school organization and administration, of educational philosophy, and of pedagogical competence. There are many thousands of persons in the Southwest whose mother tongue was Spanish, who were socially and economically disadvantaged (that is, who were in the same environmental situation as that of the Spanish-speaking children who fail miserably in many public schools today), and who did "make the grade." To attribute this to the suggestion that "they were different" does not accord with statistics on the distribution of intelligence. The fundamental difference between them and their unfortunate fellows was the quality of the school. Good schools—and by this we do not mean anything extraordinary, just good schools as judged the country over—take the "problem" of the Spanish-speaking child in stride. In the others we are confronted not with handicapped children but with handicapped schools.

III Conservation of Spanish in the Southwest

It should be clear that the retention of the Spanish language by Americans of Spanish-Mexican descent in the Southwest has been the function of default, rather than of any concerted popular or institutionalized effort. The Spanish-speaking whom the United States acquired through the American occupation of the nineteenth century were almost totally illiterate. As noted in *Forgotten People*[20] and in the works of numerous other students, little was done for the Americanization of this population group in the nineteenth century or in the twentieth, for that matter, in some of the areas where the Spanish-speaking population existed in large concentrations.[21]

The educational level of this group is extremely low, as reference to the latest figures of the United States Bureau of the Census will show. One would expect a fairly low level of linguistic proficiency among this population. Oddly enough, but not inexplicably so, their Spanish is of good quality. This is a result in large part of their isolation from the dominant, English-speaking group. In part, too, it is a result of the strange phenomenom that has made Mexico, as Don Federico de Onís once said, the country where, on the whole, the best Spanish is spoken.

The Mexicano, whether in Mexico or in the United States Southwest, has had a flair for the Spanish language, whether he were literate or not. Of course, many in the Southwest fall into barbarisms that are the result of a meager vocabulary, of English-named articles and practices for which there are no Spanish equivalents, and of the almost total lack of formal tutoring in the language. In some parts of the Southwest, as in the mountains of Kentucky and Tennessee, many archaic expressions are still common—for the same reasons in both places, isolation and lack of education.

One could point to the feeble efforts of the Spanish-language press, or to those of organizations of Spanish-speaking people, or to the fact that Spanish is an official language in New Mexico and was widely used in politics and in the Legislature until recent years. Credit is due these, of course, but the fact remains that, in the Southwest, Spanish has been retained as a major language primarily by the default of the institutions of social incorporation. This default, although producing unfortunate results in other spheres, could be turned to tremendous advantage. Some suggestions are made in this paper. Others will occur to those who recognize bilingualism and multilingualism as of great value not only in our relations with the rest of the world, but also in the enhancement of the human spirit, in the development of the highest order of humanism.

REFERENCES

I

Gilberto Cerda, Berta Babaza y Julieta Farías, *Vocabulario Español de Texas*, University of Texas Hispanic Studies, Vol. V (Austin:

The University of Texas Press, 1953). See pp. iv–v for listing of similar studies elsewhere in the Americas.

Ernesto Galarza, *Strangers in Our Fields* (Washington, D. C.: Joint United States-Mexico Trade Union Committee, 1956).

Galarza, *Merchants of Labor* (Private publication: 1031 Franquette Street, San José, California, 1965).

Charles F. Marden and Gladys Meyer, *Minorities in American Society*, 2nd ed. (New York: American Book Company, 1962); see especially ch. 6.

George I. Sánchez, *Mexico—A Revolution by Education* (New York: Viking Press, 1936).

George I. Sánchez, *Forgotten People* (Albuquerque: The University of New Mexico Press, 1940).

Carey McWilliams, *North from Mexico* (Philadelphia: Lippincott, 1943).

II

1. Sam Frank Cheavens, "Vernacular Languages in Education" (Unpublished doctoral dissertation, University of Texas, 1957).
2. *Ibid.*, pp. 50–51.
3. Bruce S. Meador, "Minority Groups and Their Education in Hays County, Texas" (Unpublished doctoral dissertation, University of Texas, 1959).
4. Norman R. F. Maier, *Frustration: The Study of Behavior Without a Goal* (New York: McGraw-Hill Book Company, 1949).
5. A. H. Maslow, *Motivation and Personality* (New York: Harper and Brothers, 1954).
6. Cheavens, "Vernacular Languages," pp. 516–517.
7. W. E. Lambert and Elizabeth Peal, "The Relation of Bilingualism to Intelligence," *Psychological Monographs: General and Applied*, No. 546, 76, 27 (1962).
8. George I. Sánchez and Howard Putnam, *Materials Relating to the Education of Spanish-Speaking People in the United States —An Annotated Bibliography* (Austin: The Institute of Latin American Studies, The University of Texas, 1959).
9. Texas Education Agency, "Handbook for the Instructional Program for Preschool-Age Non-English Speaking Children" (First Draft, 1960).
10. Texas Education Agency, *Preschool Instructional Program for Non-English Speaking Children* (1960).
11. George I. Sánchez, "Concerning Segregation of Spanish-Speaking Children in the Public Schools," Inter-American Educational Occasional Papers, IX, University of Texas, December, 1951.
12. Louis Alexander, "Texas Helps Her Little Latins." *The Saturday Evening Post*, August 5, 1961, pp. 30–31, 54–55.

13. Texas Education Agency, *The Texas Project For Migrant Children* (1964).
14. *Ibid.*, p. 11.
15. *Ibid.*, p. 4.
16. Texas Education Agency, *Report of Pupils in Texas Public Schools Having Spanish Surnames, 1955–56* (August, 1957).
17. George I. Sánchez and Charles L. Eastlack, *Say It The Spanish Way* (Austin: The Good Neighbor Commission of Texas, 1960).
18. Eli Ginzberg and Douglas W. Bray, *The Uneducated* (New York: Columbia University Press, 1953).
19. United States Bureau of the Census, *U. S. Census of Population: 1950*, Vol. 4, Special Reports, Part 3, Chapter 6, "Persons of Spanish Surname" (1953); United States Bureau of the Census, *United States Census of Population: 1960*, "Persons of Spanish Surname," Final Report PC(2)-1B (Washington, D. C.: U. S. Government Printing Office, 1963); Robert H. Talbert, *Spanish-Name People in the West and Southwest* (Fort Worth: Leo Potishman Foundation, Texas Christian University, 1955).

III

20. George I. Sánchez, *Forgotten People* (Albuquerque: University of New Mexico Press, 1940).
21. George I. Sánchez, "The American of Mexican Descent," *The Chicago Jewish Forum*, 20, 2 (Winter, 1961–62).

ii: The Role of the Christian Church

REV. JOHN A. WAGNER

In an age of awakening social consciousness, affluent American religious denominations are taking a long, hard look at well-to-do pastorates and are seeing beyond the well-dressed congregations of the comfortable homes, plentiful food, and well-paying jobs to the barely clothed, barely fed, woefully underpaid minority groups. The largest minority group whose mother tongue is other than English is the Spanish-speaking.

According to the *Yearbook of American Churches for 1963*, edited by Benson Y. Landis, church membership in the United States in 1961 was 63.4 per cent of the total population. Allowing the Roman Catholic Church an estimated 15 per cent of the Spanish-speaking population and the Protestant churches an estimated 5 per cent as regular church members, there remains an estimated 80 per cent who have no active church affiliation.[1] Protestant and Catholic church groups are both realigning a fertile field for missionary work among the Spanish-speaking.

Although this particular minority has long been with us, the organized, concerted effort for the conversion of souls and the relief of bodies is comparatively recent. The large economically deprived group of Spanish-speaking people is the target for church activity in the Southwest. However, the churches realize that converting the Spanish-speaking is not simply a matter of reaching them with the Gospel and baptism. Religion per se is not going to put a better roof over one's head, food in one's stomach, or impart health to one's children. Thus the fundamental needs of the Spanish-speaking poor must be met first, and this the churches are attempting to do in the sixties.

To review, however briefly, the history of religious conversion among the Spanish-speaking is to review the conquest and, in some instances, subsequent colonization of North and South America and the Caribbean Islands. The present southwestern part of the United States was for a long time New Spain and later a part of Mexico. Early exploration was conducted under the flag of Catholic Spain for God and King, and missionary priests were never far behind the conquerors, if not side by side with them.

> With rare exception, the attitude of the early Roman Catholic missionaries toward the Indian aborigines was one that accepted the Indian as a child of God, sought his conversion to Christianity, dealt mercifully with him, and tried to protect him from brutal exploitation by his Spanish conquerors.[2]

Thus in time the conquered peoples were converted to Catholicism. However, the inhabitants rarely left their former religions completely for Catholicism, but more often incorporated the ritualistic teachings of the Church into the native forms of spiritualistic worship.

> Outwardly, the lands settled by the Spanish were Roman Catholic at the end of the three centuries of colonization. Inwardly—in the beliefs and practices of the great masses of the people—the religion of New Spain was a mixture of Christianity and the superstitions and primitive customs of the native Indians. To this mixture was added in some places the animism and voodooism imported by Negro slaves from Africa. Under the impact of the acculturating forces at work in all the vast Spanish-invaded area, there developed a conglomerate religion that had all the externalities of Roman Catholicism.[3]

Religion came easily to the native inhabitants. In his book, *Profile of Man and Culture in Mexico*, Samuel Ramos provides valuable insight into the nature of the Spanish-speaking person.

> The real motivation for our culture, given the nature of our psychic activity since the time of the Conquest, is religiosity. . . . In other words, one can say that Mexican history, especially in its spiritual sense, is a matter of the affirmation or negation of religious sentiment. Whichever branch of our ascendancy is considered—that of the Indian or that of the Spanish conqueror—the most notable resultant characteristic is our exalted religiosity.[4]

Ramos describes the romantic, sentimental, poetic characteristics of the Mexican as basically a consuming and pervading
religious attitude toward life. Even the defiance of religion,
such as the cults of atheism and rebellions against the church,
are often expressions of the Spanish-speaking person's intense
spirituality and his repudiation of mechanistic concepts of life.
Whether or not he is formally religious, the Mexican's whole
being, says Ramos, oozes religiosity.

Understanding the material, social, spiritual background of
the Spanish-speaking in the United States is fundamental
for those who wish to help them. The Spanish-speaking have
many material needs: housing shows extensive deterioration,
lack of bath and toilet facilities, and overcrowded conditions;
frequently health services are nonexistent; educational achievement is notably lower than Anglo and nonwhite; unemployment rates are high and income is low; migratory labor streams
include thousands (127,000 from South Texas alone); English
is a foreign language; lack of effective indigenous leadership
accounts for lack of communication with community services
and schools; employment barriers are intensified by lack of
vocational counselling, apprenticeship, and job training; school
dropouts are high since motivation for education is lacking;
pride, optimism, and social participation are dormant in the
disadvantaged neighborhoods; poverty, personal and social
depression, and aimlessness destroy initiative; and the vicious
cycle of ignorance and poverty continues to enslave.

By way of illustration, Villa Coronado, a community in
southwestern Bexar County, is a study in the abject poverty of
the Spanish-speaking. Two hundred and seventy-five house-
holds, representing 1579 people, were contacted. Of these
families 59 per cent had a median family income of $37.85 per
week; 40 per cent of the total population was unemployed; 1
per cent was on old-age or social security assistance. Many of
the families in the area are migratory farm workers. At the
time of the survey fifty-two families were already gone, and
another twenty-six families were not at home. Of the 584
adults surveyed, 136 did not know how to write either English
or Spanish; only 134 persons knew some English whereas
only three did not speak Spanish; 34 adults were not American
citizens.

Nine hundred and ninety-five of the total population are

children under twenty. The extreme youthfulness of the population is indicated by the fact that 125 are under two years of age, 243 are between two and five years of age, and 208 are in the first to the third grade but only forty are of high school age. There are thirty-four school dropouts from fourteen to eighteen years of age.

Although the families are large, seven of the houses have only one room, 101 have only two rooms (the term room includes kitchen and toilet if any). Forty-three houses have indoor toilet facilities, 203 have outdoor privies, and 29 have no toilet facilities whatever. Only 18 of the houses have any kind of indoor bath facilities. Twelve have no electricity; 46 have no running water. There is no garbage collection, public transportation, fire protection, or sewage, recreational, or medical facilities. The public school to which the children must go is about seven miles from the community. Payments on homes or rent of homes averages between $10 to $25 a month. One comment from a survey taker was "Twenty-two persons living in three rooms need help badly. They have little food and clothing for the children . . . medical care is needed for most of the family. Only one person is working, earning $35 a week. Hope to get assistance immediately."

Where the Spanish-speaking in the Southwest are concentrated there is poverty with all its associated problems. This is especially true in the southern part of Texas, which stands almost apart from the rest of the nation in the extent of its problems. Within this area the problem of overwhelming poverty is the problem of a people and the problem of a nation. But an area far greater than South Texas feels the effect, for not all of the poverty spawned here remains. Part of it has been carried permanently into distant agricultural communities by farm workers seeking a less hostile existence.

The ministry of the churches to the Spanish-speaking becomes more involved when one considers the migrant farm workers. Practically all agricultural migrants from Texas are Mexican-Americans. The following chart indicates how many states are visited by the Texas migrant:[6]

Alabama	2,838	Colorado	3,778
Arizona	998	Delaware	54
Arkansas	2,402	Florida	1,724
California	2,346	Georgia	27

Idaho	12,479	North Carolina	30
Illinois	13,364	North Dakota	3,342
Indiana	15,474	Ohio	22,378
Iowa	2,697	Oklahoma	3,563
Kansas	291	Oregon	5,880
Kentucky	370	Pennsylvania	39
Louisiana	40	South Carolina	252
Michigan	26,166	South Dakota	1,448
Minnesota	12,433	Tennessee	1,313
Mississippi	78	Utah	1,913
Missouri	2,458	Virginia	335
Montana	3,844	Washington	5,611
Nebraska	2,186	Wisconsin	19,596
Nevada	10	Wyoming	3,642
New Mexico	328		

Surveys of two Mexican-American communities in Bexar County, Texas, made by the National Council for the Spanish-speaking reveal that the majority of the Spanish-speaking still call themselves Catholic but that others are reached by a variety of churches. Many, however, appear to be in a state of indecision.

Religious Affiliation in Two Communities in Bexar County, Texas

	Villa Coronado	Linda Vista
Number of families surveyed	275	198
Total number of persons visited	1579	1169
Catholic families	225	155
Non-Catholic families	50	43
Baptists	9	1
Jehovah's Witnesses	9	1
Pentecostal	3	7
Assembly of God	3	4
Alleluia	1	
Protestant	3	1
Mexican Baptist	2	
Church of Christ	1	1
Mormon	1	
Church of God		1
Evangelist		3
Methodist		3
Presbyterian		1
No religious affiliation	7	2
Incomplete information	11	18

Source: Survey, National Council for the Spanish-Speaking.

The social background of the Spanish-speaking leaves much to be desired also. Too often the American dream of justice and equality for all is just that—an unattainable dream for the minority groups. The Spanish-speaking are racially distinct in the United States.

Although most of these people are Caucasians and are classified as such in the United States Census, they nevertheless have the racial visibility of a special family of Caucasians. The Spanish American is nominally a Christian, and formally he usually speaks of himself as a Roman Catholic, an affiliation that does not endear him to the predominantly Protestant Anglo-Americans who meet him at the border. His first language, even though he and his forefathers may have been in this country for generations, is Spanish rather than English. His customs, literature, history, and habits of thought are not those of the great majority of American people. Moreover, like his cousin, the Indian, he is descended from a people conquered by the United States.[7]

Discrimination against the Spanish-speaking is often the hardest to combat because it is very subtle. Ralph Estrada, former president of La Alianza Hispano-Americana, cited an example at a 1959 conference.

Then one might say that discrimination is pretty much a thing of the past in such cities as Tucson and Phoenix. One can point to Mexican-Americans who have risen to great heights in their communities. They are admitted to the country clubs. They live in the best residential sections. They associate with high society. And yet I can point to any number of examples of a continuing discrimination in both of those communities. For instance, in Tucson it is an interesting fact that within three or four blocks of San Augustin Cathedral, which has a largely Mexican-American congregation, is another Roman Catholic church, the boundaries of which conveniently exclude virtually all the Mexican-American residential areas in that part of the city. Thus we have two churches just three or four blocks apart, one serving the Mexican-Americans and the other serving the Anglos.[8]

Social discrimination manifests itself in a variety of ways: refusing service in barbershops, soda fountains, cafes, drive-ins, beauty parlors, hotels, bars, and recreation centers; segregation in housing, movies, schools, churches, and cemeteries, as well as in public buildings and public toilets; reluctant service in hospitals, colleges, social welfare offices, and courts; and even refusing to permit Mexican-American hostesses in USO's. Sometimes there will be signs, "No Mexicans Allowed," "Mexicans Will Be Served in Kitchens Only," or "We Do Not Solicit Mexican or Negro Trade"; more often it is the less obtrusive but equally understood "We Retain the Right to Refuse Service to Any Customer."[9]

Too often the Spanish-speaking are not welcomed to the homes or social functions of Anglo-Americans because such mixing isn't acceptable to Anglo society. Marriage between Spanish-speaking and Anglo is frowned upon by both sides in many places in the Southwest. When faced with the fact of segregation of the Spanish-speaking, Anglos rationalize: "The Spanish-speaking prefer living in a ghetto," or "Ghettoization is true of any minority group that has not become assimilated into the American mainstream of life," or "The Spanish-speaking feel more secure among members of their own ethnic group who speak the same language, have the same problems." However, the Anglo cannot console himself with saying that the Spanish-speaking prefer to live in poverty with little means of bettering themselves. It is up to the dominant Anglo population to lend a helping hand to the ghettoized Spanish-speaking to speed assimilation into the rest of society. Even though economic and social barriers must first be broken down, the relationship with the churches (and the Catholic Church in particular) can be effective in bringing about a better situation. Even more than the Irish of yesteryear, the Spanish-speaking expect guidance from the Church, not only in religious but also in social and family matters. It is a sad commentary on the churches that more has not been done to better the lot of the Spanish-speaking.

The American Catholic Church with predominantly Anglo attitudes has compassion on the poverty stricken but often fails to identify with the individual Spanish-speaking. This situation was the subject of comment by Stan Twardy.

A wandering and vagabond Christ is being spurned every day by millions of church-going and otherwise devout American Catholics.

He comes to them as a hungry, ragged and socially ostracized Spanish-speaking citizen or immigrant. He meets them across the whole width and breadth of these United States and sometimes he brushes shoulders with them in church on Sundays.

But after these fleeting encounters He withdraws to the unspeakable migrant slums of Texas, the Puerto Rican Harlems of New York, the Cuban refugee encampments in Florida, the filthy shacks and shanties of Oklahoma cotton gins and all the other barns, chicken houses, pigsties and barracks where Spanish-speaking migrant workers live during the cotton, fruit and vegetable picking season.

In these gutters of misfortune He wonders how the fingering of beads, novenas and parish bingos can be construed by so many as a substitute for charity, feeding the hungry and clothing the poor.

With an estimated 8,000,000 Spanish-speaking Catholics in this country, nearly two-thirds of whom are living in the most abject poverty and degradation, American Catholicism is only slowly awakening to the social and religious challenge presented by these people.

The steady Spanish influx, estimated at 230,000 Mexicans, 20,000 Puerto Ricans, and over 100,000 Cubans in 1961, combined with the higher than average birth rate among those already in the U.S., is rapidly changing the complexion of American Catholicism. . . .

Other Americans fail to understand their sentiments, feelings and aspirations and they [Spanish-speaking] cannot understand why in this prosperous land they must remain entrapped in an impoverished and sub-human existence. . . .

In their day to day struggle for survival amid the preoccupation with the crushing burdens of hunger and illness, it is hardly surprising that so many of these overworked and illiterate people have received little or no instruction in religion.

In fact most Latins have a deeply ingrained faith in God. They see and feel Him in the midst of their poverty, and in their pressing needs they turn to Him with a fervor and humility seldom equalled by many who attend Mass every Sunday. Theirs is a living religion, with Christ personally and instantly approachable and interested in their problems.

Amid the growing secularization of today the consciousness of a living God in our midst, brought by many of the Spanish-speaking, may be the best enrichment of American religious life and the most effective antidote to secularism in the Anglo middle-class culture of America.[10]

In 1863 Lord Acton wrote of the Catholic Church: "From

time to time a very extensive revision is required, hateful to conservative habits and feelings. Crisis occurs and new alliance has to be formed between religion and knowledge, between the Church and society." This indicates the Church must be different according to different people in various ages and different circumstances. Outside of the basic framework, Peter and the Apostles—the pope and the bishops, the Christian community cannot look the same today or as it did yesterday. This is the ever recurring problem of the articulation of Christ in the world, the always thorny problem of the Christian community and the world.

There is something very basic lacking in the American Catholic Church, which makes it possible for thousands of Spanish-speaking to leave the Church each year to embrace an alien form of worship. Every indication points to the fact that many more Spanish-speaking leave the Church each year than the Church gains in converts. Large numbers of Spanish-speaking Catholics are looking to other religions for something they cannot find in the Catholic religion. Perhaps the American Catholic Church has become so solidified that it will accept membership only on its own basis and only as long as the individual conforms to its proper development. Basically, this would mean that to be regarded as a good Catholic in the American Church one would have to be in the middle income economically, be able to send his children to the Catholic school, be able to support the structure which is called the parish. Since the Spanish-speaking are not in this position, they have one of two choices: either to forsake all of their background and become as legalistic as the Catholic Anglo or find their expression somewhere else.

In a survey of five hundred adult Spanish-speaking patients conducted by Rev. Joseph Crosthwait in 1960 at John Sealy Hospital in Galveston, Texas, 12.3 per cent indicated they were Protestant. Of these only 1.2 per cent had been so from birth; 85 per cent had become Protestant in the last twelve years. Of those who had been baptized Catholic and left the Church, 79 per cent had never made their Communion and only 10 per cent of those who were married before leaving the Church had been married according to Church law. Some excuses given for leaving the Church were: "The Protestant Church helped me with food and clothing so I felt I owed it to them to join their

Church. . . . Our priest was too 'regañon' (impatient or ill-tempered), and we were afraid of him. . . . We could not get married by the Church because we could not find all the papers. . . . My parents were not married by the Church and when my father died the priest would not say any prayers for him so the Protestant minister came. . . ."

Religious groups working among the Spanish-speaking are divided between Catholic and Protestant. Individual Protestant denominations will be discussed in turn. Catholic organizations most active are the Bishops' Committee for the Spanish Speaking, National Council for the Spanish-speaking, and the Confraternity of Christian Doctrine. Individual work by various other interested Catholic groups is not included for lack of information.

Realizing the need for a Spanish-speaking apostolate as early as 1944, the late Samuel Cardinal Stritch spoke to prelates at the Annual Meeting of the Catholic Hierarchy in the United States in Washington, D. C., about the need for a unified and coordinated program of welfare work among the Spanish-speaking people in the Southwest. Cardinal Stritch asked approval of a grant from the American Board of Catholic Missions for this purpose. The matter received unanimous approval from the Catholic hierarchy of the United States. Cardinal Stritch also suggested that a committee composed of the Archbishops of Los Angeles, Santa Fe, San Antonio, and Denver be appointed to call and plan a conference of the bishops of the Southwest to study the needs of the Spanish-speaking. Thus the Bishops' Committee for the Spanish-speaking was established. Programs of this Committee are sponsored by the American Board of Catholic Missions through an annual grant. The programs have varied according to the needs of the dioceses. One of the most important services of the Committee has been the establishment of eight infant and maternity clinics for the Spanish-speaking people in San Antonio. The Committee has also promoted credit unions and housing cooperatives, youth programs, vocational guidance institutes, leadership training, and programs in citizenship and basic education. It also conducts surveys, keeps up-to-date reports on all matters that affect the welfare of the Spanish-speaking people. Experimental programs are conducted frequently and if proved practical, they are recommended to the clergy in the Spanish-speaking territories.

Working closely with the Bishops' Committee is the National Council for the Spanish Speaking. The purpose of the Council is to promote and aid the welfare and interests of the Spanish-speaking people of the United States, to engage in all necessary and expedient measures to help them share in the benefits of this democracy as rightful recipients of the fruits of society, and to enable them to make their cultural contribution to the welfare of the nation. Membership is open to all, regardless of race, religion, or nationality, who are interested in bringing the two groups (Spanish-speaking and Anglo) together in the best joint community effort. The NCSS is the only national organization embracing all the Spanish-speaking in the United States—Mexican-American, Puerto Rican, Cuban, Hispano, Latin-American, and others—and dedicated to carry out its programs on the community level. It is also the only national organization dedicated to this group that has a national office enabling it to extend its influence throughout the nation. The NCSS action programs, which have been tested on the local level and proved successful, are orientated to community cooperation and to working with those who are being given an opportunity to help themselves to a better life. Included in the NCSS action programs are the leadership training program, neighborhood councils, adult education for adults with no previous education, vocational training and job placement, literacy classes for adults, tutoring classes for elementary school children, preschool classes, and health classes.

The Confraternity of Christian Doctrine is also very active in work with the Spanish-speaking. The purpose of the CCD is to instruct Catholics in the tenets of the faith. A great amount of work is done among children of the Spanish-speaking who are unable to receive religious instruction in school.

One of the most imaginative and effective religious movements carried on by the Catholic Church among the Spanish-speaking is the Cursillo Movement.

The first Cursillo de Cristiandad was held in 1949 in the monastery of St. Honoratus on the island of Majorca. Basic doctrines of the Church were explained in an atmosphere of dynamic learning whereby the group, stimulated by the inter-action of charity, was strengthened as a vital Christian community. . . . The methods employed in these three days of intensive learning have proven to be a marvelous blend of natural means vitalized by a supernatural effectiveness. The use of techniques of group dynamics coupled with generous prayer and sacrifice was no accidental discovery. The methods of the Cursillo were the fruit of long years of study and experimentation carried on within the framework of Catholic Action by the priests and laymen in close collaboration with Bishop Hervas, the Ordinary of the Diocese of Majorca. As he states in his book, *Cursillos de Cristiandad,* two main objectives occupied their attention: the superstructure of a religious climate which would facilitate the true and authentic practice of the faith, and a study in depth of the truths of the faith as the vital force to reform society.[11]

Cursillos were first introduced to the Southwest in 1957 in Waco, Texas, by two Spanish airmen, on temporary military assignment to this country, together with a Franciscan priest originally from the island of Majorca. Started as parochial projects, Cursillos were soon given diocesan approval in nearly all of the dioceses of the Southwest.

Because of inadequate statistics on individual Protestant churches, those mentioned here are illustrative of the work being done among the Spanish-speaking by Protestants but not all inclusive. The largest Protestant sect among the Spanish-speaking is the Southern Baptist Convention.

> This denomination reports 580 missionaries (husbands and wives) working among Spanish Americans in the United States. Most of these missionaries are pastors of the 510 Spanish American congregations in the Southern Baptist Convention. These congregations are affiliated with local Baptist associations, state conventions, and the S.B.C. As would be expected from the large number of Spanish Americans in Texas, New Mexico, Arizona, California, and Florida, the largest Spanish American work of this denomination is in these states.[12]

In most of the Southern Baptist Convention churches English is used in Sunday Schools and other organizations dealing with young people. However, the preaching services are in Spanish. The number of churches using English for the sermons with simultaneous translation into Spanish is increasing. Although the Southern Baptists produce and use a great amount of Spanish-language literature, the church expects an early disappearance of Spanish-speaking churches as the younger, bilingual generation of Spanish-Americans replaces the older monolingual generation. The younger generation is more disposed to acculturation and the Southern Baptist Convention reports a large and increasing number of Spanish-Americans in the Anglo-American churches of the Southern Baptist Convention. The 1964 Baptist General Convention of Texas, in its annual meeting in Fort Worth, approved an evangelism campaign among Spanish-speaking in that state. In an address to the convention, the Rev. Carlos Paredes of Austin suggested that the greatest mission field for Texas Baptists was in their own state among Spanish-speaking. Mr. Paredes is president of the Mexican Baptist Convention of Texas.

The Methodist Church conducts a similarly large work among the Spanish-speaking. Of the 150 Spanish Methodist Churches most are concentrated in the Southwest: Texas (77), California (29), Arizona (15), and New Mexico (13). Twenty-five per cent of the 150 churches are self-supporting; the remainder are supported in varying degrees by the Methodist Churches' Division of National Missions.[13]

The Methodist Church's concern with the Spanish-speaking is twofold. Although it is not unmindful of the spiritual needs of these people, it also seeks to better their socioeconomic level.

In the United States there are 14 Methodist clinics for Spanish Americans directed toward the dual purpose of guarding the health of the people and educating them in diet and sanitary measures. In addition to these clinics the Methodist Church owns and operates 31 Spanish American settlement houses that provide citizenship classes, religious services, day nurseries, Boy and Girl Scout troops, home economics and craft classes, pastoral counseling, and vocational guidance. Like the clinics, these settlement houses are heavily concentrated in Texas and California and minister mainly to Mexican Americans. The Methodist Church also provides four boarding schools, one home for girl students, and a special program for Spanish American theological students at the Perkins School of Theology, Dallas, Texas. Apparently one of the show pieces of this denomination's Spanish American work is Lydia Patterson Institute in El Paso, Texas, which in 1962–63 had 467 junior high and high school and other students engaged in a program to train Spanish American Methodist ministers, church workers, and laymen. Methodist sources report that this is the only educational institution in the United States given over solely to Spanish American youth.[14]

A third type of Protestant ministry to the Spanish-speaking

is the Pentecostal churches, the largest of which is the Assemblies of God churches. "Ardently fundamentalist, literalist in scriptural view, given to speaking in tongues, this denomination has a zealous and effective Spanish American mission disproportionate to its size." The Assemblies of God churches publish a weekly, *The Pentecostal Evangel*, which appears bimonthly in Spanish as *Poder*, meaning power. Spanish-language materials are distributed to all of the Spanish-speaking Assemblies of God churches in the United States and Puerto Rico.

The Protestant Episcopal Church is preparing for ministry among the Spanish-speaking through conferences. The first of the two conferences held so far was under the auspices of the church's Division of Racial Minorities. The subject was "Latin American Relations in the Southwest." Held in Austin, Texas, in 1959, such experts on the Southwest's Spanish-speaking culture as Carey McWilliams, Ralph Estrada, and George I. Sánchez spoke and helped formulate recommendations for the improvement of the church's ministry to the Spanish-speaking in the Southwest.

The Presbyterian Church is becoming involved in community development programs in Spanish-speaking areas. It is experimenting with two "Social Ministers" in San Francisco, sponsoring a community development program in Guadalupe, a village south of Phoenix, Arizona, and is contemplating an experimental project involving the Spanish-speaking and the Negro in San Antonio, Texas. This religious group also sponsored a seminar in Phoenix, Arizona, in 1964, on "The Role of the Church in the Civil Rights of the Spanish Speaking."

Although most Protestant denominations minister to the Spanish-speaking under the auspices of their own churches, the Protestant churches realize that the field is too large for individual labor alone. Recognizing this situation as early as 1920, missionary-minded women formed a group to work with migrant Negroes in New Jersey; this work grew, spread, and was adopted by the Home Missions Council of North America. In 1950 the Home Missions Council became part of the Division of Home Missions of the newly formed National Council of Churches, and a National Migrant Committee was organized to promote and supervise this specialized ministry. In 1953 the national committee adopted the following Statement of Purpose:

In the Migrant Ministry the churches are united to serve men, women and children who are following the crops. This program is centered in the Christian faith and seeks to share that faith with the migrant, and to develop in him a sense of his personal worth, belonging, and responsibility. It seeks to awaken the community to the opportunity and obligation of sharing equally all the protective benefits and warmth of community life. It challenges the local churches to include these seasonal neighbors in their concern and full fellowship. It calls on the state and nation to apply Christian principles to the economy in which migrants live and work.[15]

This purpose points out the four-directional movement essential to a migrant ministry to the Spanish-speaking: toward the migrant, the community, the local churches, and the state and national governments. The symbol of the Migrant Ministry —the nation, the cross, and the people encircled by the words, "The Churches Working Together"—expresses the ideal Protestant witness and service to Spanish Americans.[16]

The scope of the Migrant Ministry is defined in a listing of national organizations for migrant farm workers and their families compiled by the United States Department of Labor. The Division of Home Missions of the National Council of Churches defines the following programs for migrant Spanish speaking:

. . . integration of migratory workers with the community where they are temporarily located; Sunday schools, vacation church schools, week-day religious education, and worship services all geared to the background, needs, and understanding of the people; service to infants and young children needing special care and protection; child care centers, well-baby clinics, health services; activities for school-age children and summer schools to supplement interrupted education; fellowship, recreation, and pre-vocational training and guidance; family night activities, both recreational and educational; counseling; interpretation of the needs of the people and the Migrant Ministry through speeches, radio, newspapers, television; enlistment of the services of local, state, and national agencies.[17]

Considering the slow but sure awakening of the churches to the needs of the Spanish-speaking, prospects for the future cannot help being brighter than in the past. Churches of all denominations realize that a basic ministry to the Spanish-speaking is twofold: to provide spiritual aid and to alleviate

socioeconomic problems in whatever way possible. Means of
providing spiritual aid have already been discussed. We turn
now to means of hastening social justice for the Spanish-speaking. Churches are becoming more politically sophisticated in
petitioning government agencies for aid for their various
flocks, and are supporting legislation and passing resolutions,
and testifying before pertinent Congressional committees as a
group; when the American Baptist or Southern Baptist Con-
ventions or the National Council of Churches or the National
Council for the Spanish Speaking makes a statement, legislators are aware that the support of thousands of people is behind the respective organization. In 1961 the American Baptist
Convention adopted the following resolution on migrant labor:

> In our relatively affluent society it is a tragic fact that half a mil-
> lion migratory American workers earn a meager living in seasonal
> agricultural work. Recognizing legitimate manpower needs, it
> remains that exploitation of migrant workers is in no sense reason-
> ably meeting these needs. Use of migrant workers for business
> profit which results in substandard education, wages, transporta-
> tion and housing is unchristian.
>
> To rectify these situations we urge:
> a. In the area of education:
>   1. That the federal government formulate and implement
>   plans by which the special educational needs of the chil-
>   dren of migrants may be met.
>   2. That American Baptists support federal legislation to pro-
>   vide financial aid to local public school districts in meeting
>   their responsibilities to educate the children of migrants.
> b. In the area of housing we urge American Baptists to support
>   both federal and state legislation to provide adequate stand-
>   ards of housing for migrants.
> c. In the area of wages we urge compliance with existing laws
>   designed to protect such agricultural workers.
> d. In the area of recruitment we urge the provision of national
>   crew leader registration supervision to protect migrants from
>   the unscrupulous practices of some crew leaders and labor
>   contractors.
> e. American Baptists have for many years worked cooperatively
>   through the Migrant Ministry to bring to migrant workers and
>   their families opportunities for fellowship, worship, pastoral
>   care, health and welfare services. Increasingly these efforts
>   have enlisted volunteers from local congregations to serve as

members of migrant committees, as teachers, and as super-
visors of child-care centers. In order to extend these services
more effectively and to meet continuing needs we recommend:

1. That members of local churches become aware of the pres-
   ence of migratory workers in their vicinity and assist in
   providing these services through a ministry to migrants.
2. That members of local churches make sure that the health
   and welfare services of the community and state are made
   available to the migrants. If legislation is needed to make
   these services available, we urge that church members work
   for the passage of such legislation.

The National Council for the Spanish Speaking, at its conference in 1962, went on record as supporting the following
pieces of legislation: Child Labor Bill, Education Bill, Crew
Leader Bill, Health Bill, National Advisory Council Bill, Sta-
bilization Bill. The NCSS also presented a statement to the
Subcommittee on the National Service Corps regarding the
needs of disadvantaged citizens, particularly the Spanish-
speaking.

In ministering to the Spanish-speaking of the Southwest
today, the basic role of the churches should be to give voice to
disadvantaged people as they try to move into the mainstream
of American life. The churches must endeavor to impress upon
the citizens as a whole the need for breaking every yoke that
unjustly binds any human being to misery and hopelessness,
to impress upon the community the necessity for sharing its
bread with the hungry, sheltering the homeless, and clothing
the naked. Love is not sectarian. A hungry Protestant is as
hungry as a hungry Catholic. Whether a man's hunger is re-
lieved by a co-religionist or by a member of a rival faith makes
no difference either to the hungry man or to God. There was
a time when love and employment were administered strictly
along sectarian lines. A Catholic was expected to employ Catholics and Protestants to do likewise.

A new spirit is beginning to grow in our time. It is closer to
the Christian teaching than the long-cherished sectarianism.
It makes no difference whether a priest or a minister or a rabbi
is leading some effort for justice or social betterment, it is the
effort that counts. The churches as a whole must protest every
exploitation of our fellowman, support every good cause for
human betterment, take leadership in bringing success to the

pattern of a good society. The churches must be committed to the realization that every individual wants his rights, wants his standards as an American. The revolution of the churches is directed not to the overthrow of the system but against the system so all may enter it. Moreover, churches must continue to be dedicated to this revolution as long as injustice, economic oppression, lack of equal education, neglected health needs, substandard housing, lack of credit, and a spirit of neglect prevail. The churches' role is to be a voice in the community, to make known to one and all the unjust treatment, misery, and needs of so many of our Spanish-speaking citizens. To accomplish this demands a greater involvement between the churches and the Spanish-speaking; churches must be concerned principally with the rights and duties of persons as human beings created by God and endowed with intelligence and free will. These rights, universal and inalienable, are the right to life and a worthy standard of living, the right to moral and cultural advantages, the right to religious freedom, the right to work, the right of assembly and association, the right of movement, and the right to political participation.

That involvement in the ministry and betterment of the life of the Spanish-speaking is the task of all churches is obvious from our Lord's own words, "As long as you did this to these, the least of My brethren, you did it to Me." If the challenge is not acknowledged, the churches may well be accused of crucifying Christ in the twentieth century by nailing His Spanish-speaking to the cross of their misery with the nails of apathy, complacency, selfishness, and irresponsibility.

REFERENCES

1. Kyle Haseldon, *Death of a Myth* (New York: Friendship Press, 1964), p. 103.
2. *Ibid.*, p. 21.
3. *Ibid.*, p. 22.
4. Samuel Ramos, *Profile of Man and Culture in Mexico.* Translated by Peter G. Earle. (Austin: University of Texas Press, 1962), p. 77. (Published in Spanish in 1934.)
5. *Loc. cit.*
6. Figures represent total number of persons—men, women, and

children—on whom records were kept in the Texas Employment Commission or the Bureau of Labor Statistics. To these figures on "known" migrants may be added about 20 per cent to cover "free wheelers" who migrated without contacting either department.

7. Haseldon, *op. cit.*, pp. 51–52.

8. *Summary of Conference on Latin-American Relations in the Southwestern United States* (New York: Division of Racial Minorities, The National Council of the Protestant Episcopal Church, 1959), p. 18.

9. John H. Burma, *Spanish-Speaking Groups in the United States* (Durham: Duke University Press, 1954), pp. 107–108.

10. Stan Twardy, "The Changing Complexion of American Catholicism," *Oklahoma Courier*, Oklahoma City, 1962.

11. Rev. Victor Goertz, "Brief History of the Cursillo Movement" (paper delivered at the Conference of the National Catholic Council for the Spanish Speaking, Milwaukee, Wisconsin, 1962).

12. Haseldon, *Death of a Myth*, p. 105.

13. *Ibid.*, p. 106.

14. *Ibid.*, p. 106.

15. *Ibid.*, p. 115.

16. *Ibid.*, p. 116.

17. *Ibid.*, p. 117.

iii: Leadership and Politics

JOHN R. MARTINEZ

The most obvious result of the political activities of the Spanish-speaking in the Southwest is the fact that they have three Congressmen and one United States Senator. Of the five southwestern states only Colorado and Arizona have not succeeded in electing Spanish-speaking persons to Congress. Yet Arizona's Spanish-speaking population exceeds New Mexico's. Except for New Mexico, none of the states had elected anyone to Congress before World War II. In fact, the phenomenon of the three Spanish-speaking Congressmen occurred only in the 1960's. Henry B. Gonzalez of Texas won his House seat in a special election in 1961, Edward Roybal of Los Angeles in 1962, and De La Garza, also of Texas, in 1964. These Congressmen were all of the Democratic party.

New Mexico does not quite fit into the political pattern of the other southwestern states.[1] Its unique political tradition is revealed in that the Hispanos have participated more fully in politics than have the Spanish-speaking in any other area of the United States. It has been traditional for the Spanish New Mexicans to share in the elective and appointive offices of their state.

Despite the role Spanish New Mexicans play in their state's public life, the processes of integration and assimilation have not entirely erased their Spanish heritage and culture. I stress this because in other areas large numbers of Spanish-speaking are being urged to assimilate to the point of extinguishing all features that are non-Anglo-Saxon. Resistance to such attempts emerges in the form of idealizing La Raza.[2]

New Mexico, however, shows that assimilation does not necessarily bring with it annihilation of the past. In a sense

47

this essay is a comparative study of the Spanish-speaking's struggle for solutions to socioeconomic as well as political problems. The realization that politics is an important means of achieving the goals of the Spanish-speaking in this country has led to the rapid and dramatic emergence of political organizations and political leadership since World War II. Politics is a social instrument for improvement, which is now viewed not only as a means to achieve certain ends, but also as a shield against abuses, exploitation, and encroachments by the dominant society.

On the one hand, politics is a means to certain rewards. On the other, it conditions this group to depend on these rewards from one political party. It tends to neutralize the zeal for change and reform. The political potential of the Spanish-speaking is only in its initial stages. In political activity a minority not only expresses its wants and needs but also provides the outlet for its potential leadership. This leadership is symbolic of the whole group. The leader's achievements are the group's achievements. His problems, his responsibilities are to fulfill himself and, at the same time, to reflect the group's aspirations.[3] For the Spanish-speaking this is particularly difficult because of the individualistic nature of Hispanic peoples, which vitiates against group action.

Also, politics provides the arena and the rules of the game in which this ethnic group can match its wits against those of the dominant group. It is a superb challenge to beat the Anglos at their own game.[4] This, of course, is a manifestation of the underlying sense of inferiority imposed by a color- and culture-conscious society in the United States.

As a whole, the Spanish-speaking resist being categorized as a minority. This is due to the depth and breadth of their culture in the Southwest. The obvious Spanish-Mexican motifs in architecture, religion, law, food, and language make it difficult to refer to them as a minority in an area in which they feel so much at home. The fact that in an area discovered and colonized by their forefathers they are discriminated against and relegated to the lowest economic and social position constitutes a motivation for political activity.

The remarkable aspect of this situation is that the will to overcome this status has taken so long to assert itself. World War II has been mentioned as a turning point for this population. The opportunities for employment, the new horizons acquired from military service, and the educational opportunities through the G. I. Bill of Rights meant that for the first time large numbers of Spanish-speaking moved into the skilled, business, and professional classes. It follows that new voices were soon heard; the educated began articulating and analyzing the plight of their ethnic group. The response was a political awakening of great numbers of people.

The rise in the educational level was an important factor in this awakening, but it is still apparent that the professional and business people and university graduates are not exclusively, or even largely, the new leaders.[5] To be sure, some of the Spanish-speaking leaders are drawn from this class, but this class has not consciously or premeditatively assumed the responsibility of leadership.

Two other factors may be responsible for the increased interest of this ethnic group in political activities. The first is the civil rights movement. Although discriminated against in public and private places, the Spanish-speaking rarely reacted overtly. In the last decade the Negro has moved to overt action as well as legal recourse. All minorities have benefited from these efforts. The rewards politically and economically, therefore, were oriented to the Negro. In comparison, the Spanish-speaking were left relatively unrewarded and their passivity underscored.

Since the Kennedy administration, the Spanish-speaking have regarded Negro assertiveness as a threat to themselves. Yet they could not bring themselves to identify with civil rights' demonstrations. Employment opportunities were more available to Negroes than to Mexican-Americans causing the potential friction between the two ethnic groups to increase.

Thus the Negro movement stimulated a crystallization of miscellaneous discontents into organized form. Only by sharp contrast with Negro efforts did the Spanish-speaking see themselves politically silhouetted. This did not provide the guidelines, but it did indicate the necessity for political acitivities.

In fact, the very nature of the new political activities tended to polarize themselves around a racial problem. For the Spanish-speaking, it posed dilemma. On the one hand, the Anglos were not solicitous, and on the other, there was a great reluctance to join the Negro. *La Raza*, therefore, became a rallying point as it never had been in earlier times in this country for the Spanish-speaking. Even Congressman Gonzalez, an assimilated, thoroughgoing American type, used *La Raza* as a base of his early campaigns.[6] His candidacy was portrayed as a move to unite *La Raza*. In Phoenix, Arizona, a politically minded group has organized a club called *Raza* made up of a small number of Democrats who wish to illustrate by their club's name that they are conscious of the appeal of this ethnic term.[7]

The other significant factor stimulating civic activities among the Spanish-speaking has been the Economic Opportunity Act. This is a by-product of the Negro civil rights movement, although it is considerably more broad in its application. The Spanish-speaking quickly discovered programs in which they could participate and even direct if they organized. Many organizations among them had never functioned effectively for lack of funds, but with the EOA it has become possible to finance programs.

Those Spanish-speaking who were already involved in political activities or were on the periphery of them, moved easily into programs provided by the Economic Opportunity Act.[8] However, it is certainly possible that political activities would have emerged anyway as the chief means of expressing the group's desires and needs. The essential point is that the relative effectiveness of political activities did not emerge until these two factors came into being.

For example, the existence of many organizations among the Spanish-speaking has been both advantageous and disadvantageous for political activities. Their existence defined to both the civil rights movement and the War on Poverty the problems of the group. Such organizations as the League of United Latin American Citizens (LULAC) had for decades debated the main problems of the Latin Americans.[9] The issues were clear and well stated even though remedies were not available.

These organizations were a training ground for the new leadership, who after World War II brought into being new organizations to deal more specifically with political and economic problems.

The new organizations, such as the Mexican American Political Association (MAPA) of California and Arizona, the Political Association of Spanish Speaking Organizations (PASO) of

Texas and Arizona, American Coordinating Council of Political Education (ACCPE) of Arizona, and the G. I. Forum of Texas and California, grew out of the need for direct action. The traditional organizations were, in the main, nonpartisan. LULAC, for example, specifically excludes politics.[10] It was precisely due to the nonpolitical basis of most of these organizations that the new leadership moved to organize its own groups. The leaders of these organizations were members of the older organizations and knew the impossible task of trying to reorient them to politics.

Nevertheless, the new leadership was concerned about old problems and new approaches. The new leadership belongs to a variety of the older organizations that were interested mainly in educational, fraternal, social, and recreational activities.[11] Those who devoted themselves to political activities found, however, that the very existence of these organizations (75 in Arizona alone) was one of the greatest obstacles to political cohesion. There were too many organizations, too many leaders, too much in-fighting.[12]

The difficulty of overall coordination has been the common denominator of Spanish-speaking political activities throughout the Southwest. This may be only a temporary problem, or it may persist because of the absence of powerful personalities or issues to unite *La Raza.*

On a practical basis the fragmentation in this ethnic group manifests itself in the lack of sufficient funds with which to support their candidates for office or promote political programs. In his race for the San Antonio City Council Gonzalez' largest single contribution was $50.00—from a Japanese restaurant owner![13]

The lack of support for political activities among the Spanish-speaking is not due to the group's lack of money. There are those of wealth among them. But the business and professional class has not identified itself with political activities. Moreover, the educated wealthy of this group have hung back in suspicion of the politically oriented.[14]

This is accounted for by the lack of political activists to persuade the educated wealthy that they are personally qualified and meritorious of support. These leaders often are not of that class and may even be tainted by histories of double-dealing among their own people.

Neither the Democratic nor the Republican party has sub-sidized Spanish-speaking political activities, for more or less the same reasons that the educated wealthy of their own group have held back. Even though the Democratic party would en-large its membership by encouraging the Spanish-speaking in politics, it has been slow in this activity for fear of having to share positions and policy-making processes with them. The Democratic party is not yet convinced that the Spanish-speak-ing are good for it.

Of course there are instances in which these ethnic leaders have worked closely with the Democratic party and vice versa. But the overwhelming fact is that the new, politically struc-tured Spanish-speaking organizations are either nonpartisan or bipartisan and not particularly Democratic. In fact, specific attempts by Mexican-American Democrats to bolt their party have been made in Colorado and Arizona.[15] One of the reasons for Mexican-Americans organizing outside the political parties is that the parties eschew this minority's leadership. As Dr. Hector Garcia has said, "My feeling is that nobody in this country of ours wants us to get organized."[16] Spanish-speaking Democratic workers have warned the Arizona American Co-ordinating Council of Political Education leaders that any attempt to make ACCPE a Democratic party organization would result in their separating the local chapters from the state organization. The stated reasons for organizing the ACCPE were that county Democratic leaders refused to let Spanish-speaking into important positions in the party. ACCPE was the minority's only means of illustrating that they had some power that, if not recognized, would be used against the party.[17]

The failure to gather money for political activities stems from "Juan Tortilla's" apathy. The average Spanish-speaking person has been uninvolved, lied to, and exploited so that he is not responsive to appeals. His suspiciousness is matched by that of the educated wealthy of his ethnic group and by Anglos of his same party. Although where Juan Tortilla has been worked with, talked to personally, and where sincere efforts have been made to involve him meaningfully, the results have been successful. Edward Roybal's courses in Los Angeles are a good case in point.

The function of the new organizations has not yet been

clarified. Although they all have constitutions and by-laws, their work is hampered by the fact that their objectives are too comprehensive. Almost all of these organizations, old and new, propose the need for improvement of the social, economic, and educational welfare of all the Spanish-speaking. The non- or bipartisan structure of these organizations casts too wide a net. It takes in members of all parties; the main emphasis is on the advancement of the Spanish-speaking regardless of party affiliation. When specific issues arise, they often call for a partisan response; this causes an internal struggle. Those who advocate partisan measures are met by arguments that the organization was not created to solve the problems of the Democratic party. Either no action at all is taken or the organization is split into factions.

As Eugene Marín points out, in Phoenix the Mexican Democrats Club welcomes Mexicans of all parties. Yet the president of the club has publicly stated that he would not support a Republican even if he were a Mexican.[18]

Henry B. Gonzalez has obviously avoided dependence upon organization support, and his personal independence has been the mainstay of his success and popularity. He did appeal to the Spanish-speaking organizations for support, but that was not his exclusive source of votes.[19] The Texas Congressman's breakthrough should illustrate a pattern. Anglo votes were needed for his election and they were got. To have used his ethnic background as the only reason for his candidacy would have meant certain failure. Since his earliest attempts to gain elective office, Gonzalez' Anglo support has increased far beyond the heavy Mexican-American districts of San Antonio. The alliance of Spanish-speaking, Negroes, labor, and "liberal Anglos" has been helpful to Gonzalez and has been useful for success in other areas.[20] This pattern, apparently developed disconnectedly, occurred in Phoenix in 1963 in the city elections and in the primary and general elections of 1964. At that time there was no knowledge of what had been done in San Antonio; circumstances brought the coalition into being.

The experience in Crystal City, Texas, has been influential, too, especially at the city level. In Crystal City 85 per cent of the population is Spanish-speaking, and the mere awareness of what could be done led to an all Spanish-speaking city council. It took work, of course, but, as Albert Peña, Jr., reports, once the people were persuaded to pay their poll taxes and register to vote, the outcome was inevitable.[21]

Important improvements were made, but the next election saw the initially successful Spanish-speaking weeded out. Two things account for this: (1) the in-fighting among the first city council of Spanish-speaking led to discrediting the council itself and (2) cast doubt on any ethnic council's ability to administer city problems responsibly. And although PASO had been instrumental in the success of these councilors, it was powerless two years later in the face of the "establishment's" slate, which included two Spanish-speaking persons.

Here again we see an anomaly of the political activities of this group in a two-party situation: the tendency of Spanish-speaking to run against others of their group. In every area of the Southwest where Spanish-speaking organize for action they are met by some of their own who for sincere reasons or because they have been "bought" are prepared to side against them.

Peña, nevertheless, asserts that the victory in Crystal City was a lesson that will never be forgotten. His hope is that more Crystal Cities will occur. More concretely, the fact that in the long run votes are the only force that brings results was amply illustrated. Despite the fact that PASO has been instrumental in getting an all Spanish-speaking city council in Crystal City, it was not capable of continuing its success. PASO, like many other Mexican-American organizations, grew and expanded quickly in the early 1960's. It was organized in Phoenix following the election of John F. Kennedy to the presidency. The Viva Kennedy Clubs were, in fact, the forerunners of this interstate group. However, before the Viva Kennedy Clubs, any number of Spanish-speaking persons devoted much time and effort to political activities in all five of the southwestern states. The people are truly responsible for the groundwork that has resulted in the present-day sophistication.

PASO national officers called the first ACCPE meeting. Their intent was to found an Arizona chapter of PASO. But in the Phoenix meeting, PASO was set aside for an organization more suited to the needs of the Arizona Spanish-speaking.[22] Several factors in the formation and development of ACCPE typify what has occurred in other organizations like it. Choosing the name of the organization occupied a large part of the debates and was one of the most fiercely fought issues. The younger members of the organization's convention championed some inclusion of Mexican in the title. The others argued its exclusion, with emphasis on American. The younger delegates repeatedly moved for Mexican over American and even opposed Spanish or Latin. Moreover, these advocates warned that the average person of Spanish-speaking background would react negatively to the title American Coordinating Council on Political Education. The opposition pointed out that it was high time that this ethnic group took its place in American society, that they were not, in fact, Mexicans and that the name should express full commitment to American approaches.

This view prevailed, and ACCPE spread rapidly throughout Arizona. The potential Mexican-American leadership grasped its meaning and applied its principles quickly. Within two years 2500 paid members were enrolled. Important chapters functioned in ten of Arizona's fourteen counties. ACCPE organizations were successful in winning various city council posts for Mexican-Americans where members of this group had never even been admitted to city swimming pools. ACCPE's most dramatic success was in Miami, Arizona, where five out of the seven city councilors elected in 1962 were Mexican-Americans.

By the 1964 elections ACCPE, like so many other organizations of its type, had come up against problems that brought its initial dynamism to a slowdown. Its successes at school board and city council levels could not be translated into victories at county, state, and federal levels. The seemingly obvious reasons were that the latter positions are partisan, whereas school board and city council offices are not. The Democratic and Republican organizations are not associated with these local positions, hence no real divisive influences.

Since ACCPE, MAPA, PASO, G. I. Forum and LULAC are bipartisan or nonpartisan, they confront themselves with impossible dilemmas when partisan issues and candidates are considered. Even though most of the membership of these organizations is Democratic the problem persists, because they refuse to commit themselves to either party. They fear being taken for granted. They fear loss of leverage. Bernie Valdez of Denver reports how a group of Spanish-speaking Democrats deserted their party and voted Republican with immediate rewards after the Republican victory.[23] In Arizona, Bob Robles of Yuma and Joe Benites of Phoenix both were given responsible assignments by the Republican party in the 1964 campaign.[24] There are countless instances like these.

This refusal to be incorporated into one party or the other theoretically allows these organizations a flexibility they otherwise could not enjoy. It permits primary endorsements, for example, that official party members and organizations are precluded from making. In many areas if no selection is made at the primary level, little or no choice would be available later, since the strength of one party or a given candidate is such that the opposition will provide only token opposition.

Hence the argument that these organizations must retain the freedom to make primary endorsements. This position also permits them to put up their own ethnic leaders without violating party regulations to support only party candidates. It is here that the Spanish-speaking organizations may be able to perform their most important function: the selection and support of talented and qualified candidates from their group.[25] As yet, however, these organizations have not contributed significantly in this way. A partial explanation is the newness of the organizations, most of which have come into being since 1945. This political inexperience has a demoralizing effect in that many of the ethnic leaders and groups have not been able to leap over the partisan barriers.[26] The hoped-for successes have not been realized merely by organizing the Spanish-speaking.

The potential is there but it must be searched out, financed, and worked for before continuous victories can be achieved. Gonzalez, Roybal, De La Garza, Montoya, and others indicate the possibilities for the future.

The bipartisan nature of the organizations, although it theoretically provides more political freedom, in practice denies the Spanish-speaking the very leverage they seek. The Democratic party, to which most of them belong, has not provided services and funds for these organizations since they are not part of the system. The party only recognizes and rewards its own. Moreover, Democratic party leaders are confident, and elections have proved, that the minorities tend to vote for the Democratic candidates anyway. Since no important part of the Spanish-speaking have voted otherwise, ethnic leaders have had little influence in convincing the Democratic party to reward them. The Republican party has shown little inclination to woo ethnic votes. The result is that ethnic leaders are up against political realities that neutralize their altruistic motives.

Congressman Gonzalez illustrates a possible compromise. His record presents a consistent support of Democratic (really Administration) issues. His vote in Congress has been 98 per cent in support of Democratic-sponsored bills. Yet Gonzalez enjoys widespread respect for his political individuality.[27]

Given America's two-party system, it is difficult to envision an influential role for ethnic political groups outside the framework of either of the parties. To gain credits for patronage loyalty to the party in power is a prerequisite. However numerous an ethnic group may be, in the long run its influence can only be exercised within the structure of one of the two parties.

If the strategy of siding with one party and then the other is adopted to gain short-run rewards, the suspicions of both parties are aroused, the dependability of the ethnic group is in serious question, and a situation of "votes to the highest bidder" develops. Moreover, a splintering of the ethnic groups might result. Always precariously unified, these groups tend to disintegrate in the face of serious issues to which the membership is not fully committed.[28] The ease with which these groups can be organized makes the solution of important issues difficult.

The Spanish-speaking also confront the financial problems involved in political activities. At any level of politics a certain amount of money is necessary. Mere work by numbers of Spanish-speaking and their organizations has not proved enough to put their candidates in office.

In city elections an expenditure of several hundred dollars per candidate to reach those eligible to vote is not unusual. And where newspaper, radio, and television coverage is necessary, it may run into the thousands. If the city is not divided into wards or districts, the Mexican-American candidates must run at large. Valdez reports that "subdistricting" of the legislative areas in Colorado was advantageous to the Mexican-American candidates. And when these candidates ran for city or county offices, they were successful mainly where there was a 30 per cent or more Spanish-speaking voting population.

County-wide elections increase all the problems inherent in

a city election. In addition to mailings and personal contacts
with ethnic organizations and neighborhoods, there is the need
to appeal to voters not of the ethnic group. In most instances
the cost of selling a minority candidate becomes prohibitive.

Some of the most successful approaches have been "alli-
ances" of Spanish-speaking, Negroes, labor, and liberal Anglo
groups, as in Texas and Arizona. The advantages have also
brought derogatory charges of "leftism," "socialism," and "pro-
communism" for the leaders of these political conglomerations.
The problems for the Spanish-speaking are nearly the same as
those they face when deciding whether they will work within
or without the political party system. There are two consequences: first, to make political advances, a de-emphasis of
La Raza must take place in a coalition; second, the freedom to
select their own candidates and the means by which to elect
them must be compromised. Compromise itself is difficult for
Spanish-speaking leaders. Weakening of their role in coalitions
is a factor that makes cooperation difficult.

But the need for financing campaigns persists. The traditional organizations cannot and will not provide funds for
these purposes. Their constitutions forbid this, and they actually do not have the money.

The emerging leaders have discovered no consistent way to
finance their newly created organizations, let alone finance
campaigns. The usual way of raising funds is by membership
dues of $1.00 to $5.00 per year per member. At the outset the
members of the organizing group usually pay this amount.
The second annual dues are more difficult to collect, and expansion of membership does not solve the problem either.

Parties, barbecues, dances, "tamaladas," rafflles, and fairs
are also used to raise funds. These are not altogether unsuccessful, but there are so many organizations, political and
otherwise, doing the same thing that this is not a reliable
source of income.

There are two other sources of income. One is the solicita-
tion of funds from wealthy persons of the same ethnic group.
However, the educated wealthy have not responded gener-
ously. People of this class do not have confidence in the solicit-
ing group, or they are already oversolicited, or they simply do
not believe in the efficacy of politics. The only other approach
is to try to persuade the leaders of either of the two major

political parties that Spanish-speaking political activities be subsidized. This, however, implies that a particular ethnic leader represents a substantial part of the ethnic community and that he pledges the group to support the party solicited. In many instances the response is negative. Most ethnic leaders of integrity and respect never make requests on such a basis. But even when they do the results have been more harmful than helpful. The party cooperating on this basis inevitably is disappointed with lack of votes delivered and talk that the ethnic leader is all the richer for the bargain.

Fund-raising is one of the most serious obstacles to ethnic organizational growth, but it is not entirely due to the lack of money among Mexican-Americans. It is the lack of defined objectives worthy of achievement that prevents money from flowing into the treasuries of those organizations sponsoring candidates or issues. Neither a theoretical position nor a theoretical spokesman of this ethnic group has arisen to inspire Juan Tortilla to dig deep into his pocket for political activities. The Spanish-speaking leaders have taken one step in voicing the widespread feeling that something ought to be done about lack of education, poverty, crime, delinquency, ill health, and lack of employment. But it is one thing to describe the problems and quite another to solve them.

Specific not general remedial action is needed, and the ethnic leadership is divided precisely along those lines. Those who seek specific action, the "radicals," are temperamentally not suited to working with the "diplomats." The radicals want to drive hard to get results. When there is discrimination against fellow Spanish-speaking they are ready to mobilize against the establishment. They endear themselves by energetically seeking employment for "their people." They are outspoken; they consider that there is a war on and that there is an enemy that must be brought into the open, identified, and demolished.

The diplomats, as the name implies, are not unaware of the problems confronting the ethnic group. But they are not sure which route to take in solving them. They appear to be constantly in a dilemma. The radicals accuse them of being incapable of action and, therefore, not the best representatives of the Spanish-speaking people.

However, the diplomats are the only ones who can communicate with the world outside the ethnic group. Because of their education, their professional or business positions, they are in daily contact with the leaders of the dominant society. They are the bridge over which no one travels. That is the tragedy of this group. The diplomats come from the poor and uneducated, they strive to rise and improve themselves, and then they do not know what the next step is. As in Plato's Allegory of the Cave, should one return into the darkness to help lead out the unfortunate or remain in the light of day, separate and aloof.

This is a serious ethical problem in political activity. The diplomats alone have the ability to articulate the needs of their ethnic group, and with study and dedication they could devise the means to achieve political action. However, going among the Spanish-speaking of lesser education and social status can cool the ardor of the most stout-hearted reformer. He is almost never completely understood by his ethnic brethren and is usually under sharp attack from ethnic leaders of lesser education.

The diplomat chooses one of two alternatives. Either he tries to work within the structure of the existing organizations and leadership, or he attempts to organize yet another group. In any case, the radical leadership regards the diplomat as a threat and a Johnny-come-lately. And unless the diplomat has wealth and power or easy access to it, his efforts are neutralized by the problems that obstruct the other leaders and their organizations.

This aspect of the problem of the Spanish-speaking is perhaps the most crucial. The discussion of leadership presented here is only cursory and preliminary. This is the least researched and least understood aspect of ethnic life in the United States.[32] All political activity among the Spanish-speaking ought to be studied more thoroughly. The fact that some work has already been done and certain projects are now underway ought not to preclude further research. As a result of a variety of studies by different persons and groups we will learn what constitutes irreducibly Spanish-speaking problems. Enlightening action programs for this large and important minority will not be forthcoming without this basis.

The question of leadership and research leading to a better understanding of it extends into several areas. For example, there ought not to be any reluctance to finance research that could lead to training Spanish-speaking leadership for fear that it might become political or controversial. Instead, providing training in the techniques and concepts of leadership would be an important contribution to American society.

Some of the emerging leadership inevitably will concern itself with political activities. On the other hand, the leadership may very well orient itself to combating lack of education, delinquency, economic and health problems. The point is that there is a pressing need for leadership. Each of the problems involved in political activities of the Spanish-speaking in the Southwest should be more thoroughly investigated, and present conclusions should only be tentative.

REFERENCES

1. Bernard Valdez, "Political Participation of Spanish surnamed in Colorado," a report submitted to Dr. Julian Samora, 1965.
2. Sister Frances Woods, "The Ethnic Leader," *Mexican Ethnic Leadership in San Antonio, Texas,* pp. 63–66.
3. *Ibid.,* pp. 85–88.
4. *Ibid.,* pp. 68.
5. Sister Frances Woods, *passim.*
6. Eugene Rodriguez, Jr., "*Henry B. Gonzalez, a Political Profile*" (Unpublished master's essay, St. Mary's University, Texas, 1965).
7. Eugene A. Marín, "The Mexican-American in Arizona Politics," a report submitted to Dr. Julian Samora, 1965, p. 14.
8. *Ibid.,* p. 25.
9. Rodriguez, master's essay, p. 27.
10. Albert A. Peña, Jr., "Politics and the Mexican-American in South Texas," a report submitted to Dr. Julian Samora, 1965, p. 4.
11. Sister Frances Woods, pp. 87–88.
12. Marín, p. 6.
13. Rodriguez, p. 55.
14. Sister Frances Woods, *passim.*
15. Valdez, p. 7.
16. Marín, p. 12.
17. *Ibid.,* pp. 12–13.
18. *Ibid.,* p. 14.
19. Rodriguez, *passim.*
20. Peña, p. 5.
21. Peña, pp. 4–5.
22. Marín, p. 12.

23. Valdez, p. 7.
24. Marín, p. 22.
25. Rodriguez, pp. 153–157.
26. Sister Frances Woods, *passim.*
27. Rodriguez, *passim.*
28. Sister Frances Woods, pp. 85–87.
29. Valdez, p. 5.
30. Peña, p. 3.
31. Sister Frances Woods, pp. 69–74.
32. Sister Frances Woods, pp. 74–80.

iv:The Migrant Worker

REV. WILLIAM E. SCHOLES

The Problem

In a "totem-pole" economy it is necessary by definition that
someone has to be at the top and someone else at the bottom.
Where muscle and manual dexterity are in greater supply than
the demand, they are considered to be at a lower purchase
level than the skills of the bookkeeper or clerk or machine
operator. Moreover, in an area of our economy where many
costs are fixed, where one of the few variables is the price of
labor, the pressure has always been to have available a supply
of labor under conditions that make possible its purchase at
the lowest possible rate.

Its History

In the early days of our country, along the eastern seaboard,
Negro slaves filled the need for cheap labor. Later, as a result
of economic, religious, and political upheavals in Europe,
wave after wave of immigrants approached this country full of
hope and ambition. As each group arrived, with cultural differences and language problems, its people were forced to accept
the most menial and lowest paid tasks as cooks, dishwashers,
dock hands, stokers, and railroad laborers. Concomitant results
were poor housing, poor health facilities, difficulties in education, and social isolation. With the coming of each new group
the prior one took a step up the ladder. Thus the slum areas
of our large cities have been occupied by a succession of ethnic
groups.

However, where there were large numbers of Negroes,
immigrants were not needed and pressure was not exerted

upward by new arrivals. Other factors related to racial distinctions, prejudice, and the economic sterilization of the South in the years after Emancipation united to make the American Negro the general exception to the normally expected assimilation and economic progression.

Whereas the great need for cheap labor in the Northeast was in heavy industry, the need in the South and West was for agricultural labor. The need in the Southeast was filled by former slaves and their children. On the West Coast, however, the need was filled by the Chinese, in numbers great enough to be an eventual threat to domestic labor. Therefore, the 1882 Exclusion Act was passed, drying up this source. The Chinese were followed by Japanese in West Coast farm labor until 1906, when this source also came to an end. Since then Filipinos have been used but not to the extent that they have influenced our agricultural economy.

Another group that has played a major role in the agricultural labor story has been the Anglos who were forced out of Oklahoma, Arkansas, and Missouri when their small farms failed from erosion in the dust-bowl era and during the economic crises of depression years. Their plight was highlighted by Steinbeck and by a succession of exposés up to and including the CBS production of "Harvest of Shame." However, those still available as seasonal farm laborers present much the same picture as that made famous by Steinbeck. Although the vintage of car has changed and greater education is available, the families of these people are still a major source of seasonal farm labor. They are agriculturally oriented and have not stepped up the economic ladder as quickly as one might have supposed, although within the migrant agricultural labor force they tend to think of themselves as the favored group and are somewhat selective about their jobs, tending to concentrate in the harvesting of fruits and berries.

In the western part of the United States Indian Americans have also been used as seasonal farm laborers. In some areas they are used only as a last resort because they are considered unreliable. In other areas they are sought after as the best help available. There are few areas where they have been used in overwhelming numbers; rather they are scattered through most of the fields of the far West. The greatest exception to this is in the State of Washington where our own American

Indians, plus Canadian Indians, make up a large percentage of the work force.

However, the most important group within our seasonal agricultural labor force has been Spanish-speaking persons. Unfortunately, people of Spanish-speaking heritage have too often been considered as a homogeneous group. This is a most erroneous assumption, for they are no more all alike than are all English-speaking persons. They represent different origins and different cultures, with language background being the only common denominator. Even this is not too common, for the Spanish of the Mexican or the Mexican-background American, or the Cuban, or the Puerto Rican varies almost as widely within groups as it does among groups.

The recent Cuban immigration has shown clearly that relatively few of the refugees were agriculturally oriented, and therefore most were not acceptable as farm laborers. The recent heavy influx of Puerto Ricans from the urban centers of the Island has been to the urban centers of the mainland, bringing us to the point at which there are more Puerto Ricans in New York City than in San Juan. On the other hand, the rural-oriented Puerto Rican has been used in the farm labor market of the Northeast very successfully since about 1950. A carefully worked-out program of farm labor has always given the Puerto Rican the kind of stability and control of working conditions that was seldom available to other people in seasonal farm labor groups. Controls on wages and working conditions enforced by representatives of Puerto Rico have made their conditions more tolerable than those of others.

Spanish-Speaking Agricultural Migrants of the Southwest

By far the largest group of domestic seasonal farm workers is the Mexican-Americans or Texas-Mexicans (the choice of terminology depends entirely upon the area). These are the people who have been a backbone of the seasonal agricultural labor force in the Southwest for over 60 years, and as a group they have not taken the anticipated step up the economic ladder for many reasons.

First, they have come primarily from the rural areas of our own country or Mexico and have been more admirably suited to farm work by tradition and cultural pattern than many previous groups.

Second, because of the 1924 National Origins Act there was consequent diminishing of immigration from Europe. Later World War II virtually eliminated immigration. Existing farm labor went into military service or higher paying war industry jobs, leaving the agricultural labor market in the Southwest to the Spanish-speaking population, who could not qualify for war industry because of language difficulty, discrimination, lack of skills, or lack of citizenship. The Bracero Agreement of 1942 with Mexico and the "wetback" took up most of the labor shortage (see Table 1).

Third, no new immigrant group was seeking the unskilled and semiskilled jobs, and enough labor was available directly from Mexico to prevent any radical shortage that might have increased wages. Thus the economic and social status of the migrant worker of Mexican background remained unchanged.

In recent years there has been a concerted attempt by Mexican seasonal farm laborers to become a part of settled life patterns. In the central and western parts of the United States almost every city and town has its slum area just outside or near the city limits, occupied by those Spanish-speaking people who are trying to improve their economic position by settling down. The factors mitigating against them are tremendous, such as lack of adequate education, lack of machine skills, etc. Important also is the fact that these people are still needed in the work of surrounding agriculture and thus the community tries to hold them available for seasonal farm work. Employment offices will not recommend them for other jobs. "Once a farm laborer, always a farm laborer" is the damning and unjust stereotype.

When any number have been able to make the climb over the barriers, their places have been taken by new arrivals from the Mexican-American border or from Mexico itself, so that we have a group that may slowly climb, but is replaced by others of similar background. With no immigration quota for Mexico, this source seems to be almost inexhaustible.

It must be remembered that parts of our country were part of Mexico up until relatively recent times and that those areas still share a strong cultural affinity with Mexico itself. Thus sections of Texas, New Mexico, Arizona, and California are most comfortable areas for newcomers from Mexico. Here the arrival from Mexico finds people who speak his language,

Table 1

SEASONAL AGRICULTURAL WORKER SOURCES, 1948–1965*

	Total Mexican Bracero Use	Peak Braceros Use	Wetbacks	Domestics
1948	35,345	–	193,852	–
1949	107,000	–	289,400	422,000†
1950	67,500	–	469,581	403,000†
1951	192,000	121,000	510,355	–
1952	197,100	125,473	531,719	352,000†
1953	201,380	159,174	839,149	–
1954	309,033	194,534	1,035,282	365,000†
1955	398,650	232,297	242,000 (est.)	–
1956	445,197	276,893	72,000 (est.)	427,000†
1957	436,049	260,522	44,000 (est.)	427,000†
1958	432,857	274,525	37,000 (est.)	–
1959	437,643	291,515	30,000 (est.)	303,000‡
1960	315,846	234,171	–	293,100‡
1961	291,420	208,511	–	–
1962	194,978	111,414	–	–
1963	186,865	90,142	–	–
1964	177,736	82,140	–	264,000‡
1965	–	–	–	278,000§

* Figures in Columns 1, 2, and 4 are from the Bureau of Employment Security, U. S. Department of Labor, as reported by U. S. Senate Sub-Committee on Migratory Labor, 2nd Report. Figures in Column 3 are from the U. S. Immigration Service in terms of illegal entrants apprehended and returned to Mexico. Many were returned more than once and many were never apprehended, so all figures here must represent only estimates of numbers of actual workers.

† From "The Hired Farm Working Force," Agricultural Marketing Service, U. S. Dept. of Agriculture *total* rather than *peak* figures.

‡ U. S. Dept. of Labor *peak* figures for July on use of Domestic Migrant Labor.

§ February 1965 peak. July peak would be higher.

understand his way of thinking, and generally treat him with warmth and friendship. But these are also the areas of high seasonal unemployment.

The Texas-Mexicans leave the rural areas of Texas in overwhelming numbers to move north with the cultivating and harvesting seasons. Towns such as Asherton in Texas may have a population of 2000 people in January and a population of 10 or 20 people in July, when everyone has moved north for the harvests. Nor do they move north from the rural areas alone; great numbers move out of San Antonio, as well as Laredo, Brownsville, Victoria, Eagle Pass, and Crystal City, Texas, to fan out into states as far north as Minnesota or Washington and Oregon, and as far east as Michigan and Ohio, stopping for seasonal work in almost all the states in between. These people are found working in appreciable numbers in at least 37 states, returning to Texas in the late fall; 16.2 per cent of

Table 2

STATES IN WHICH TEXAS MIGRANTS WORKED IN 1964*

Alabama	2,426	Montana	5,265
Arizona	633	Nebraska	3,345
Arkansas	1,170	Nevada	49
California	2,806	New Mexico	188
Colorado	5,674	New York	9
Delaware	51	North Dakota	2,489
Florida	1,384	Ohio	21,921
Idaho	15,709	Oklahoma	2,946
Illinois	14,841	Oregon	6,343
Indiana	13,354	Rhode Island	75
Iowa	2,201	South Carolina	203
Kansas	458	South Dakota	1,310
Kentucky	259	Tennessee	782
Louisiana	199	Utah	2,294
Michigan	28,598	Washington	4,338
Minnesota	10,427	Virginia	364
Mississippi	64	Wisconsin	17,982
Missouri	797	Wyoming	3,974

Total number of states, 37.

* Figures taken from the 1964 report of the Texas Council on Migrant Labor and the "Statistical Profile of the Spanish-Surname Population of Texas," University of Texas.

Figures represent total number of people—men, women, and children—on whom records were kept in the Texas Employment Commission or the Bureau of Labor Statistics. To these figures on "known" migrants may be added about 4 per cent to cover "free wheelers" who migrated without contacting either department.

the Spanish-speaking population of Texas is employed in farm labor.

Agricultural seasonal laborers were previously thought of as completely migrant, having their homes where the crops were ripe. However, the realization has grown that almost without exception each family has a home base, most probably in Texas, Arizona, or California. There they possibly own a "ranchito" of a half-acre in an area known to the community as the "colonia." They often have a small shack with few or no modern facilities, but it is "home" and in *that* community they *belong*. Most of them would like to stay there the year around, but there is relatively little work for them in Texas. Even though south Texas is a remarkable area which can grow at least two and sometimes three crops a year, the agricultural jobs have for the most part been traditionally usurped by the "wetback," the Bracero, the "green-carder" (resident alien), or the "commuter" (those with visitor's passes). Thus the most ambitious tend to be those who, after a stay at home, move north again with the crops in search of better income and something better for their families.

Most would be willing and eager to remain in the Rio Grande Valley of Texas year around if wages, working conditions, and stability of employment could be offered. Oddly enough, those who have been considered the finest agricultural labor for Michigan and Ohio, Wisconsin or Minnesota are not considered steady workers by the Texas farmer. They are deemed undependable because they are likely to walk out in the middle of a season and head north. But the reason for going north has been the pull of an hourly wage of 90¢ to $1.25 in the North as against a possible 45¢ to 70¢ in Texas. It has never been necessary for the Texas grower to compete with the higher wage from the North because of the existence of an abundant supply of labor from across the border.

The Wetback

During the years between 1945 and 1955 the great competition to Spanish-speaking farm labor came from the wetback, persons who crossed the Rio Grande River illegally to work on the United States side of the border. During the peak year of 1954, 1,035,282 separate deportations were recorded (see Table 1). Since many were deported more than once and others never apprehended, this indicates that a half million to a million individual wetbacks entered illegally from Mexico, flooding the labor market of Texas and California, finding their way as far north as the Canadian Border.

The Braceros

During World War II extra labor had been imported from Mexico on a temporary basis. Congress formalized the agreement with Mexico in 1951 under Public Law 78, with 190,745 Braceros contracted that year. The cost of this program to the general public in nineteen sixty-two alone was $3,168,000.[1] The numbers gradually increased until during the years 1956 through 1959, over 400,000 were contracted each year (see Table 1). Thus the domestic Spanish-speaking worker still had uncontrolled competition for his labor with no alternative but to migrate north.

The law insisted that no Nationals (braceros) could be employed as long as domestic labor was available. But availability depends on working conditions, and there are countless ways of discouraging a domestic if Nationals (braceros) are under contract. For instance, if the only housing is the barracks type suitable for single men and there is no housing for family groups, of course there will be no domestic family groups "available." If a good field with a good crop is assigned to braceros and a poor field with a poor crop is assigned to domestics, there will soon be no domestics available. Public Law 78 also called for the Nationals to be paid the "prevailing wage," which does not allow for any year-to-year increase.

The crux of the matter is this: as long as an unlimited supply of labor was available from Mexico, there could be no competition in the farm labor market here. A man could be told to take whatever was offered or get out. There were always plenty of others to take his place. Therefore, as long as the growers did not have to compete for laborers it was next to impossible to improve conditions.

Finally Congress recognized the inequity in the situation and warned farm labor employers that there would soon be no more imported labor available. In December 1963 Congress extended Public Law 78 for the "last time," noting for agriculture that there would be no further extensions and that the law allowing labor importations would end December 31, 1964.

The general impression was that Congress would reconsider. The pressure was heavy to bring such a reconsideration and another extension, but Public Law 78 died with the beginning of 1965.

Early in 1965 the expected competition for labor began. Wages and working conditions began to improve as growers sought ways of attracting labor. Labor Secretary Willard Wirtz had the power to interpret our general Immigration Law to provide for some importation of labor under extreme hardship circumstances where a real and proven shortage of labor existed. But he refused to circumvent the will of Congress by using this as a backdoor method of importation. He insisted that before any consideration could be given to an arrangement for emergency help, a specific area must have proved that an honest effort had been made to recruit domestic labor, that working conditions met certain standards, and that wages should be at a certain minimum (minimums set by the Department of Labor and in each instance somewhat higher than the general minimum that had been offered heretofore).

Under these conditions loud cries of impending disaster rose from many groups of agricultural producers. However, predicted shortages of labor generally did not materialize. In response to the better wages and working conditions now offered (essentially those working conditions formerly offered to braceros), farm labor was available in greater quantity than had been anticipated. In area after area predicted shortages did not appear.

We quote from an address of Senator Harrison J. Williams of New Jersey, as printed in the Congressional Record of June 9, 1965, page 12605:

> In our free enterprise system it is impossible for an industry to prosper, grow, and expand when it is primarily dependent on a foreign labor force or when it looks to the Federal Government for a guaranteed supply of workers. What other area of our economy relies on a foreign labor force? What other area of our country looks to the Federal Government for a guaranteed supply of workers? There is no other area. That is the reason why we are trying to establish within agriculture the same healthy atmosphere of domestic employment that we have in other industries.

It is obvious to many that foreign labor is not needed in this country to any real extent. A better way of helping the workers of Mexico is to aid them in developing their own agricultural economy. This we must do. Moreover, we must be alert to prevent efforts to open the doors once again to labor importation in the agricultural areas, which depresses wages and working conditions for all.

The Green Card

Another very real source of competition was the misuse of the "green card" under Public Law 414. The green card is the identification of the resident alien, the Mexican person in this country for a specific purpose and a specified length of time. Great numbers were guaranteed specific jobs and migrated to this country to do specific work. However, once the season was over they were free to go where they wished. Moreover, as they encountered the pressure of higher costs in this country, they tended to ask for higher wages. At this point they were often dismissed and replaced with a new set of green card workers. It should also be mentioned that these resident aliens are in the same position as other domestics in that they have none of the protections that were afforded the braceros. That is, they do not have to be paid the prevailing wage; they are not guaranteed a minimum number of days' work per week; and they are not provided transportation from their previous base of employment.

The Commuter

Another person in competition for south Texas jobs is the "commuter." The women among this group make up much of the domestic household help on the American side of the border. They may return home into Mexico each evening or may come on Monday morning and stay until Friday night. They might have been in this country for only an hour, or their stay may have been much longer. The men of this group can rather easily find short-term jobs as agricultural laborers in areas domestic labor has vacated because of low wages. These people of course are less dependable than those who have come in under Public Law 78, but more acceptable because of the lack of accompanying controls.

Travel Patterns

Thus regular patterns of migration have emerged. Certain

families from Crystal City will travel to the same areas of Minnesota year after year, while the farmer of south Texas expects to fill his labor needs from the surplus of day workers or green card holders, or workers on contract under Public Law 78 if they are available.

Those who have been migrating for the greater number of years tend to stabilize their work cycle and write ahead for jobs during the following season. It is not unusual to find them start early in the spring with strawberries in Louisiana, then move to asparagus in Illinois, cherries in Wisconsin, tomatoes in Ohio, cotton in Lubbock, Texas, and thus back home before Christmas.

Transportation and Living Conditions

The mode of travel varies widely as do the relationships to employers. In many areas of the country laborers work and travel under a crew leader, who makes the contract and receives the total payment. He in turn pays each worker after deducting for transportation and other costs. The crew leader may furnish the transportation in his own truck. However, the crew leader pattern may not hold for Texas-Mexicans traveling north to the central and western states. In most instances, even if a family travels with a group, they travel in their own cars or trucks, loading in all the possessions they might need during the time away from home. If they have their own truck they may transport many more of the necessities or extras that make life in a camp bearable. If they own a television, this goes along with their mattresses and other items to make a barren cabin in some far-off state at least as livable and homelike as they can. If they own a truck, later in the job they may earn more money by renting out the trucks at the peak of the season. The families who travel in their own cars, however, can usually transport only the bare necessities.

The Spanish-speaking migrant may work directly for a farmer who has one or two living units for migrants, or he may work for a large organization through a crew leader and field boss. In this instance he will probably have one of a long row of tiny cabins. The only water available most likely has to be carried some distance, and sanitary facilities are often primitive. In some areas field sanitation may be wholly lacking, even when the family is away from base camp for the total day.

Work Patterns

It is possible during the summer season to be working on a crop where the whole family can help (such as cherries or berries). Total income may be relatively satisfactory, but whether a migrant family has a good or poor season depends a great deal on continuity of employment without too much intervening travel, plus abundant crops (where picking is faster), plus a minimum of poor weather, which might keep them idle for days at a time or ruin a crop so that they would have to move on without having had income for days or weeks. Domestic Spanish-speaking migrants have never had the protections afforded the bracero. This is especially evident in lack of guarantees for a minimum of days of work each week.

In California the pattern varies somewhat. Certainly not all Spanish-speaking in California are migrants. But from Calexico in the south to Yuba City in the north, each city or town has its Mexican population. In California 41.9 per cent of all farm laborers are Spanish-speaking.[2] Most of these people have settled in the least affluent sections of town or live in camps or little colonies on the edge of town. The first group is made up of those who have managed to find a permanent job; the latter are usually those who depend upon seasonal agricultural employment. This means that they probably travel north and south within the state of California to find as much employment as possible during the year. If the area near their home base has enough crop variety to keep them busy for most of the season, they may remain, trying to find odd jobs between crops.

The Spanish-speaking agricultural worker in California has been plagued by the same kind of competition within the labor market as that which has caused difficulty for the Texas resident. The very existence of a huge labor pool across the border, which can be called upon by growers if the workers insist upon considerations in wages and working conditions, means that social action or labor organization is relatively ineffective.

Legislation

Another of the great problems facing Spanish-speaking seasonal farm workers is the fact that very few of the accepted patterns of labor legislation apply to them. One exception of sorts has been in relation to the Sugar Act of 1937. This Act

. . . contained within it a provision for the welfare of agricultural labor employed in the cultivation and harvesting of sugar beets and sugar cane. The primary object of the Act was to protect and even to promote the production of sugar in the United States, despite a world price for sugar which would have made American production economically impossible. The instrument employed was a subsidy from the Federal Government to growers of cane and beet sugar. A condition for the payment of these subsidies was the agreement of the growers to pay a wage for each operation which was no less than the wage promulgated annually by the Department of Agriculture.

The purpose of the provision was clear. Since tax revenues collected from the whole people were to be employed for the relief of a special group, the Sugar Act of 1937 expressed, as a matter of public policy, that it would be desirable to make the benefits available in some measure to sugar beet laborers as well as sugar beet farmers and refiners. The procedures were formally democratic. The wages promulgated by the government were to be determined as the result of open hearings at which any interested party could testify. Given the negligible organization of agricultural labor and the high degree of organization of the farmers through the refineries with which they contracted, the results have scarcely been those intended by the statute. Often there has been no representation of agricultural labor at the hearings. Where agricultural labor has been represented, its spokesmen have not been competent to testify with respect to the complexities of yields, production costs, sugar content, and prices which largely govern the minimum wages set.

The result has been in a sense worse than if the gesture had not been made. The wage thus established has tended strongly to become the wage paid. Though declared as a minimum wage, it has commonly been the only wage, supported by the sanction of government action and presented often by the growers to the workers as a wage which had become mandatory by government decree.[3]

Although efforts are now being made on a national scale to extend protective legislation to this segment of the labor force, the fact remains that at the time of this writing the seasonal farm laborer has no protection under national minimum wage laws, the National Labor Relations Act, or from abuses of child labor in certain areas. Neither do we have as yet a National Advisory Committee to examine constantly the needs of and speak for this most inarticulate group of citizens.

The argument is constantly advanced that labor legislation for farm workers should be a matter of state action. Many would agree that this is an appropriate area for state action, but by and large the states where this is most needed are the states that do not and will not act of themselves. The fact is that protective legislation considered most important for seasonal farm workers is nonexistent in 12 of the United States. Yet these 12 states use 47 per cent of the total seasonal labor force, including Texas, Kansas, Nebraska, and North Dakota, states which use Spanish-speaking labor almost exclusively.[4]

Housing

Thirty states have mandatory regulations for housing and sanitation in farm labor camps. Six additional states have either advisory or limited enforcement standards. Great strides toward the provision of good sanitary housing have been made in a few states as a whole and in isolated instances in almost every state. Housing codes, whether enforced or not, generally state that the camp site shall be properly graded and drained, and have structurally sound shelters. They provide that there shall be an adequate supply of water for drinking and bathing, properly constructed toilets or privies for both sexes as well as provision for proper disposal of garbage, waste water, and refuse. Screens are important, as are adequate laundry facilities.

Much progress has been made in the areas where better housing already exists and where there is some competition for labor. Moreover, the expiration of Public Law 78 on December 31, 1964 increased the need to improve housing in order to attract domestic labor. But it is obvious to those who are close to the situation that the mere existence of a law on the statute books does not mean that appropriations have been made or authority given for enforcement. The bulk of the housing remains relatively unchanged—it is still a disgrace.

There is wide variation in housing arrangements. In sugar beet country, where work is scattered, housing usually is in old farmhouses. In fruit and vegetable country the concentration of workers frequently makes large camps necessary. Often this housing is free to the worker, but in some states, such as California and Arizona, there is a charge for housing. It must be remembered that this work is in isolated areas where housing must somehow be provided, with or without charge. There seems to be little relation between the charge and the condition of the housing.

One of the great criticisms by growers is that seasonal farm workers do not take care of the housing provided. It is true that the workers sometimes damage housing and other facilities. Some of this is due to cultural factors, a fact that makes clear the need for an educational program. If a family does not understand the purpose of screens they may not care for them as they should.

Spanish-speaking people who understand what is expected of them tend to respond accordingly, and if the attitude of the owner is one of understanding, he tends to receive understanding in return. If a sanitary facility adequate for one family must do for twenty families, with no provision for cleaning and maintenance, the facility soon looks as if it has been dreadfully abused. Garbage cans are not always provided, but when they are, if there is no provision for them to be emptied periodically, we are asking for abuses. On occasion a grower provides housing but does not go near it from the beginning of the season until the end, and then is shocked by what he sees. But by and large the grower who provides reasonable maintenance of the housing, grounds, and sanitary facilities, who takes a personal interest, finds that he has less difficulty, and when isolated abuses occur he does not blame all migrants for them.

Greater efforts need to be made in every state, with the cooperation of the growers themselves, for the appropriation of funds for the enforcement of the existing housing laws.

Health

In 1962 the 87th Congress passed the Migrant Health Act, which was the first break-through nationally in legislation dealing with migratory farm workers. Through this Act Federal grants pay part of the costs for state and local projects to improve health services and health conditions among migrants. Under the Migrant Health Act the Public Health Service has assisted 60 county or multicounty projects in 29 states and Puerto Rico. The projects vary from one locality to another in the nature and scope of their services. They provide medical treatment for illness or injury, immunizations, casefinding and treatment of communicable diseases, pre- and postnatal care, and other services. Family health service clinics to provide medical and, in some instances, dental care have been established in or near farm labor camps; public health nurses have been employed to visit families in the camps on a regular schedule; sanitarians have joined projects to work with the migrants and with property owners to upgrade housing and environmental conditions; and health educators have been hired to work with the migrants to develop better understanding of modern medicine and good health practices.

Many farm worker communities and migrant camps are so isolated from the general community that doctors are not readily available, especially when the laborer is not able to take time off from work. If time is taken a day's work is given up, and the migrant may not have the money to pay for the services. Clinics are sometimes available but often at great distances, only during daytime, and only for residents. Therefore, more often than not, Spanish-speaking seasonal farm workers have had little or no medical services as a result of working hours, lack of funds, or lack of residence.

To these people the Migrant Health Act has been a Godsend. The careful management of meager funds has stretched the services as far as possible. Seldom has so little in public funds gone so far to relieve physical suffering and illness and to attack their causes. With doctors giving time on a reduced fee basis, with volunteers from the community plus the use of community health aides from among the seasonal workers, and with the generous use of the time of public health nurses, maximum numbers have been served. It is.not unusual for a mobile clinic with hours from 6:00 to 9:00 P.M. to run until 11:00 P.M. because of the great number of patients needing service. Moreover, the attitude of the public with respect to migrant health is improving. A report from the Laredo Migrant Health Project states in part:

> Migrant health workers and migrant programs should start with the knowledge that migrant workers are *people*. They do not have to be invited to the Country Club, but unless their treatment, and their social and living conditions are improved, the sanitation and public health needs of the migrant will continue to increase regardless of all the migrant health programs conducted, and this is the first real assistance they have ever received.

Education

School attendance is difficult for children of farm workers. They move so often that they are often behind in class. If they are in a community for a very short time the community often feels that it is not worth while to enroll new children and to take them through the process of accommodation and adjustment for only two or three weeks' stay. Often school districts into which children move are overcrowded, and even if they are accepted and urged to attend, the teacher may be too busy to give them the individual attention they need. If great numbers of seasonal workers move into an area for a short time they may completely overtax the local school system unless special arrangements are made.

There is also the problem of language. Especially among the very young children relatively little English may be understood and spoken. Cultural adjustment must also be made and cultural understanding is necessary if the educative process is to work.

Teachers have long held that children of Spanish-speaking seasonal farm laborers, given equal opportunity, show as much native intelligence and ability as children from other cultural and economic backgrounds. In a series of interviews with teachers and principals, these children were rated highest in truthfulness, cooperativeness, citizenship, and respect for law.[5] Yet in a study of 665 Spanish-speaking migrant families in Texas some few years ago only 32 per cent of the children had 30 weeks of schooling.[6] It is not surprising, then, that they show up poorly in scholastic achievement and are increasingly retarded in the higher grades regardless of native ability and desire for education. But attempts to provide good education for these young people can and are being made in some instances.

First, the community must care enough to urge the Spanish child to go to school, even if for a very short period of time. Special summer schools are being conducted in many states. Through the efforts of citizen groups in cooperation with local, state, and federal agencies, some real progress has been made toward improving the lot of the agricultural workers' child. In California and in Texas special attention has been given to the education of migrant children in the areas where they have their home base. Special efforts in California have been made in the area of curriculum. Operation "Head Start" may gradually help small children to enter prepared to meet the beginning years of school on an equal footing with children of other families who have had help at home or have gone through some preschool educative experience.

Second, parents must be urged to stay at home base for as much of the school year as possible. The State of Texas is now experimenting in the Rio Grande Valley with a special arrangement in migrant home base areas whereby an accelerated curriculum, longer school days, with fewer holidays, is attempting to give a full year of schooling to each child between the time he returns to home base with his parents and the time they take off again.

Third, communities into which migrants move are experimenting with effective methods of helping these young people. By hiring retired teachers or young mothers for the weeks of the crop season, special classes are occasionally provided. As often as possible these special teachers understand at least some Spanish, especially if they are working with the younger children who have little facility in English. This special attention may seem to be another form of segregation, but it need not be so if the necessary individual attention is given these children and they are moved into regular classes as rapidly as there is room and continue to receive a normal amount of attention and help.

Fourth, authorities in some areas, recognizing that children of Spanish-speaking agricultural workers may, in subtle ways, be discouraged by overcrowded school systems, are striving to find ways to assure their receiving the best integrated educational opportunities.

Welfare

Another difficult problem for migrant families is that of welfare. In most communities, counties, and states, residence laws are rigid. Families in financial difficulty often are not eligible for welfare since they move with the crops and seldom have long enough residency to qualify. They must depend upon emergency aid, if that is available. The same difficulty is experienced in the most instances in the availability of county health services. The elimination of residence requirements in general would be of great help. Spanish-speaking people, however, do as much as they can to help each other in difficult circumstances, and as a rule the seasonal agricultural worker is not the drain upon our welfare services he is normally thought to be. Preliminary reports tend to confirm our belief that requests for welfare services have diminished since the end of Public Law 78. A report from the Welfare Director of Monterey County, California showed that since the end of imported labor, greater opportunities have been afforded domestic farm labor. In April, 1965 only 77 families received welfare aid as compared with 313 families in April, 1964 because, "these men have found work picking crops which a year ago were picked by *braceros* from Mexico."[7]

Crew Leader Legislation

There has been a real attempt toward the registration of crew leaders.

> Farm labor contractors or crew leaders are responsible for placement of many of the migratory agricultural workers in farm jobs. Usually their duties are to contract with growers to recruit and supply workers, and, for these workers, enter into agreements with the growers as to wages, transportation, housing, and working conditions. Generally they receive a fee for such services, sometimes paid by the grower, sometimes by the workers. They may also supervise the work, control and distribute the wages, and make arrangements for board, lodging, and transportation of the migrants.
>
> Because this relationship of the farm labor contractor or crew leader with the migratory farm worker has led to some undesirable practices, eight States and the Federal Government regulate the activities of farm labor contractors or crew leaders.[8]

These laws are designed to minimize abuses, to assure prompt payment of wages when due, and to assure the worker that true information has been given about the terms and conditions of employment.

Transportation

At times workers have been crowded into farm trucks and transported over long distances under intolerable conditions. At present the Interstate Commerce Commission does regulate the transportation of three or more farm workers traveling at least 75 miles across state lines. They are authorized to check the safeness of the equipment used, to see that the drivers are properly licensed and do not drive for excessive periods of time, and to see that all passengers have seats, and to make certain that there is at least an eight-hour rest stop every 600 miles. Only eight states have their own laws relating to such transportation; these are California, Oregon, Colorado, New York, Connecticut, Pennsylvania, West Virginia, and North Carolina.

Child Labor

Under the Federal Fair Labor Standards Act a child under 16 years of age may not work in agriculture during school hours. The Federal Sugar Act prohibits the employment of children under 14 at any time. However in 18 states specific laws set a minimum age for children who work in agriculture. Together these laws are beginning to change the picture of child labor in agriculture, but much improvement is needed.

One of the difficulties comes from the seasonal farm worker families themselves. Because of the very meager income in seasonal agriculture, families want children to work with them as soon as possible to supplement the family income. Because of difficulties in school, children may become discouraged and feel they would rather work with their parents. Patterns of family organization among the Spanish-speaking people of the Southwest tend to encourage the practice of the whole family working together.

Minimum Wage

As yet no states have general laws that effectively apply a minimum wage to all seasonal agricultural labor. The only control at the moment is over those who would use the state employment services to recruit domestic agricultural help. This domestic help must be paid a going minimum wage if there is to be any consideration of requests for foreign labor during domestic help shortages. Wages have been as low as 35¢ or 40¢ an hour in some states, and as high as $1.75 in another. Generally speaking, 75¢ or 80¢ an hour has been considered normal in the south-central states. With the end of Public Law 78 and the consequent drive for domestic help, wages generally are rising toward $1.25 per hour. This may seem like the millennium to some, but it must be remembered that for a 50-hour week this would bring a total of only $62.50. We must also remember that for the seasonal agricultural worker there are rainy days when no work is available, and there are idle weeks between crops, and time must be taken out for travel. Also, no worker can find such a perfect crop rotation that he has 12 months' work. It is pretty well acknowledged that any agricultural worker is fortunate to have 35 weeks of work per year. This means that if he is one of the fortunate and rare few to work an average of 50 hours a week for 35 weeks at $1.25 per hour, his income is a little under $2200, or only two-thirds of the accepted poverty level for this country. Before this occupation becomes a stable one the wages must go way beyond $1.25 per hour, with contracts *guaranteeing a minimum number of hours per week and minimum number of weeks per year.*

Social Security

Seasonal agricultural workers are covered under Social Security, provided the laborer works for one employer 20 or more days in a year for cash wages figured on a time basis or if the employer pays him $150 or more in cash wages during the year. One of the difficulties has been the tremendous educative job to convince the workers of the importance of Social Security for them and to convince them that the money deducted from their wages is not going into the pocket of the employer. The second problem has been to be sure that wages so deducted are actually turned over to the government as Social Security payments and recorded accurately under the right name and number. The third problem is establishing who is the employer. The employer can be either the farmer or the crew leader. Neither is particularly anxious to undertake the extra work involved in record keeping. But as each year goes by a greater number of seasonal workers are regularly covered under Social Security.

Workmen's Compensation

Workmen's compensation is important in an occupation which is so hazardous.

As the agricultural industry increases its use of mechanical devices for sowing and harvesting crops, it becomes more evident that an ever-growing number of agricultural jobs involve hazardous conditions. In most hazardous occupations, industrial workers are covered by workmen's compensation laws, which, in case of a job injury, provide them with benefits to help make up for loss of wages, as well as with medical services, and, in a number of states, with some rehabilitation benefits.[9]

However, only 10 states now have laws applicable to the Spanish-speaking farm laborer. These include California, Wisconsin, and Ohio, states which use Spanish-speaking people from the Southwest. Only California provides benefits for agricultural workers under temporary disability insurance laws.

Continuing Legislation

Many other efforts in national migrant legislation which were unsuccessful, bills generally under the sponsorship of Senator Harrison Williams of New Jersey, have found acceptance through the Economic Opportunity Act of 1964. Through this Act funds are now available for special educational programs for adults and children, as well as day care centers for children. It is also possible under Title III-B of the Economic Opportunity Act to establish rest camps on the migrant routes and to experiment with field sanitation and camp facilities. Much of what was to be made available through specific legislation can be accomplished through this Act if communities are concerned enough to make the effort.

At the time of this writing new efforts are being made for specific national legislation that would establish a National Advisory Council on Migratory Labor; which would make effective for migrant farm labor certain of the child labor provisions of the Fair Labor Standards Act; which would provide the machinery for a national voluntary farm placement program; which would set piece rates to guarantee a minimum hourly wage; and which would guarantee to seasonal agricultural workers collective bargaining rights under an extension of the National Labor Relations Act. The last two are most basic and critical and will need every support possible.

Labor Organization

Probably the most important development affecting seasonal

farm labor among Spanish-speaking people of the Southwest has been the recent gains in labor organization. Over the years there have been sporadic attempts to organize farm labor, and from time to time important strikes have been called. However, in spite of real issues and concentrated leadership efforts, the opposition usually has been powerful enough to defeat these efforts. Some thought that the organization of farm labor could not be accomplished in the foreseeable future. Organizing efforts were too costly in time, manpower, and money.

However, Filipino workers who had been working in the 1965 grape harvest in the Coachella Valley of California at $1.40 per hour plus incentive were disappointed upon returning to the Delano area for the grape harvest to find that their wages for the same work were to be only $1.25 per hour plus a smaller incentive. They had lived and worked in the Delano area for years and felt that the area could pay wages at the same level as those offered in the Coachella Valley.

With the help of the Agricultural Workers Organizing Committee, they determined to do something about the situation. Letters were sent to employers asking for an opportunity to discuss wages, working conditions, and contracts. The letters were not answered, and there was no alternative but to strike on September 8, 1965. Mr. Al Green, with offices in Stockton, was directing the activities of the AWOC. The local organizer in Delano was Mr. Larry Itliong, who had been a resident of Delano for six years. At that time about 600 to 800 farm workers, mostly Filipinos, were involved.

Eight days later, on September 16, 1100 Mexican-American farm workers met and voted to join the strike. This was actually a meeting of the National Farm Workers Association, a grass-roots organization of Mexican-American workers. The Director of the National Farm Workers Association is Mr. Cesar Chavez, a former migrant, who had previously worked for the Community Service Organization of California. He has spent the last four years building the National Farm Workers Association as an indigenous organization completely supported by its membership.

On September 19, 1965 the Agricultural Workers Organizing Committee and the National Farm Workers Association created a joint strike committee. By September 20 more than 1200 Mexican-American farm workers had joined the Filipinos on strike, making a total of over 2000 workers who had left the fields.

Employers refused to recognize that a strike existed. Since farm workers had no recourse to the National Labor Relations Board, the growers were under no compulsion to recognize either the strike or the organization that sought to represent the workers. Their answer was to step up recruiting of workers to replace those who had left the fields. Many of those who left the fields in sympathy with the strike also left the area to work elsewhere, but as many as could be supported by the striking organizations remained to continue picketing operations.

What had originally been an isolated struggle soon caught the imagination of citizens in California and throughout the nation. Help in the form of personnel, food, clothing, and money soon began to arrive in Delano. Support came from the broadest representation of interests. Citizens' groups, unions, churches of all faiths, students, laborers, clergymen, and professional people from varying walks of life joined the picket lines and offered personal services. Among others, the United Auto Workers of the AFL-CIO pledged $5000 per month to support the strike.

In mid-December the city manager of Delano asked the City Council to request the services of the State Conciliation Service as mediators in the strike, but since the growers did not feel mediation was necessary the City Council refused to request this service on the grounds that it would be taking sides.

On October 7, 1965 the California State Department of Employment had formally certified that Schenley workers had a legitimate dispute with the Schenley ranch, therefore the logical counteraction to refusal to negotiate was to boycott Schenley products. Boycott of the Schenley Industries began in San Francisco and quickly spread throughout the country. Moreover, picketing was continued in all areas where Delano grapes were being sold or shipped.

There have been many arrests of workers, clergymen, and students during the strike, but at the insistence of the leadership of the farm workers theirs has been a nonviolent effort.

On March 17, 1966 the NFWA and others left Delano on a pilgrimage to Sacramento, both to make their plea to the Governor of California and to make their effort known to the nationwide public. The 300-mile march took 25 days, ending in Sacramento on Easter Sunday. Marchers were limited to about 100 to keep costs at a minimum and for safety on the roads. Workers were hosted on the march by other farm workers. This most orderly demonstration received acclaim and assistance all along the way, and the workers were joined by untold numbers of volunteer supporters at their own expense. During the last Saturday of the march over 500 people were involved. Over 1500 were at the rally that night, April 9. On Easter Sunday, April 10, there were nearly 4000 marchers, and approximately 8000 attended the rally, which the Governor did not attend. However, there was a victorious spirit in the Easter rally at Sacramento which had more than a touch of religious significance. On April 6 the marching strikers received word that agreement had been reached between Cesar Chavez, Director of NFWA, and the attorneys for Schenley Products, recognizing the Association as bargaining agent and calling for negotiation within a specified period of time. Shortly after this, word was received from the largest grower, the Di Giorgio Fruit Corporation, that the company had called on the California State Conciliation Service to hold secret elections on their property to determine if workers wished to be represented by any labor union. In other words, negotiations have been called for by the Di Giorgio Corporation, but on their terms, which have not at the time of this writing been acceded to by the NFWA. The reasons for this are obvious. Negotiations are never real when limiting conditions are laid down by one party. Moreover, the Di Giorgio Farms have a minimum number of migrants working for them at this time. Many of their present help are full-time, year-round employees, or are strikebreakers. Further negotiation will be necessary before any such strike vote can be valid.

At this writing the strike still continues, and the boycott has been shifted from Schenley to Di Giorgio products. The Spanish-speaking farm laborers who carried the emblem of Our Lady of Guadalupe from Delano to Sacramento have persevered longer than anyone believed possible, and have received more support from the public than even they dreamed of. The struggle has just begun, for the local growers are not willing to follow the lead of Schenley. And even if the efforts in Delano are successful, it is only the beginning of further struggle in other areas. What has been accomplished can and ought to be the basis for an all-out citizens' effort across the nation to help all people gain protection through the National Labor Relations Act so that future efforts may not be as long and hard.

Above all, this effort has clearly proved that people can do for themselves what outside leadership cannot do. It has proved beyond doubt that when the end is important to the people themselves, they can organize effectively; can develop their own leadership; are willing to sacrifice; do accept responsibility both for their own organizations and their own actions; and will act for themselves to solve their problems in their own responsible way if given the slightest opportunity.

Prospects for the Future

There is every reason to feel that in the years to come, Spanish-speaking Americans will continue to be the basic source of farm laborers. If the income from such labor is to be raised to a level to sustain a family in decency, and if the working and living conditions associated with it are to enable a man to find pride and dignity in his occupation, concerted action toward a minimum wage is imperative. But the tendency is for the minimum wage to become the maximum wage unless the Spanish-speaking farm workers join in indigenous unions or farm labor cooperatives that can negotiate contracts. And any such efforts will be relatively ineffectual if there is a resumption of the importation of foreign labor. When a foreign labor force is easily available there can be no real competition for labor, and farm workers have no bargaining position. Efforts of workers to improve their lot will also be relatively ineffectual until farm labor is included under the protection of the National Labor Relations Act. Even if a foreign labor force is *not* available it will be important that Spanish-speaking American farm laborers have the protections of the Labor Relations Act to support their position and to insure bargaining in good faith. When a man is able to put a value on his own labor, he becomes a person rather than a human machine. When he is able to put a value on his labor, he becomes a person of worth in his sight and in the sight of God and man.

Many groups are trying to help the Spanish-speaking in this area of personal development. In California alone there are a number of groups working to help. Notable is the previously mentioned work of Mr. Cesar Chavez, who has been attempting to gather Mexican-American farm laborers into their own strong labor cooperative under indigenous leadership, as a union without controls from other organizations. The work of the American Friends Service Committee in community development and self-help housing has produced interesting results. The Communities Service Organization has been helping the Mexican-American people of various communities to find self-expression as registered citizens and in small organizations for community improvement and opportunity. The Migrant Ministry of the Northern and Southern California Councils of Churches has been serving the Mexican-American migrant population for many years. In recent years it has attempted to identify community leadership among the farm labor population, encouraging them in all efforts to find identity and creative expression as a recognized citizen group working for better wages, working conditions, and community services. Such work is based on the belief that human beings have the *ability* to make decisions for themselves and that they have the *right* to make their own decisions and to speak as a group for themselves and for their place in society.

When all has been said, we come again and again to the conclusion that the fundamental need of Spanish-speaking seasonal farm laborers is for a realistic living wage, plus security of employment under contract. It is doubtful that this will ever happen until the people themselves form strong organizations or unions with enough power to bring about change. This they must do for themselves. They will need people to help them in developing their role and purpose: people who will help them get started and then withdraw from direct leadership; people and groups who out of real concern will stand ready to help and support when the pressures from the agri-business community get rough; groups who will help them gain protection under the National Labor Relations Act. The nonfarm community must stand ready to help, but the basic job of developing labor associations with power must be theirs alone under their own developing leadership.

An electrician or a carpenter is usually proud of his trade. Farm work is a trade that also involves a specific skill. We assert that problems will continue to beset the Spanish-speaking American in farm labor until the conditions of living and working make this a dignified occupation—until he personally has come to the place where he too can hold his head high and state with personal pride the fact that he is a farm worker.

REFERENCES

1. Hearings before the Senate Subcommittee on Migratory Labor, June 19, 1963.
2. Division of Fair Employment Practices, *Californians of Spanish Surname*, State of California, Dept. of Industrial Relations, San Francisco, May, 1964.
3. Lloyd H. Fisher, *The Harvest Labor Market In California* (Cambridge: Harvard University Press, 1953), pp. 106–107.
4. Bureau of Labor Standards, "Coverage of Agricultural Workers Under State and Federal Labor Laws," a Map Series. U. S. Dept. of Labor, *Bulletin 264*, 1964.
5. Shirley E. Greene, *The Education of Migrant Children* (Washington, D. C.: The Department of Rural Education, NEA, 1954), p. 101.
6. *Ibid.*, pp. 72 and 77.
7. *"The Religious Newsweekly"* (475 Riverside Drive, New York, N. Y.), June 22, 1965.
8. Bureau of Labor Standards, "Major Provisions of State and Federal Farm Labor Contractor Laws," U. S. Department of Labor *Bulletin 275*, May, 1965.
9. Bureau of Labor Standards, *Coverage of Agricultural Workers Under State and Federal Labor Laws*, U. S. Department of Labor, Washington, D. C., 1964.
10. Harley L. Browning and S. Dale McLemore, *A Statistical Profile of the Spanish-Surname Population of Texas* (Austin: Bureau of Business Research, The University of Texas, 1964).

National Council on Agricultural Life and Labor, *Action Call Bulletins* (Washington, D. C.: June and July, 1965).
Fred H. Schmidt, *After the Bracero: An Inquiry Into the Problems of Farm Labor Recruitment* (Los Angeles: Institute of Industrial Relations, University of California, October, 1964).
National Advisory Committee on Farm Labor, *Agribusiness and Its Workers* 112 East 19th Street, New York, N. Y., October, 1963.
Mary Ellen Leary, "As the Braceros Leave," *The Reporter*, January 28, 1965.
U. S. Department of Labor, *Background Information on Farm Labor*, Washington, D. C., March 19, 1965.

Children's Bureau, U. S. Department of Health, Education and Welfare, "Children in Migrant Families," a report to the Committee of Appropriations, December, 1960.

Public Health Service, "Domestic Agricultural Migrants in the United States, Maps and Statistics," *Publication No. 540*, U. S. Department of Health, Education and Welfare, Washington, D. C., 1960.

U. S. Commission on Civil Rights, A report on "Equal Opportunity in Farm Programs," 1965.

National Council of Churches, *Ethical Goals for Agricultural Policy*, adopted by The General Board, June 4, 1958.

American Public Health Association, Inc., *Evaluatory Study on Operations of the Migrant Health Program Under the Migrant Health Act*, 1790 Broadway, New York, N. Y., 1964.

George L. Mehren, Excerpts of remarks at Grocery Manufacturers Mid-Year Meeting, White Sulphur Springs, W. Va., June 14, 1965.

U. S. Department of Labor, *Fact Sheet on the Labor Department Hearings Concerning the Importation of Foreign Farm Workers*, October, 1964.

Clarence Fuqua, *Facts, Factors, Forces and Future for the Church In Its Concern for the Spanish-speaking in Texas*, Texas Council of Churches, Austin, January, 1963.

U. S. Department of Labor, *Farm Labor Developments*, monthly publication, Manpower Administration, Bureau of Employment Security, August, 1960 and October, 1964.

————, *Farm Labor Developments*, "Employment and Wage Supplement," January, February, March, and June, 1965.

————, *Farm Labor Developments*, "Review and Outlook," January, 1965.

Citizens for Farm Labor, "Farm Labor—Equal Rights for Agricultural Workers," P. O. Box 1172, Berkeley, California, II, 6 (1965).

Bureau of Employment Security, "Influence of Harvest Labor Wages on Retail Prices," Statistical reports of the U. S. Department of Labor, July 12 and July 27, 1965.

Public Health Service, "Interim Report on Status of Program Activities Under the Migrant Health Act," P. L. 87-692, by Department of Health, Education and Welfare, June 30, 1964.

Julian W. Mack, "Memorandum on Hired Agricultural Labor to Delegates to 1961 Convention, American Veterans Committee," San Francisco, California.

Ernesto Galarza, *Merchants of Labor* (San Jose, California: The Rosicrucian Press, Ltd., 1964).

The President's Committee on Migratory Labor, "Mexican Farm

Labor Program Consultants Report," Washington, D. C., October, 1959.

Farm Placement Service, "Mexican Workers, for Employers of Contracted Mexican Workers in United States Agriculture," U. S. Department of Labor, 1956.

The President's Commission on Migratory Labor, "Migratory Labor in American Agriculture," Report of the President's Commission on Migratory Labor, Washington, D. C., 1951.

"News from U. S. Department of Labor," July 1, 1965, USDL–6672; December 19, 1964, USDL–6642.

National Advisory Committee on Farm Labor, "Poverty on the Land," a Report on the Public Hearings held by the National Advisory Committee on Farm Labor, Washington, D. C., May 18–19, 1964.

Samuel Ramos, *Profile of Man and Culture in Mexico*, trans. Peter G. Earle (New York: McGraw-Hill Book Co., 1963).

Leo Do Nieto, *Religious Profile of Spanish Surname Population in Austin and Travis County, Texas, 1965*, Texas Council of Churches, Austin, March, 1965.

The National Committee on the Education of Migrant Children, "Report of the National Workshop on The Education of Migrant Children," 145 East 32nd Street, New York, N. Y., 1964.

———, "Report of the Texas Farm Labor Conference," Texas Committee for Migrant Farm Workers, 5511 San Pedro, San Antonio, Texas, 1964.

California State Department of Health, "Review of Bureau of Health Education in the Seasonal Agricultural Workers Health Program," May–October, 1961.

Public Health Service, "Selected Films for Migrant Workers," Publication No. 869, revised 1964.

Bertha Blair, Anne O. Lively, and Glen W. Trimble, *Spanish-Speaking Americans*, The National Council of Churches, 475 Riverside Drive, New York, N. Y., 1959.

U. S. Commission on Civil Rights, "Spanish-Speaking Peoples," staff paper submitted February 5, 1964.

Bureau of Labor Standards, "Standards for Good Day-Haul Practices," U. S. Department of Labor, Washington, D. C., 1964.

Bureau of Labor Standards, Bulletin 274, "State Committees of Seasonal Agricultural Labor," U. S. Department of Labor, Washington, D. C., June, 1965.

Samuel A. Snyder, Jr., "Statement at Hearing of the Agriculture Committee of the U. S. Senate on Criteria for Importation of Foreign Farm Workers under P. L. 414," Washington, D. C., January 15, 1965.

Bureau of Labor Standards, "Status of Agricultural Workers Under

State and Federal Labor Laws," U. S. Department of Labor, Washington, D. C., Fact Sheet No. 2, January, 1965.

Texas Council on Migrant Labor, "Texas Migrant Labor: The 1964 Migration," San Antonio, Texas, April, 1965.

National Advisory Committee on Farm Labor, "The Case for the Domestic Farm Worker," 112 East 19th Street, New York, N. Y., April, 1965.

Fay Bennett, "The Condition of Farm Workers in 1963," and "The Condition of Farm Workers in 1964," Annual Reports to the Board of Directors of National Sharecroppers Fund, 112 East 19th Street, New York, N. Y., 1963–1964.

Senator Harrison J. Williams, "Migratory Agricultural Workers," The Congressional Record, 89th Congress, First Session, June 9, 1965.

National Council on Agricultural Life and Labor, "The Farm Labor Policy of the Federal Government, With Special Reference to the Mexican Farm Labor Program (Public Law 78)," 1751 N Street, N.W., Washington 6, D. C., May, 1960.

National Council of Churches, "The Fifth Decade," Report of National Study Conference on The Church and Migratory Farm Labor, 1961.

Daniel Panger, "The Forgotten Ones," reprinted from *The Progressive*, by National Advisory Committee on Farm Labor, New York, 1963.

Industrial Union Department, "The Forgottenest," reprinted from IUD Agenda, May, 1965, by Information Center, AFL-CIO, 815 Sixteenth Street, N.W., Washington, D.C.

Lloyd H. Fisher, *The Harvest Labor Market in California* (Cambridge, Mass.: Harvard University Press, 1953).

Marketing Research Service, "The Hired Farm Working Force," Department of Agriculture, Washington, D. C., 1964.

Ben H. Bagdikian, "The Invisible Americans," reprinted from *The Saturday Evening Post*, December 21–28, 1963.

William Madsen, *The Mexican-Americans of South Texas* (New York: Holt, Rinehart and Winston, 1965).

Migrant Ministry Dept. of the National Council of Churches, "The Migrant Ministry Annual Report," 1963, 1964, 1965, New York.

Migrant Ministry Dept. of the National Council of Churches, "The Migrant Ministry Today, A Self-Evaluation of Direct Services and Progress Toward Legislative Goals," New York, 1960.

United States Senate Committee on Labor and Public Welfare, "The Migratory Farm Labor Problem in the United States," U. S. Government Printing Office #68037, 1961.

U. S. Senate Subcommittee on Migratory Labor, Report No. 1225,

"The Migratory Farm Labor Problem in the United States," U. S. Government Printing Office, March 1, 1962.

Truman E. Moore, *The Slaves We Rent* (New York: Random House, 1965).

Elmer Kelton, *These Are Braceros,* The San Angelo Standard, Inc., 1958.

Louisa R. Shotwell, *This Is The Migrant,* National Council of Churches, 475 Riverside Drive, New York, N. Y.

Bureau of the Census, *"United States Census of Population 1960— Persons of Spanish Surname,"* U. S. Department of Commerce.

Texas State Federation of Labor (AFL), *What Price Wetbacks?* American G. I. Forum of Texas, Austin, Texas.

v: The Right to Equal Opportunity

LAWRENCE B. GLICK

Two ethnic, or racial, groups in the United States are currently distinguished by their inferior economic status as compared with the nation as a whole. These are the Negroes and the Spanish-speaking. It is not surprising that these two groups, however dissimilar, have in common histories unlike those of any other groups in the nation. The Negroes have endured slavery in the United States, and the Spanish-speaking have suffered defeat in battle with the United States.

From these histories comes the heritage of civil inequality and social prejudice that are, in large part, the basis for present economic deprivation. The struggle for Negro civil rights has focused attention on a past in which such rights have been denied. Little attention has been given to the history of the Spanish-speaking, and their civil rights have largely been ignored.

The status of the Spanish-speaking has never been rigidly fixed by statute and ordinance as was that of Negroes in the states of the South. Nevertheless, the unwritten laws of many communities in Arizona, California, Texas, New Mexico, and Colorado established a degrading system of segregation and social inferiority that insured a subservient status for them. Many communities, with at least the tacit approval of local government, enforced the segregation of this group in schools and in housing, restricted their level of employment, and prohibited their participation in public affairs such as service on juries and police forces. Moreover, in many communities the police have failed to provide protection for them or, in fact, have singled them out for harrassment.

The object of this paper is to indicate briefly the historical basis for the status of the Spanish-speaking group, the current situation, the programs in progress to improve the situation, and some views of the prospect for the future.

Education

In the school segregation cases of 1954, *Brown* v. *Board of Education*, (347 U. S. 483), the United States Supreme Court held that the segregation by race of children in public schools is a deprivation of their basic right to equal educational opportunity. To what extent Spanish-speaking children have been denied this right through the process of enforced segregation is difficult to estimate. However, that such segregation existed is clearly shown by suits as early as 1930 and as recently as 1957 to require school officials to cease the practice of segregating Spanish-speaking children solely on the basis of their ethnic origin.

In *Independent School District* v. *Salvatierra* (Texas Civ. App. 33 S.W. 2nd 790 (1930)), it was alleged that Spanish-speaking children were denied equal protection of the laws under the Constitution because a separate school was maintained for Spanish-speaking, mostly migrant children. The court held the maintenance of separate facilities to be constitutional if the good faith purpose was to solve the children's language and educational retardation problems. It was held to be unlawful discrimination to the extent that it applied only to Mexicans and without any consideration of each child's abilities. Thus it is clear that there is no legal basis for the segregation of Spanish-speaking pupils in Texas, unless for the legitimate purposes of special education reasonably designed to overcome educational deficiencies, particularly those of language.[1]

Apparently the Salvatierra case did not end the practice of segregation in Texas. In 1957, three years after the school segregation cases, another suit was brought in behalf of Spanish-speaking children to achieve their admission to school on a nonsegregated basis. In this case, *Hernandez* v. *Driscoll* (Civ. No. 1384, U.S.D.C. So. Dist., Tex., Jan. 11, 1957, 2 *Race Rel. L. Rep.* 329), the plaintiff contended that the Driscoll school district deprived Spanish-speaking children of equal protection of the laws under the 14th amendment by maintaining separate classes and an educational system that required a majority of the children to remain in the first two grades for three years. The court found that it was reasonable to group "in good faith" children with language deficiencies for the first year but only after examination by school authorities. The practice of segregating Spanish-speaking children for any other reason was held to be contrary to the 14th amendment. Suits brought on similar grounds and with similar results in Arizona, *Gonzales* v. *Sheely* (96 F.Supp. 1004, D.Ariz. 1951) and California, *Mendez* v. *Westminster,* (64 F.Supp. 544, aff'd, 161F.2d 774, 9th Cir. 1946) are recorded testimony of the extent to which segregation of Spanish-speaking children has been commonplace in the schools of the Southwest.

Physical segregation, however damaging it may be, is not the only impediment to a child's success in the American scheme of education. When cultural and linguistic differences exist (ignored by the school systems) as well as segregation, the result is a basic inequality of educational opportunity.

Studies of the culture of the Spanish-speaking emphasize the significance of loyalty to the Spanish language as the mother tongue and the resistance to the use of English. Furthermore, residential segregation of this group, whether voluntary or not, reinforces their commitment to Spanish as the primary and favored language. In such a community, a child can and frequently does reach school age knowing only Spanish and having had no contact with what is to him the foreign world of the Anglos.

For many children entrance into the public school brings the first confrontation with the English language.[2] The inability of the non-English-speaking pupil to understand or respond in the language of instruction results in academic failure and an accompanying diminished self-image.[3]

As may be expected, Spanish-speaking children communicate with each other in Spanish. In the attempt to force the children to learn English, the schools usually prohibit the use of Spanish in the classroom or on the school grounds.[4] When Spanish is suppressed and its use is treated as misconduct subject to punishment and as a mark of inferiority, it becomes identified as the language of the conquered, the poor, and the ignorant.[5]

Early in his school experience the non-English-speaking

pupil is confronted by testing and classification procedures that play a large role in his school career. Such procedures are designed for the English-speaking child, who is not inhibited by language difficulties from scoring at his highest potential level. The Spanish-speaking child facing tests given in what is to him a foreign language can hardly be expected to score well, regardless of his innate intelligence and ability.

At a Congressional hearing held in Los Angeles in 1963,[6] there was testimony that because of the language barrier, testing procedures used by the schools are inherently discriminatory against Spanish-speaking children. An elementary school teacher of many years experience stated:

> Sometimes these children—and many of them were in the primary grades—were placed in lower achievement groups. Sometimes they were tested and found to be retarded. Sometimes they were passed along to the next grade with barely passing grades.[7]

The results of such testing procedures for Spanish-speaking children was described as follows:

> . . . Once the child has been classified as below a certain I.Q. level or mentally retarded, the schools then set the schedule to service this type of student, and the schedule will usually encompass vocational or industrial arts training, so that in fact they are segregating this particular ethnic group of Mexican-Americans into an economic group which is in fact a vocational type of worker-laborer who is not afforded the opportunities of higher education.[8]

In a report submitted at this same Congressional hearing it was alleged that some counselors tend to guide Spanish-speaking children into vocational study, believing this to be a "realistic" course of action.[9] Similarly, in a survey of the Denver public schools, it was reported that counselors assume all too frequently that Spanish-speaking pupils will probably not go to college and therefore provide a minimum of guidance.[10]

A factor influencing education of these children is the cultural distance between the Spanish-speaking and Anglo communities. This has been described as a function of de facto residential segregation. Little positive contact exists between the schools and the parents in the Spanish-speaking community. The parents want the best education for their children but feel that the school is not part of the community.[11] Observers in Los Angeles have stated that school principals and their staff run the PT A meetings, are patronizing with the parents, and communicate the feeling that the Spanish-speaking community, not the school, is at fault for "not wanting to better itself."[12]

Although gerrymandering of school districts to create or maintain educational segregation is no longer common, the residential concentrations of Spanish-speaking have served to return these pupils to the depressed economic milieu from which they came. Culturally and linguistically handicapped, these children are tested and classified by Anglo standards, shunted into the nonacademic vocational school environment, and, at best, face a limited economic future.

But if the educational picture for urban children is bleak, it is vastly better than that for the children of migrant farm workers. Migration to the northern states begins in the spring, before the school term ends, and return to the Southwest is not until months after school has reopened in the fall.[13] The migrant child may move every few days or weeks.[14] It has been said that the schools in some Texas counties are so overcrowded by the influx of migrant children that some are denied admission.[15] Other schools have refused to accept these children on the ground that they were nonresidents of the state and not entitled to its educational facilities.[16]

Even when a child is permitted to enroll in school in each district to which migration takes him, he may be handicapped by difficulty in transferring records, differences in the methods and level of instruction, lack of proper food and clothing,[17] age-grade retardation, and economic pressure to take field jobs as they become available.[18] It has been estimated that more than 50 per cent of the 100,000 school-age migrants in the nation are from one to four years behind in school by the time they reach the age of fourteen.[19] Seventy-five per cent of the 3800 school-age migrants in Colorado each farm season are Spanish-speaking;[20] 67 per cent or more are retarded in age-grade status;[21] 95 per cent are socially retarded;[22] and 90 per cent of them need to make up school work.[23] Almost three-fourths of these children speak Spanish as the chief language in the home,[24] and 14 per cent do not speak English at all.[25] In Texas approximately 80 to 90 per cent of the migrant children know little English.[26]

Although late in season, there is a growing realization

among educators and legislators in the Southwest that the special needs of these children of school age have not been met. In California, Texas, and Colorado special programs for Spanish-speaking pupils and migrant children are underway. To what extent these programs will repair a hundred years of neglect is difficult to estimate. However, it may be projected with reasonable certainty that if these programs and those supported by the federal government prove to be inadequate, the endless cycle of poverty among the Spanish-speaking cannot be broken. What this cycle means in terms of the employment levels of the Spanish-speaking is the theme of the next section of this paper.

Employment

In proportion to their populations, four times as many Anglos are found in professional and technical occupations as Spanish-speaking. One-third of the Spanish-speaking men are engaged as laborers or farm workers. Only 7 per cent of Anglo men are so employed.[27] Of nearly 450,000 federal employees in the five-state area in 1964, 8 per cent were Spanish-speaking, and they were concentrated in the lower-paying jobs.[28] The same pattern prevails in employment by federal contractors,[29] and state employment follows a similar course.

Of all workers, Spanish-speaking farm workers occupy the lowest rung on the employment ladder in the five states. Nationally, 586,000 Spanish-speaking Americans were listed as part of the civilian labor force in 1960.[30] Nearly half were engaged in agricultural labor. More than 80 per cent of this farm group was located in the five southwestern states.[31]

Spanish-speaking work more days for less pay and have a higher rate of unemployment than other farm workers. In 1960 the average income of a Spanish-speaking farm worker in the Southwest was $1256 for 183 days of work. In an area designated as the "Southern region" by the United States Department of Agriculture—mainly Texas—farm workers worked only 115 days and earned an average of $656.[32]

There is evidence suggesting that discrimination because of ethnic origin plays a part in their employment plight, but the degree is difficult to fix. It cannot be said that any governmental agency maintains an official and avowed policy of discrimination. The relative status of the Spanish-speaking, while generally low, varies without predictable pattern from area to area in the Southwest. One Texas congressman has stated that "racial discrimination in job opportunities and wages is not unusual." But, he added, "education is a substantial part" of the problem.[33]

Federal Employment

Spanish-speaking are under-represented on federal employment rolls in California, Arizona, and New Mexico in terms of their percentage of the total population in those states. In Texas and Colorado the proportion who are federal employees is about equal to their share of the population. In all five states, the greatest percentage of Spanish-speaking in federal employment hold blue-collar jobs paying $5000 a year or less.

The figures showing the quantitative percentages vary widely from state to state. In California, Spanish-speaking hold 3.8 per cent of the federal jobs but represent 9.1 per cent of the total population. The comparable percentages for Arizona are 7.6 and 14.9; for New Mexico, 21.1 and 28.3; for Texas, 14.8 and 15.2; and for Colorado, 9.0 and 8.9.[34]

Overall, 41.8 per cent of the Spanish-speaking federal employees make $5000 or less per year.[35]

Similar patterns were found in a study of federal employment in four southwestern communities. Spanish-speaking constitute 3.4 per cent of the federal employees and 9.3 per cent of the total population in Los Angeles. Spanish-speaking comprised 4.6 per cent of those who inquired about and 5.4 per cent of those who competed in federal employment examinations, as compared with 45.8 and 39.2 per cent, respectively, for Negroes. Negroes represent only 13.5 per cent of the population.[36]

The U.S. Civil Service Commission reported that several leaders of the Spanish-speaking community offered as reasons for the seeming disinterest in government employment "a cultural aversion to having more contact with government than is necessary," a generally low level of education, language difficulties on written examinations, a lack of interest in office work of the women, and the belief, widely held among well-educated Spanish-speaking, that they have a greater potential in private then in public employment.[37] What might be added is the reluctance of proud people to subject themselves to a possible rejection because of prejudice or discrimination.

In San Antonio Spanish-speaking represent 36.2 per cent of the federal employees and 37.4 per cent of the total population.[38] The federal government is a major employer of the civilian labor force of the city. As an equal opportunity employer, it is ranked ahead of the city government and private business.[39]

United States Senator Joseph Montoya of New Mexico has related to U.S. Commission on Civil Rights investigators that Roswell, New Mexico, is the one city in the state that has traditionally discriminated against Spanish-speaking.[40] Nearby Walker Air Force Base has followed Roswell's example, the Senator said; Walker has 420 civilian workers, 80 of whom are Spanish-speaking. Only 27 of the 80 are in white-collar classifications, and only four of these earn more than $6000 a year.[41]

The federal government is one of Denver's largest employers. There, Spanish-speaking constitute 4.8 per cent of federal employment and 6.5 per cent of the population. The majority of these employees are at the lower wage board and classified levels.[42]

Despite various programs for minority recruitment, firm non-discrimination policies, and a rise during 1962–63 of 2.8 per cent in total federal employment throughout the Southwest, employment of Spanish-speaking by the federal government increased by only one per cent. However, when in 1963–64, the number of federal jobs in the five-state area declined 2.8 per cent, those held by Spanish-speaking rose 8.3 per cent.[43] The programs apparently have borne some fruit, although the percentages are less impressive than the total number of jobs gained for Spanish-speaking—1945 in 1963–64.[44]

State Policies and Actions

Four of the five southwestern states have adopted legislation to eliminate job discrimination, including the establishment of machinery for hearing and handling specific complaints. The laws of California, Colorado, and New Mexico cover both private and public employment. Arizona covers only public employment. Texas has enacted no laws in either area.[45]

Relatively few Spanish-speaking have filed complaints of discrimination.[46] Language problems, ignorance of the statutes, distances between their residence and government offices, a

tendency to avoid and distrust Anglo government, and an unwillingness to equate their problems with those of Negroes —all these have been cited for the relatively low incidence of complaints from the Spanish-speaking.[47]
An official state document of California says that:

> If you are a California Negro, you are almost twice as likely to lose your job as a white person—and if a Mexican-American nearly half again as likely to become unemployed as other whites.

The same document attributes this situation to lack of education and job skills, language handicaps, seasonal employment, and "out and out racial discrimination."[48] The California State Employment Service has set up a minority group program to seek out "qualified minority applicants for . . . employers who are actively trying to integrate their work forces."[49] Yet Spanish-speaking, who represent 8.3 per cent of the insured labor force, filed 12 per cent of all new unemployment claims during the last half of 1963.[50]
During 1963 the state conducted an ethnic survey of its more than 100,000 employees. It showed that the state employed 89,904 "Caucasians," 5467 Negroes, 3190 Orientals, 2409 Mexican-Americans, and 720 "other non-whites." Significant findings of the survey were:

1. The high concentration of minorities in the urban area limits the types and salaries of state jobs available to minority group applicants.
2. Urban minority concentrations also influence the choice of occupations.
3. Mexican-Americans and Negroes dominate the low-skill jobs; relatively few occupied the crafts, trades, or professional jobs.
4. Minority representation in law enforcement is low.
5. Better representation of minorities in policy and management levels would make state government better able to deal ". . . with many of the cultural, economic and educational problems peculiar to minority persons."[51]

In California, as well as in other states, citizenship requirements tend to exclude otherwise qualified Spanish-speaking from public employment. Inadequate state support for adult education classes inhibits the ability of resident aliens to prepare themselves to meet the literary and other requirements of citizenship.[52] However, it has been said that the most significant factor in greater Spanish-speaking representation in public employment at the policy level would be to create a better image and inspiration for young members of the community.[53]

A survey by the Los Angeles County Commission on Human Relations has shown that of 42,583 county employees, 1973 are Spanish-speaking, 10,807 are Negro, and 28,584 are Anglo. The remainder is divided among Orientals and "other non-white." In every job level, Negroes far outnumber the Spanish-speaking.[54]

From the high percentage of Negro employment, particularly in professional and secretarial work, it would appear that racial or ethnic discrimination is not an inhibiting factor in employment. The Los Angeles Commission on Human Relations has not, however, offered any analysis of the relatively low numbers of Spanish-speaking employees. Yet this agency has stated that there is a lack of reliable statistics defining their problems in the Los Angeles area.[55]

Other California counties and cities have been surveyed either by other governmental agencies or U.S. Commission on Civil Rights staff. Available data do not show discriminatory hiring practices. Studies in the City of Los Angeles by the Civil Service Department revealed no evidence of discrimination. However, the Department resisted requests by the California FEPC to make a "head count."[56]

U.S. Commission on Civil Rights investigators found significant numbers of Spanish-speaking employed by the California cities of Montebello, Santa Fe Springs, El Centro, Monterey Park, and Pico Rivera.[57] The California FEPC reported that hiring practices in San Diego are not inherently discriminatory, but nevertheless the city had not projected a strong image of equal employment opportunity.[58]

Few Spanish-speaking are found in law enforcement work, although most of the cities surveyed by the Commission had some Spanish-speaking police officers. In Los Angeles City there are 180 such officers in the police department, which numbers 4700.

San Diego employs a police force of 833, of whom 27 are

Spanish-speaking. According to the chief of police of this city, the high entrance requirements weed out approximately 92 per cent of all applicants. He also stated that newspaper advertisements were being used to seek out applicants to fill what he considered a need for more Spanish-speaking on the force.[59]

In other states of the Southwest, municipal employment patterns appear to be determined by factors unique to each area. In Texas employment opportunities are greater in the larger cities where the size of the Spanish-speaking population is substantial. An exception is Austin, where only 6.5 per cent of city employees are Spanish-speaking.[60] In Corpus Christi, Laredo, Edinburg, Crystal City, and San Antonio, representation in municipal employment is more closely related to their percentage of the population.[61] The director of personnel for El Paso, Texas, pointed out that 62.8 per cent of the municipal employees were Spanish-speaking compared with 35.1 per cent Anglo. Although the majority of the former are in custodial or other low level jobs, a substantial number occupy senior positions in professional and supervisory capacities.[62]

Allegations have been made that the Texas Highway Patrol and the Texas Rangers practice employment discrimination against Spanish-speaking.[63] Whether or not this is true is difficult to determine. However, it is clear that few Spanish-speaking are employed by state law enforcement agencies. Of a total force of 1119 Highway Patrol officers, eight are Spanish-speaking, while none are employed by the Texas Rangers among the 62 officers.[64]

No allegations of discrimination against persons of Latin heritage have been made with respect to public employment in New Mexico. A prominent leader in the Latin community of New Mexico indicated that the only discrimination that may exist would be in private employment and in a subtle way that would make it difficult to prove.[65]

The city manager of Las Cruces, New Mexico, has stated that in his opinion discrimination is very limited if it exists at all. Indeed, the municipal government is dominated by Latin-American personnel from supervisory to custodial. The city has had an antidiscrimination ordinance for about three years, but there have been no tests of the law to date. Las Cruces is said to be not unusual among New Mexico municipalities.[66]

Public employment opportunities have apparently improved

for Spanish-speaking in Denver, Colorado. Currently the director of the City Welfare Department and the deputy undersheriff are Spanish-speaking. Public and private employment opportunities are said to be much more restricted in Colorado Springs, Colorado. Of a total 1200 persons employed by the city, only 107 are Spanish-speaking. The police and fire departments have employed no Spanish-speaking, the explanation being that few apply and that those who do have difficulty meeting minimum height qualifications! None are employed in the City Hall and few are employed in other white-collar or administrative jobs.[67]

Colorado counties outside Denver and Colorado Springs apparently have few job opportunities for Spanish-speaking except in farm work or menial labor. It is reported that in some counties (Adams, Bent, Boulder, Otero, Rio Grande, and Weld) unemployment is a serious and chronic problem for Spanish-speaking.[68]

Although Spanish-speaking workers in urban areas of the Southwest generally occupy a low economic status, the status of agricultural workers is almost invariably lower. Agricultural workers generally earn less than any other group and experience a high rate of unemployment. Many farm workers occupy housing without electricity, heat, running water, or sanitary facilities. Agriculture ranks third among occupations in the number of accidental deaths.[69] Nearly 400,000 children of agricultural workers in the United States work in the fields with their families.[70] Farm laborers are generally exempt from federal legislation providing for minimum wages, unemployment insurance, and workmen's compensation.

Housing

In housing, as in education and employment, the Spanish-speaking have had a different experience from that of the majority of the community. In many parts of the Southwest, housing for this minority has traditionally been restricted to well-defined sections of city or town. Historically, almost all the towns of the lower Rio Grande Valley in Texas were divided by the Missouri Pacific Railroad tracks into Anglo and other sections. In some of these cities, in Colorado and California, the railroad tracks remain the physical dividing line between Anglo and Spanish-speaking. In large urban centers of the Southwest there is a marked degree of housing concentration. More than one-half of the approximately 700,000 Spanish-speaking residents of Los Angeles are concentrated in the central portion of the city. In San Antonio, Spanish-speaking, comprising almost 40 per cent of the city's population, are largely concentrated on the west side of the city. In Phoenix, more than half the Spanish-speaking people are located in a single section called the "inner city."

Housing segregation of this population is not a declining phenomenon. In 1964 the executive director of the Los Angeles County Commission on Human Relations testified that "the City of Los Angeles in particular is becoming a much more highly segregated community than it has ever been before."[71]

Today more than 80 per cent of the Spanish-speaking inhabitants of the Southwest live in urban areas. Although poor housing is a natural consequence of their low income status, in many areas residential restriction has also been a direct cause of poor housing. Confinement to a specific residential zone results in ever increasing demand on a limited housing supply. As a result, the housing dollar of Spanish-speaking buys less than the housing dollar of other whites. In California, they pay more and live in lower quality housing than other whites.[72] In Texas and California these families occupy worse housing than any other ethnic group,[73] and the housing situation of the Spanish-speaking population of Texas is the worst in the Southwest. In 1950 more than four-fifths of the Spanish-speaking families of Texas were housed in substandard dwellings.[74] In 1960 in some major Texas metropolitan areas, six times as many dwellings of Spanish-speaking as other white were overcrowded, and from 19 to 39 per cent were deteriorating.[75] In other southwestern cities, including Phoenix, Tucson, Albuquerque, Denver and Los Angeles, deterioration, dilapidation, and overcrowding are common characteristics of the homes of Spanish-speaking.[76]

Not infrequently Mexican-American residential areas in the Southwest have been excluded from the usual municipal services. Commission staff investigation has found a number of instances in which local governments have failed to provide Mexican-American sections with the municipal services provided for the predominantly Anglo sections. In Weslaco, Texas, the Spanish-speaking residential area north of the railroad tracks has almost no paved streets, sidewalks, or curbing.[77] A similar situation prevails in Crystal City, Texas,[78] and in Cotulla, located in the Upper Rio Grande Valley.[79]

In South Tucson, Arizona, where there is a 60 to 70 per cent Spanish-speaking population, it is reported that the city sanitation codes are not enforced and that little police protection is provided in their section of the city. Moreover, it has been alleged that refuse collection is regular on the north side, but rare on the south side.[80]

It cannot be denied that the residential segregation of Spanish-speaking in the Southwest is to a certain extent self-imposed and the existence of "barrios" is in part a matter of choice. Such clustering of ethnic group members in particular parts of urban areas is found throughout the country. In many cities of the Southwest there are no artificial limitations on the sections in which Spanish-speaking with adequate financial resources find housing. However, there is evidence that neither choice nor economic inadequacy is solely responsible for the inability of this group to find adequate housing. In the past restrictive covenants were used to bar this group from Anglo neighborhoods. An officer of the Los Angeles chapter of the National Association for the Advancement of Colored People has commented, "Nowhere in the Nation were there as many of these restrictive covenants which included Negroes, Orientals, and Mexicans, as in California."[81] Even after the 1948 United States Supreme Court decision holding that restrictive housing covenants excluding persons because of race are unenforceable, these convenants were applied to Spanish-speaking.[82] Housing officials in Phoenix have reported that restrictive covenants were used to bar Spanish-speaking as recently as 1954.[83]

Real estate brokers in the Southwest have played a role in restricting the housing available to Spanish-speaking. Article 5 of the Code of Ethics of the National Association of Real Estate Boards states: "A realtor should not be instrumental in introducing into a neighborhood a character of property or use which will clearly be detrimental to property values in that neighborhood." Although this article contains no reference to race or ethnic group, it is commonly interpreted by local boards of realtors to prohibit the introduction of persons into areas in which their race or ethnic group is not traditionally housed. Brokers' application of this exclusionary policy to Spanish-speaking is reportedly still common in Los Angeles, San Diego, Denver, Austin, and a number of small Texas cities.[84]

Real estate brokers in Denver allegedly hang up the telephone on callers who speak with a Spanish accent. For those who have no accent but whose name is typically Spanish, the brokers make appointments that are never kept. It is alleged that such practices are common enough to be a factor in maintaining definite "Mexican areas in Denver.[85]

Correspondence received by the U.S. Commission on Civil Rights from a member of the state legislature of Texas from San Antonio enclosed a complaint from a Spanish-speaking constituent who alleged that a broker had refused to rent an apartment in Austin to her son because of his ethnic background. The representative stated that he had received "many similar complaints."[86] In Weslaco, Texas a Spanish-speaking physician who tried to purchase a home in an Anglo section in 1961 was informed by a real estate broker that he could not do so because the area was "restricted."[87]

It has been charged that financing institutions such as banks and loan associations also play a part in restricting the housing market for this group. In 1964 a Spanish-speaking realtor in Los Angeles stated before the California Advisory Committee to the U.S. Commission on Civil Rights that it was difficult to place loans for Spanish-speaking who wished to buy homes in certain areas.

One factor playing a generally unspoken but significant role in housing discrimination against Spanish-speaking is skin color. Those who are *trigueño*—"dark" in skin color—are more apt to meet discrimination than those who are more fair-skinned.[88] Such discrimination has been reported in Oakland, California[89] and in some areas of Colorado and Texas.[90]

It was reported that in 1960 a light-skinned Spanish-speaking who purchased a home in an Anglo neighborhood in Harlingen, Texas, referred another darker-skinned acquaintance to the same broker, who told him, "I'm sorry, you can't buy that house; the neighborhood is restricted to Anglos."[91] A Spanish-speaking woman with an Anglo name who resides in Los Angeles stated that she received a cordial reception from realtors on the telephone and an invariably unfavorable reaction to her obviously Latin appearance upon meeting them in person.[92] In late 1964 a biweekly English-language Los Angeles newspaper that is directed to the Spanish-speaking community charged that the president of a realty board had instructed members not to sell to dark-skinned Spanish-speaking, and that a prospective buyer had recently been told by a broker over the telephone, "If you are light-skinned, we have several homes available, but if you are dark-skinned, don't waste my time."[93]

Law Enforcement

No discussion of the Spanish-speaking of the Southwest in a civil rights context would be complete without reference to law enforcement and the relationships of police and this minority. Although it is dangerous to generalize from the experience of only two urban areas, it is clear that if Los Angeles and Denver are typical, this minority and the police are at arms length. Undoubtedly, the poor are more subject to harassment by law enforcement officers than others, and it becomes difficult to separate poverty from ethnic origin as a basis for the unsatisfactory relationship of this group with the police. If the now well-known remarks of Chief William H. Parker of Los Angeles are indicative of a general attitude, it is obvious that the ethnic factor is germane. At a hearing held by the U.S. Commission on Civil Rights in Los Angeles in 1960, Chief Parker stated:

> So we keep the record straight, the Latin population that came in here before us and presented a great problem because I worked over on the East Side, when men had to work in pairs . . . and it's because of some of those people being not too far removed from the wild tribes of the district of the inner mountains of Mexico. I don't think you can throw the genes out of the question when you discuss behavior patterns of people.

An assistant to Governor Edmund Brown has stated that much of the unrest and racial problems complicating police-community relations in Los Angeles are the result of police attitudes typified by Chief Parker. He also claimed personal knowledge of arrests, both of individuals and groups of youths on their way to perfectly legal activity at their neighborhood youth center. These arrests were alleged to be without proper cause and the juveniles were later released without prosecution.[94]

Harassment of Spanish-speaking, particularly young persons, by police rather than physical brutality is the major source of conflict in Los Angeles. Although cases in which physical brutality is involved do occur, these are difficult to prove and the Spanish-speaking victims are usually unwilling to compound their difficulties by seeking redress through legal processes. A particular problem confronting these youths in Los Angeles is the police practice of arrest on suspicion. This has been described as arresting everyone in sight or in reach when a crime has been committed. The result of this is that many young men accumulate long arrest records without even being tried or convicted of a crime. An arrest record, with or without convictions, is difficult to overcome in future educational or employment opportunities.

In Denver, as in Los Angeles, there are unsatisfactory relationships between the Spanish-speaking community and the police. Here the view of the minority would appear to be that the police have little concern for the right of citizens to be free from assault under the guise of official conduct. The attitudes of both police and members of minority groups in Denver are well illustrated by the Salazar case in 1964, which also may serve as an illustration of why members of the Spanish-speaking community tend to distrust officialdom.

On March 10, 1964 a 19-year-old youth named Alfred Salazar died of a brain injury caused by a skull fracture.[95] A policeman had struck him on the head while breaking up a fight.[96]

On March 12 the American GI Forum and *Los Voluntarios*, both organizations of Spanish-speaking, joined the family in demanding a full investigation by the mayor into the death of the youth.[97] A police investigation produced no evidence of police brutality. The Congress of Racial Equality asked for a public hearing into the circumstances of the death of Salazar.[98]

On March 23, 1964 the district attorney announced that there would be a grand jury investigation of the death of Salazar.[99] The district attorney said that conflicting statements by witnesses to the fight were contained in the report prepared by the police. He said the "grand jury should review the entire matter to determine who has told the truth."[100]

On March 30, 1964 the Colorado Committee Against Police Brutality branded the grand jury investigation as "an attempt to silence widespread public criticism and still do nothing."[101]

On April 16, 1964 civil rights organizations sent a letter to

Governor Love calling on him "to take aggressive and constructive steps to spot what can now only be interpreted as retaliation against Spanish and Mexican-Americans by the Denver Police Force."[102] The Governor said he would defer to the Denver grand jury in its investigation of the alleged police brutality.[103]

Officials of CORE, *Los Voluntarios*, GI Forum, and the United Mothers Club asked the president of the city council to introduce an ordinance to set up a 12-member commission to investigate complaints of police brutality. The draft of the ordinance was referred to the judiciary committee of the city council. The president of the city council said that the Police Internal Affairs Bureau and the Mayor's Commission on Community Relations were adequate to take care of any disciplinary action in the police department.[104]

On May 11, 1964 the grand jury filed its report on the Salazar case and on other allegations concerning the police department. It was found that Salazar was struck at least twice in the fight, once by a participant and once by a policeman. The grand jury found that he complained that his head hurt, but refused medical attention; that when it was recognized that medical aid was necessary, it was provided; but that "due to the abnormal thinness of his skull, no medical treatment could have offset the effects of the fatal blow"; and that no evidence of the use of excessive force on the part of police officers was found.[105] The grand jury recommended that police training be improved to include: training in public relations in the understanding and handling of minority groups; that the Internal Affairs Bureau of the Police Department be abolished; that no citizens' complaints should be handled by any department of the police concerning allegations of police brutality or improper treatment;[106] and that a citizens' board be established by a charter amendment with its members to be appointed by the mayor.[107]

By the time the grand jury handed down its report, the Colorado Anti-discrimination Commission had begun special hearings on equal enforcement of the law in Denver. There were six sworn charges of brutality to Spanish-speaking made against the police department.

The safety manager and the city attorney advised 29 Denver policemen under investigation not to appear at a Commission hearing on May 16, 1964. The mayor reiterated his position that the Colorado Anti-discrimination Commission had no legal responsibility for looking into accusations against the police department of Denver.[108]

This tangled story of charges and denials is difficult to evaluate, but it is clear that there are serious and continuing problems between the Spanish-speaking and the police in Denver and that cases such as that of Alfred Salazar are not unique.

Jury Service

Of particular concern throughout Colorado is the issue of jury service. In recent years Spanish-speaking have served on the juries of six Colorado counties (Adams, Bent, Boulder, Otero, Rio Grande, and Weld) very infrequently. The United States Supreme Court in *Hernandez* v. *Texas*[109] held that Spanish-speaking people may not be systematically excluded from jury duty. Later, in a Colorado case,[110] the Supreme Court of Colorado held that these people had been systematically excluded from the juries of Logan County, Colorado. It was proved that although there were persons with Spanish surnames on the tax rolls of the county who were qualified to serve, no Spanish-surname person had appeared on the jury lists in eight years. According to the arguments in the Montoya case, a finding of systematic exclusion requires that a substantial segment of the population, some of whose members are eligible to serve as jurors, must be absent from juries for a substantial period of time. By these criteria, the Colorado counties have not engaged in systematic jury exclusion because a few Spanish-surname persons have appeared on juries in all of the counties for most of the years surveyed. However, the number of Spanish-surname persons serving has been extremely small and has not been in proportion to the numerical strength of the Spanish-speaking people in these counties.[111]

In all six Colorado counties the proportion of Spanish-speaking appearing on jury lists or juries was much smaller than their proportion of the total population. In Bent County, where the Spanish-speaking constitute more than 25 per cent of the population, less than 9 per cent of this group appeared on the 1964 jury list. Over a five-year period from 1959 to 1963, only 17 of the county's more than 1500 Spanish-speaking residents served on juries. In 1961 there were no such persons on the juries of Bent County. Rio Grande County has a Spanish-speaking population of more than 34 per cent. Between 1959 and 1963, only 3 to 8 per cent of the persons on the final jury list were from this population.

Over 20 per cent of the population of Otero County is Spanish-speaking. Between 1959 and 1964 Spanish-speaking persons on the jury lists ranged between 4 and 9 per cent, and only 2 and 6 per cent of those were summoned. In 1959 and 1961 no Spanish-speaking persons served on juries in Otero County. For the rest of the years examined, approximately one-half to one per cent of the jurors were Spanish-speaking (with the exception of 1960, when the percentage was 4). In five years, the total days served on Otero County juries by this group was about 36.

In Boulder and Adams Counties Spanish-speaking have appeared on juries. The Spanish-speaking population of Boulder is about 4 per cent, in excess of 2 per cent of which have appeared on the jury list during the past five years. Adams County, with less than 10 per cent Spanish-speaking, had substantial numbers of these on the jury list.

There are almost 9000 Spanish-speaking persons in Weld County, approximately one-ninth of the population. In five years, about 50 such persons were summoned for jury service. Only 16 of them actually served. Eleven of those served in a single year, 1963. According to a local official, in that year, an attempt was made to include as many Spanish-speaking names as possible on the jury list. One-thirtieth of those summoned were Spanish-speaking.

The relatively small number of Spanish-speaking people appearing on juries, particularly in Bent, Rio Grande, and Otero Counties, may be influenced by the means of jury selection in these areas. In Bent, Rio Grande, and Otero, prospective jurors are taken from the county tax lists. Colorado law permits counties to compile jury lists from tax rolls and other documents that may provide the names of persons eligible to serve. Spanish-speaking people are property owners less often than other whites and so are less likely to appear on the county tax rolls. In Otero County a questionnaire is sent to the prospective juror to establish eligibility to serve. This questionnaire poses a question which could be used to disqualify a Spanish-speaking juror: #22. "Can you read, write, and understand English?" It is important to note that Colorado law does *not* require a juror to *read and write* English. It states only that he may be challenged for cause if he cannot *speak or understand* the English language.[112] In Rio Grande the list goes to the county commissioners, who present the court with a final list of "chosen jurors." Colorado law provides that the jurors shall be summoned by chance, drawing from a box of statutory specifications.

Boulder and Adams Counties, with relatively larger numbers of Spanish-speaking persons on their jury lists, take the names from voter registration lists (Adams) and election records (Boulder), send out a questionnaire to establish eligibility, and then summon eligible jurors by drawing their names from a wheel. A Boulder County judge admits that the county has been under close scrutiny in its jury selection practices for several years (probably since the Montoya case) and that attorneys keep a sharp eye on procedures. The Boulder, Adams, and Weld Counties' questionnaire ask the prospective juror whether he owns real estate in the county. The relevance of the question is not apparent.

In conclusion, to discuss the Spanish-speaking in the context of equal protection under the laws as we speak about Negroes is to put the discussion in an improper context. In the Southwest there have never been especially established mechanisms, operated through state agencies (from the governor to the highway patrol), *based in law* that have established the Spanish-speaking as an inferior group such as was true of the Negroes in the South. To be sure, as has been pointed out throughout, there have been many instances of prejudice and discrimination directed at the Spanish-speaking and involving education, employment, housing, police brutality, public accommodations and jury service. These, however, have been instances of individual prejudice or of local practice and not denials of equal protection under the laws. It is this point that is important to bear in mind, and which is devastating to deliberate discriminatory practices.

REFERENCES

1. The current policy of the State of Texas Educational Agency (T.E.A.) is cited in the *Handbook for Local School Officials*, T.E.A. Revised, Nov. 1963, p. 131: "The intent of state law is

that the public schools of Texas be operated in such a way that equal educational opportunity is provided for all children. The separation of children of Latin-American descent from children of Anglo-American descent in the public schools is contrary to law."

2. Mildred Boyer, "Texas Squanders Non-English Resources," in the *Bulletin of the Texas Foreign Language Association*, 5, 3 (October, 1963), 1. Similarly, a teacher of the Anaheim (California) city schools has commented that ". . . (t)he Spanish-speaking child may never have heard English spoken or have spoken it himself until he enters school. (He) often comes to the first grade knowing little or no English. He is given a directive to forget his Spanish and to learn how to understand, speak, read, and write English, *which to him is a foreign language*. The irony is further heightened by the fact that the reading-readiness program has been planned for English-speaking children." Remarks of Miss Delia Gomez, quoted in California State Department of Education, Bureau of Elementary Education, *Report of the Orange County Conference on the Education of Spanish-speaking Children and Youth*, Garden Grove, Calif., Feb. 14–15, 1964.

3. Victor Sumner, Research Director, Texas Education Agency, quoted in the *Bulletin TFLA*, 5, 3, 4.

4. An interesting example of Mexican-American children's attitude toward Spanish is an essay written by a seventh grade pupil in San Antonio (sent to Dr. Bruce Gaarder, U. S. Office of Education under cover of a letter from Mr. Alonso M. Perales, San Antonio, dated October 13, 1964).

"When I entered Elementary school we weren't allowed to speak spanish, sometimes I got mad and said inside myself 'why shouldn't we speak spanish?' it's our language. In the second, third, and fourth grades we talked spanish without teachers getting mad at us. Since the first grade, I can remember her getting after us. I was moved twice in the first grade to other first grade rooms; and in each we couldn't talk spanish. In the fifth grade while playing outside we were talking spanish, and a teacher heard us from inside, and said if we kept on talking spanish we would (go) down to the office, several times it happened. Our real teacher though, didn't think that at all. She said that while we were outside, we could talk any language, except bad words. In the sixth grade the teacher always got mad(e), because she said if we didn't stop talking she wouldn't let us have the special privileges others had. But everything that has been told to me has gone into one ear and out the other, I guess, because I still like to talk spanish everywhere."

5. For a full discussion of the educational implications of the suppression of Spanish, see *Language Loyalty in the United States,* Office of Education, U. S. Dept. of Health, Education and Welfare, Vol. III, 1963.

6. Hearings Before the Select Subcommittee on Education of the Committee on Education and Labor, U. S. House of Representatives, 88th Cong. 1st Sess., Los Angeles, August 12, 1963.

7. Statement of Mrs. Ninfa Nieto, Hearings, August 12, 1963, p. 26.

8. Statement of Rudolph Rivas, Hearings, August 12, 1963, p. 14.

9. Hearings, August 12, 1963, p. 65.

10. *Report and Recommendation to the Board of Education, School District Number One,* Denver, Colorado (A Special Study Committee on Equality of Educational Opportunity in the Denver Public Schools), March 1, 1964, C-34.

11. Statement of Lillian Aceves, Higher Horizons Program, August 12, 1963, p. 14.

12. Hearings, August 12, 1963, p. 25.

13. Metzler and Sargent, "Income of Migratory Agricultural Workers," *Texas* Agricultural Experiment Station 6 (March, 1960).

14. Potts, "Roadside School Bells Are Your Challenge," *Proceedings of Western Interstate Conference on Migratory Labor,* Phoenix, Ariz., April 10–13, 1960, p. 17. One-third of a group of Colorado families travelled to one work area during the season, one-half to two places and the rest to three or more locations. Potts, "Providing Education for Migrant Children," Colo. State Dept. of Education, Denver, 1961, p. 2.

15. Texas Council on Migrant Labor, "Texas Migrant Workers 1963, Summary of Data," March, 1964, p. 2.

16. Potts, note 15, 51. Colorado law permits school boards to deny educational facilities to nonresidents. Colo. Rev. Stat. 123-10-22 (1953), 123-21-2 (1953).

17. Calif. Senate Fact-Finding Committee on Labor and Welfare, *supra* note 79 at 48.

18. Potts, note 15, p. 63.

19. Senator Williams, "For A National Task—A National Program," *Proceedings of Western Interstate Conference on Migratory Labor,* p. 10.

20. Potts, note 15, p. 53.

21. Potts, p. 1.

22. Potts, p. 35.

23. Potts, p. 37. Almost three-fourths of the parents of these children did not go beyond grade school; p. 62. Almost one-third of the mothers and about one-fifth of the fathers speak only Spanish; p. 60.

24. Potts, p. 61.

25. Potts, p. 60.
26. Texas Education Agency, *Proposed Curriculum Program for Texas Migratory Children*, 1963, 3.
27. *Persons of Spanish Surname*, U. S. Census of Population 1960, Final Report PC(2)-1B.
28. President's Committee on Equal Employment Opportunity, *Report to the President*, 1964.
29. "Total and Spanish-American White Collar and Blue Collar Employment by Government Contractors in Five Selected States," July 1, 1964. Source: Standard Form 40, Prepared by: LR, 10/7/64. Letter from N. Thompson Powers, Executive Assistant to Secretary, U. S. Department of Labor to the U. S. Commission on Civil Rights, Oct. 15, 1964.
30. U. S. Department of Labor, *Manpower Report of the President and a Report on Manpower Requirements, Resources, Utilization and Training*, March, 1964, 120.
31. U. S. Department of Agriculture, *Economic, Social and Demographic Characteristics of Spanish-American Wage Workers on U. S. Farms*, 1963, p. 5.
32. *Ibid.*, pp. 5, 11.
33. Statement of Representative Henry B. Gonzalez, *Hearings Before Subcommittee on Employment and Manpower, Relating to the Training and Utilization of the Manpower Resources of the Nation*, U. S. Senate Committee on Labor and Public Welfare, 88th Cong., 1st Sess. Prt. 4, 1963, pp. 1250–1254.
34. Source: President's Committee on Equal Employment Opportunity: *Minority, Employment Survey* 1964, and U. S. Census of Population 1960: *Persons of Spanish Surnames*, Final Report PC(2)-1B.
35. President's Committee on Equal Employment Opportunity: *Minority Employment Survey*, 1964.
36. U. S. Civil Service Commission: *Los Angeles Community Review*, 1964.
37. *Ibid.*
38. Source: President's Committee on Equal Employment Opportunity and U. S. Census of Population, *supra*, note 10.
39. U. S. Civil Service Commission, *San Antonio Community Review*, 1934.
40. Interview with Senator Joseph Montoya, *Investigation Report No. 64-01-77*, July 22, 1964. N.B. The author has examined the files of the U. S. Commission on Civil Rights. All references to interviews refer to material in the files of this Federal agency.
41. Interview with C. C. Robinson, Director of Civilian Personnel, Walker Air Force Base, Roswell, New Mexico, *Investigation Report No. 64-01-98*, Sept. 11, 1964.

42. Source: President's Committee on Equal Employment Opportunity and U. S. Census of Population, *supra*, note 10. See also U. S. Civil Service Commission, *Denver Community Review* 1963.
43. President's Committee on Equal Employment Opportunity *Minority Employment Surveys* 1963 and 1964.
44. *Ibid.*
45. Arizona Revised Statutes, Title 23, 373-375, *Equal Public Employees Opportunities Act*, 1955; 44 Ann. Calif. Code, sec. 1735 and 1410-1435, *The California Fair Employment Practices Act*. Colorado Revised Statutes, 80-21-1, 2, *Colorado Labor on Public Works;* Colorado Revised Statutes, 81-19-1, 18-19-8, *The Colorado Antidiscrimination Act of 1951*. New Mexico Statutes Ann. 59-4-1, 59-4-14 (1949), *Equal Employment Opportunities Act*.
46. Letter held in U. S. Commission on Civil Rights files from John Hope II, Director, Federal Employment Program, President's Committee on Equal Employment Opportunity, Sept. 2, 1964. See also State of California FEPC, *Discrimination Complaints by Persons of Spanish Surname,* Sept. 18, 1959–June 30, 1964.

Mexican-American leaders are reported as saying that the California FEPC was doing a "dismal" job for their people in California and demanded representation on the State Personnel Board, programs to train or retrain Mexican-Americans in rural areas, and that Mexican-Americans be hired for positions which deal with the Spanish-speaking public (Los Angeles *Times,* Nov. 11, 1964, p. 28). Nevertheless, between September 1959 through June 1964, the California FEPC received only 200 employment complaints from Mexican-Americans. Of these, 111 showed either no discrimination or insufficient evidence; 26 were satisfactorily adjusted; the remainder were either dropped, discontinued, or did not fall within FEPC jurisdiction.
47. E.g., letter from staff member, California FEPC to the Commission, Aug. 4, 1964.
48. California Department of State, *Document* DE-NR-366, Feb. 5, 1964.
49. Woods, "Employment Problems of the Mexican-Americans," *Assembly by Subcommittee on Special Employment Problems at East Los Angeles College,* Jan. 10, 1964.
50. California Department of Employment, "Racial Characteristics of New Claimants of Unemployment Benefits in California, July–December, 1963."
51. *Press Release—LH* #838, Governor Edmund G. Brown, Nov. 27, 1963.

Governor Brown directed appropriate department heads to make a detailed analysis of the census, "the first step towards

meeting our objective of complete equality of opportunity. . . ."
Other steps promised by the governor were: (1) a conference of
educators to study educational practices as they pertain to State
and private employment, with special reference to counseling
practices, curricula, and educational policy to determine if we
are properly meeting our obligations . . . especially (to) members
of minority groups—for employment; (2) a complete study of all
state job applications to determine whether minorities are apply-
ing for State jobs; and (3) a request to the State Personnel Board
to recommend new education and in-service training programs
specifically tailored to the needs of minority groups.

Attachments to Press Release 838, Report to Governor Ed-
mund G. Brown from Frank A. Mesple's *Ethnic Survey of
Employment in State Government,* p. 3. Frank A. Mesple is
Secretary to the Governor's cabinet.

52. Remarks of Herman Gallegos before the California Senate Fact-
Finding Subcommittee on Race Relations and Urban Problems,
San Francisco, Calif., Oct. 2, 1963, p. 2.
53. U. S. Commission on Civil Rights interview with Judge Leg-
soldo Sanchez, Los Angeles, May 15, 1964.
54. U. S. Commission on Civil Rights interview with John Buggs,
Chairman, Los Angeles County Commission on Human Relations, Los Angeles, Calif., July 22, 1964.
55. *Ibid.*
56. U. S. Commission on Civil Rights interview with Joseph Haw-
thorne, General Manager, Civil Service Dept., Los Angeles,
Calif., July 27, 1964. Memorandum to the city administrative
officer from the General Manager, Civil Service Dept. Subject:
Survey of city's employment practices, dated Oct. 8, 1962.
57. U. S. Commission on Civil Rights interviews with: Mr. Malcolm
C. Gerschler, city planner, Montebello, July 15, 1964; Robert
T. Wilson, City Manager, Santa Fe Springs, Aug. 19, 1964; Mr.
Leonard E. McClintock, El Centro, Aug. 5, 1964; Mr. Samuel
R. Norris, Finance Director, Monterey Park, July 15, 1964; Mr.
Jerrold Gonce, Administrative Assistant, Pico Rivera, July
15, 1964.
58. California FEPC, "Employment Practices, City of San Diego,"
June 23, 1964, pp. 1, 2.
59. U. S. Commission on Civil Rights interview with Wesley S.
Sharp, Chief of Police, Aug. 5, 1964.
60. U. S. Commission on Civil Rights interview with James G.
Wilson, Assistant City Manager, Austin, Texas, Apr. 22, 1964.
The vast majority of Mexican-Americans are employed in park
or custodial jobs. Of a police force of 299, seven are Mexican-
American; of 282 in the fire department, two are Mexican-Amer-

ican. Mr. Wilson noted, however, that recently of 500 applicants for the fire department, four were Mexican-American.

61. U. S. Commission on Civil Rights interviews with Benjamin Franklin, Personnel Director, Corpus Christi, Apr. 27, 1964 (of a 1680 total employed by the city of Corpus Christi, 793 are Mexican-American. In police and fire departments, Mexican-Americans number 108 of a total of 325. Most are employed in custodial work in the departments. The population is almost 55 per cent Mexican-American.); Judge E. D. Salinar, Laredo, June 17, 1964; Alfonso R. Ramires, Mayor of Edinburg, June 16, 1964; George Ozuna, Jr., City Manager, Crystal City, June 10, 1964; Frank Valdez, Apr. 3, 1964, *Field Investigation Report* No. 64-01-07 (May 18, 1964). Mr. Valdez, a professional architect stated that there were few, if any, issues of discrimination in San Antonio. On the other hand, in an interview with John C. Alaniz, Apr. 13, 1964, Mr. Alaniz, an attorney and State legislator, alleged that discriminatory hiring and promotion practices were evident in the city-owned gas and utility company. He stated that only menial jobs are available for the Mexican-American. Commission investigation (interview with J. T. Duly, Assistant General Manager, and John M. Costello, Personnel Director, Public Service Board, Apr. 20, 1964, revealed that Mexican-Americans make up 95 per cent of the unskilled; of the office force—630 total—12 were Mexican-American; of the skilled workers—1125 total—two were Mexican-American).

62. *Ibid.*

63. U. S. Commission on Civil Rights interview with John Alaniz, Attorney and Representative to State Legislature, San Antonio, Texas, Apr. 13, 1964.

64. U. S. Commission on Civil Rights interview with Homer Garrison, Jr., Director, Texas Department of Public Safety, Austin, Texas, June 3, 1964.

65. U. S. Commission on Civil Rights interview with Luis Tellez, Chairman, G. I. Forum, Albuquerque, N. Mex., Sept. 1, 1964.

66. U. S. Commission on Civil Rights interview with Fred Alvarez, City Manager, Las Cruces, N. Mex., Sept. 1, 1964.

67. U. S. Commission on Civil Rights interview with Mrs. Pauline Knopp and Mr. John M. Biery, City Manager, Colorado Springs, Colo., May 15, 1964.

68. U. S. Commission on Civil Rights Field Investigation Report by George Roybal, Special Field Consultant, August, 1964.

69. Sixty-five deaths per 100,000 workers, National Safety Council, *Accident Facts* 85 (1964). California reports 56.5 disabling injuries per 1000 agricultural workers compared with 31.9 injuries

per 1000 workers in the all-industrial average. This rate was exceeded only in construction and mining in California. California Senate Fact-Finding Committee on Labor and Welfare, *California's Farm Labor Problems,* Pt. II, 1963, p. 37.

Between 1951 and 1960 there were more than 3000 farm workers in the nation poisoned by sprays. During this time, 22 adults and 63 children died from the effects of the sprays. Bennett, "Still the Harvest of Shame," *Commonweal,* Apr. 10, 1964, p. 85.

Transportation accidents are common hazards for migrants. In 1956 the Interstate Commerce Act was amended to permit the Interstate Commerce Commission to establish safety and comfort regulations for trips exceeding 75 miles and crossing a State line. Pt. II of the Interstate Commerce Act 70 Stat. 958 (1956), 49 U.S.C. Sec. 304 (3a) (1958).

70. In 1961 there were more than 350,000 children between the ages of 10 and 13 who work in the fields of the nation, U. S. Dept. of Agriculture, *The Hired Farm Working Force of 1961,* 18 (1963) note 47, p. 85. No data available for children of a lower age. State and Federal laws permit children to work after school and during vacation. On the Federal level the child labor provision of the Fair Labor Standards Act permits children under age 16 to work in agriculture outside of school hours. Fair Labor Standards Act of 1938, 52 Stat. 1060, 29 U.S.C. (1938), 29 U.S.C. sec. 203(e), 212, 213(c) 1958. Child Labor Regulation, Orders and Statements of Interpretation, 29, CFR 1500, 123 (1951). Laws in the southwestern states limit ages and conditions of the employment of minors in agriculture but do not prohibit it. Texas Penal Code Ann. (Vernon's) Art. 1577, 1578a (1964 Supp.); Calif. Labor Code, sec. 1394; Colo. Rev. Stat. 80-8-1 (1953); N.M. Rev. Stat. Ann. 59-6-2, 59-6-3, 59-6-8 (Supp. 1963); Ariz. Const., Art. 18, sec. 2, Ariz. Rev. Stat. Ann. secs. 23-231 to 23-248 (1956).

71. Proceedings in re California Advisory Committee to the U. S. Commission on Civil Rights (Los Angeles), Jan. 13, pp. 56–57/79, Jan. 13–14, 1964 (unpublished document in the Commission Library). Hearings Before the U. S. Commission on Civil Rights, Los Angeles, Calif., Jan. 25–26, 1960.

72. U. S. Commission on Civil Rights *op. cit., supra* note 81 at 142 and Governor's Advisory Commission on Housing Problems, *Housing in California—Appendix* 129, April, 1962.

73. McEntire, *Residence and Race* (1964), pp. 126 and 131; Governor's Advisory Commission on Housing Problems, *op. cit.,* note 82, pp. 129 and 141.

74. McEntire, note 83, p. 125.

75. U. S. Census of Population: 1960, Final Reports PHC (1)

Series; U. S. Census of Housing: 1960 Final Reports PHC (1) Series.

76. *Ibid.*
77. U. S. Commission on Civil Rights Interview with Armando Cuellar, M.D., Weslaco, Texas, May 19, 1964.
78. U. S. Commission on Civil Rights interview with George Ozuna, City Manager, Crystal City, Texas, May 19–20, 1964. Crystal City is only 20 per cent Anglo. The Mexican-American section of town has long needed paved streets, street lamps, sewage service, and running water. According to Mr. Ozuna, Zavala County originally contributed $60,000 to a joint local-Federal project to construct new municipal buildings, including a jail and fire station. After a completely Mexican-American city administration was elected in April, 1963, the county government withdrew this support, on the basis that it lacked confidence in the municipal administration.
79. U. S. Commission on Civil Rights interview with William Balbour, Esq., City Secretary, Cotulla, Texas, May 25, 1964. In Cotulla, inspection by a member of the Commission staff revealed lack of paved streets and interior plumbing in the Mexican-American section east and south of the railroad tracks, and poor street lighting. Until recently, there was no trash collection. The Anglo section was generally paved and had some sidewalks. The city secretary stated that city improvements, planned to be carried out with the aid of federal funds, will concentrate on Mexican-American sections. It is expected that these funds will be used for a sewage system for the Mexican-American part of town.
80. U. S. Commission on Civil Rights interview with Luis Martinez, Tucson, Ariz., Aug. 5, 1964.
81. Hearings Before the U. S. Commission on Civil Rights, Los Angeles, Calif., Jan. 25–26, 1960.
82. *Shelley* v. *Kraemer,* 334 U.S. 1 (1948). In 1948 a California district court in the San Francisco Bay region, in compliance with the Supreme Court ruling, held a covenant barring sale to "persons of the Mexican race" unenforceable. *Matthews* v. *Andrade,* Civ. No. 13775, Dist. Ct. of Appeals, 1st Dist., Div. 1, Calif. (Oct. 13, 1948).
83. U. S. Commission on Civil Rights interview with Roy B. Yanez, Exec. Director, Phoenix Housing Authority, and Fred S. Piper, Asst. Dir., July 28, 1964.
84. Information derived from numerous U. S. Commission on Civil Rights interviews in these cities.
85. U. S. Commission on Civil Rights interview with Roger Cisneros, Esq., Denver, Colo., April 5, 1964.
86. Letter from John Alaniz, Esq., Sept. 18, 1964.

87. Interview, *supra* note 88.
88. U. S. Commission on Civil Rights interview with Mrs. Grace Davis, Los Angeles, Calif., April 8, 1964.
89. Transcript of Proceedings Before the California State Advisory Committee to the U. S. Commission on Civil Rights, Oakland, California, May 12, 1964, p. 154.
90. U. S. Commission on Civil Rights interviews.
91. U. S. Commission on Civil Rights interview with Raul Garza, Harlingen, Texas, May 26, 1964.
92. Davis interview, *supra* note 91.
93. Carta editorial, Los Angeles, Calif., Vol. II, No. 5, pp. 1 and 2 (August 1, 1964).
94. U. S. Commission on Civil Rights interview with William Becker, Special Asst. for Human Rights, Sacramento, Calif., April, 1964.
95. Denver *Post*, March 10, 1964, p. 3.
96. *Rocky Mountain News*, March 11, 1964, p. 5.
97. Denver *Post*, March 24, 1964, p. 11.
98. Denver *Post*, March 20, 1964, p. 1.
99. Denver *Post*, March 24, 1964, p. 1.
100. *Rocky Mountain News*, March 25, 1964, p. 54.
101. Denver *Post*, March 30, 1964.
102. *Rocky Mountain News*, April 17, 1964.
103. Denver *Post*, April 17, 1964.
104. Denver *Post*, April 18, 1964.
105. Report of the Grand Jury, Second Judicial District, No. 57775, June 11, 1964, p. 2.
106. *Ibid.*, p. 4.
107. *Ibid.*, p. 5.
108. Denver *Post*, May 18, 1964.
109. 347 U. S. 475 (1954).
110. *Montoya* v. *People*, 345, P.2d 1062 (1959).
111. The source for the following material on jury service in Colorado is (except where otherwise noted) from reports in the files of the U. S. Commission on Civil Rights submitted to George Roybal, special consultant to the Commission.
112. Colo. Rev. Stat. 78-2-1, 78-3-3, 78-4-3, 78-4-4 (1953).

vi: Community Participation and the Emerging Middle Class *

PAUL M. SHELDON

The southwestern states have long been the home of a large minority population that is referred to by various descriptive names. In California and to a degree in Arizona and the Midwest, there is grudging acceptance of the term "Mexican-American." With apologies and with awareness of its inaccuracy and its distastefulness to many persons, the term Mexican-American is used here because it is the simplest and most inclusive term by which to describe this portion of the American population.

Factors Which Prevent Cooperative Action

The very inability to agree on an all-inclusive name is an example of the unique heterogeneity of the roughly 4,000,000 Spanish-speaking people who live in the five southwestern states. Heterogeneity is a major factor in their inability to get together, to develop strong leadership, and to form organizations through which this large group may express its needs and desires and make itself felt in the political, economic, and social life of the broader community. It compounds the problem of self-identification that occurs among all minority groups.

To start a long discussion among Angelenos of Spanish-Mexican descent simply introduce the subject of self-identification or throw out the question, "Who are we?" It will continue

* The findings discussed in this paper are taken from a manuscript in preparation for publication by the Laboratory in Urban Culture of Occidental College under the sponsorship of the John Randolph Haynes and Dora Haynes Foundation of Los Angeles.

for hours. At a conference on problems of Mexican-American youth held at Occidental College in 1963, six discussion sections were announced for the participants. By far the largest number signed up for the section on self-definition. After meeting for several hours in the morning and again in the afternoon the section members reported that

> . . . (we) cannot agree on a single definition of Mexican-Americans. Objectively, it is determined by the attitudes of the dominant community; subjectively, it is the totality of each individual, of how each person conceives of himself. . . . The discussion has raised a number of interesting points and evoked many challenging ideas warranting further consideration . . . the group should meet again for further discussion.[1]

The often repeated complaint that "Mexican-Americans cannot get together on anything" could be explained by heterogeneity alone, without any additional complications. It is not, however, the only separating factor.

Persons of Spanish-Mexican descent in the United States are further fragmented by differences in degree of acculturation. Their or their forebears' residence extends from the earliest sixteenth-century settlements to those who arrived yesterday from Mexico. There are those who, after several generations of exposure to the English language and to Anglo mores and values, have become (at least outwardly) completely Americanized. They retain little of their linguistic or cultural heritage. Others who have been here equally long speak only Spanish, follow Mexican ways of life, eat only Mexican food. Many elderly people look forward to returning "home" to Mexico.

There are differences among people who came from one or another state in Mexico and among those who have migrated from various areas of the Southwest; there are differences in religion and in a host of subtle factors that make for lack of cohesiveness.

Social class differences are becoming increasingly significant as more and more Mexican-Americans achieve higher levels of education and move up the socioeconomic ladder without changing their identity; they remain persons of Mexican descent instead of becoming "Old Spanish," as was formerly the custom when being "Mexican" carried greater stigma.

The Mexican Tradition of Individualism

Individualism is a major characteristic of Mexican culture. Awareness of personal differences, respect and admiration for individuality are characteristic throughout Mexico, in urban as well as rural populations and in all social classes. One student has called it ". . . a country often described as 'many Mexicos,' where individual worth is held to be almost sacred and admitted conformity to the group, *any* group outside of the family, a cardinal sin."[2]

The Mexican tends to react differently toward each person, depending on their interpersonal relationships. To the Mexican, all men are *not* created equal. He may well say: "Juan is my brother, Carlos is my 'compadre,' José is my enemy, that fellow who came yesterday to my office seeking a favor is totally unknown to me. How could I possibly treat each of these the same?"

In the United States a certain amount of lip service may be paid to individuality, especially if the individualist lived a hundred or more years ago. In practice, however, conformity, the submerging of the individual to the interests of the group, is a vital part of the American heritage. "In unity there is strength" is the accepted pattern; Anglo-Americans have accepted the British tradition of working together to achieve a common goal and rallying round a common cause.

This tradition takes on increased meaning as the population becomes more highly urbanized, more concentrated in the city. We foster it in our schools under the label "adjustment." The lone voice is seldom heard in urban affairs. A major characteristic of Western society is the proliferation of voluntary associations. Urban populations may indeed be heterogeneous, as Wirth pointed out, but effective action in this country is possible only when individuals band together into political parties, labor unions, professional groups, luncheon or civic clubs.

It is not surprising that Mexican-Americans have been unable to put to effective use the tool of the mass voice to promote the common good of their group. They are in fact *not* a group; they do not speak with a common voice; they do not have mutual agreement; they are fragmented first by their heterogeneity and second by the tradition of individualism.

Other and perhaps more subtle factors militate against their forming effective coalitions or developing strong leaders: the tradition of first loyalty to the extended family; the pattern of the double standard and of clearly defined male-female roles; the rural folk distaste for individual advancement at the expense of one's peers; these and other traditional values in opposition to the mores of the Anglo-urban society place the Mexican-American at a disadvantage. They also create value conflicts in the upwardly mobile middle class.

These conflicts, not easily resolved, are evident when one aspires to a position of leadership within his own community, and especially when he seeks to form the strong organizations that are necessary if Mexican-American needs and desires are to be brought effectively to the attention of those in authority in the broad urban community.

Immigrants from Mexico to the United States have been largely but not entirely from the lower class. The few remaining descendants of the early Californios claim descent from the Spanish-Mexican settlers who developed the ranchos in the late eighteenth and early nineteenth centuries. The Manitos of northern New Mexico take pride in similar but earlier ancestry. Fugitives from the 1910 Revolution included landowners, merchants, and professional people who, although they tended to be forced into considerably lower status in the United States, passed on to their children more urbane attitudes and values.

To understand their difficulties in accommodating to the Anglo-urban way of life, especially their problems of organization and leadership, it is necessary to consider all of these traditions and, insofar as possible, to compare each with the others as well as with the mores of the new Anglo-based society.

The design for the present study took account not only of the traditional values and mores of the rural folk culture of Mexico but also of traditional and emerging values of the urban upper and middle classes, especially as they are described by Beals and Humphrey[3] and Gordon Hewes.[4] These and a few other scholars have attempted to understand the personality of the modern urban Mexicans who most nearly approximate the rising middle-class Mexican-Americans in cities in the United States.

By far the greater part of the migration from Mexico has taken place within the past 50 years and continues today. The migration from rural areas to the cities of Mexico and the United States is even more recent—much of it within the last 20 years. A majority of the families or recent in-migrants to Los Angeles came originally from the rural border provinces of Sonora and Chihuahua, often by way of Texas.

Rural folk values and mores, therefore, are still helpful in trying to understand people of Mexican descent in this country. However, we must be constantly aware that, although broadly characteristic of the majority of immigrants from Mexico and from other areas throughout the Southwest, the Mexican rural folk traditions do not apply to all groups in the urban Southwest, that they have been influenced by rapid changes taking place in Mexico as well as in cities north of the border. Modern Mexico strongly influences Mexican-American residents of Los Angeles, not only because of continued in-migration, but also because of extensive visiting back and forth across the border.

We must be cautious, then, in generalizing about so heterogeneous a group as the Mexican-American population of Los Angeles. As one said wryly, in commenting on a paper written by a local Mexican-American leader, "He lists nine different types of people of Mexican descent living in Los Angeles, but I don't see myself or my friends as fitting into *any* of these groups."

Background for the Study: The History of Los Angeles

A brief look at Los Angeles as it was and is illustrates an additional complicating factor: urban Mexican-Americans in the Southwest are forced to adjust to the alien culture of the dominant Anglo society and to the complexities of city life in cities that their forebears founded, which in essence were theirs and which were taken from them by conquest or exploitation.

Los Angeles was founded under the Spanish flag, but by indigenous from what is now Mexico. It was a Mexican town for three-quarters of a century before the influx of Anglos from the eastern seaboard overwhelmed and pushed aside the native Mexican population. Within the standard metropolitan statistical area of Los Angeles there are now nearly three-quarters of a million people of Mexican descent. This represents a 100 per cent increase since 1950. They constitute at least 12 per cent of the total residents of the area and are the largest urban concentration of persons of Mexican descent outside of Mexico.

Why is it that despite this numerical significance Mexican-Americans tend to be underrepresented in business and the professions, in politics, in government positions, and in all areas of the broader community life in which influence or power are manifest? Is it attributable to local history, cultural heritage—or are there other major causes?

The founding fathers of Los Angeles were recruited from the province of Nueva Viscaya (now the northwestern Mexican states of Sonora, Sinaloa, and part of Chihuahua). The Spanish governor of California, Phillipe de Neve, established the pueblo in 1781 to raise cattle and crops needed to supply the four presidios at San Diego, Santa Barbara, Monterey, and San Francisco. It was hoped that this and the two other pueblos, San José and Branciforte, would grow and buttress Spain's claim to California, which was being threatened by England and Russia.

The governor had requested 25 Spanish families who were sober and hard-working. His request was not granted. There were few Spaniards other than the mission priests within 2000 miles of California. Those in and around Mexico City were less than enthusiastic about leaving that pleasant situation to travel so far and face such an uncertain future.

The eleven recruits who, with their families, constituted the 44 original settlers of Los Angeles were not the hard-working, sober *pobladores* whom Governor de Neve sought. At no time in its early days did the pueblo do more than support itself and its own needs. Such extra supplies of food and other necessaries that were produced locally were primarily the results of the labors of the padres and their Indian neophytes at the Mission San Gabriel, which had been established 11 miles east of the pueblo in 1772. The Mission, the fourth in the chain of 21 founded through the labors of Father Junipero Serra, was a much more effective force in the development of the province of California.

One should not belittle the role of Los Angeles' founding fathers in setting up a village that 100 years later began the phenomenal growth that has made it one of the great cities of the world. However, when the Anglo immigrants from the

East poured into California during the Gold Rush period and thereafter, the Spanish-Mexicans ceased to be a major force in the development of the city their ancestors had founded.

The land that now constitutes the counties of Los Angeles and Orange was parcelled out by various Spanish viceroys and local governors during the years between the original settlement of the valley and the time of the Mexican War in 1846–48. Major land distribution occurred under the Mexican government following the overthrow of the Spanish colonial regime in 1822. The settlement reached its peak between 1834, when Governor Pio Pico secularized the missions, and 1849, when the United States established an Anglo government following the war between the two countries. In effect, therefore, the *rancho* period achieved fame far beyond its actual significance, in terms of the extent of its reality in time and land area. It flowered and died within one generation.

The two major missions at San Gabriel and San Fernando and the smaller mission church established in the *Plaza* as a part of the original pueblo have always been focal points for settlement of people of Mexican descent in the area—even today—although the *Plaza* enclave moved gradually east during and after the Gold Rush period. This original Mexican settlement, then called "Sonora-Town," was pushed out to the banks of the Los Angeles River and east into what was known as "The Flats." The great wave of refugees fleeing the 1910 revolution in Mexico extended this settlement even farther east into the Boyle Heights-Hollenbeck district, as that area declined from an elegant suburb to become the gate of entry for immigrants arriving from many countries.

During the twenties and early thirties, migrant labor camps grew up east of the city limits between Indian Avenue and the Mission San Gabriel. These gradually became more stable communities and as the Mexican-American population increased with the inmigration of workers needed for the developing citrus industry, the Boyle Heights area and the country area grew closer together so that today they form an area of some 40 census tracts known as "East Los Angeles."

The transfer of control from Mexico to the United States in 1846–48 had been valiantly resisted by a small group of loyalists in the Los Angeles area, but the major upheaval occurred in the wake of the 1849–50 gold rush to northern California.

Beginning around 1851 and for 20 years thereafter, Los Angeles was a rip-snorting, wide-open town famous for every kind of vice and crime.

At first the rancheros had prospered as the price of cattle driven north to the Gold country rose astronomically. The bubble soon burst, however, when top-quality beef cattle were brought in from the Plains states to found breeding farms in the Sacramento Valley. By the late 1850's there was little demand for the scrubby range cattle from southern California. One after another the overextended rancheros, who had mortgaged their lands to take advantage of the cattle boom, lost their entire holdings through foreclosures or inability to pay the taxes assessed by the new government. A disastrous, prolonged drought in the 1860's ended the attempts of the remaining few Spanish landowners to recoup their losses by raising sheep, and thus the Spanish-Mexican ranch period ended.

Some of the ranch owners returned to Mexico; others moved into the cañons above the surrounding valleys. Only the "American Mexicans" remained, the Anglo immigrants who, beginning in the 1820's, had acquired large land holdings either by marrying into the families of local rancheros or by dubious purchases at tax or mortgage foreclosure sales.

The early history and the Mexican influence of Los Angeles were forgotten during the succeeding years. Those whose parents or grandparents had been the dashing *vaqueros* and *caballeros* became manual laborers, field hands, or, in some instances, bandits who were either driven into Mexico or executed by the Anglos. The ranch hands either worked for the new owners or drifted to one or another of the Mexican enclaves. Some of the group probably remained in Sonora-Town or in The Flats to the east during the coming of the railroads and the subsequent mass immigration of Anglos during the boom of the 1880's, through the development of the Los Angeles Harbor and the amazing growth of the great Anglo metropolis, but they are not mentioned in official records.

During this period the large landowners in the San Joaquin and Imperial Valleys began to encourage immigration of seasonal farm workers from Mexico to harvest the crops. It was commonly thought that these workers returned to Mexico at the end of the picking season. Actually, many of them "returned" to Los Angeles for the winter. From 1910 on, whole blocks in Chavez Ravine and East Los Angeles were emptied of people in April and repopulated in October. These people were looked down on by the more stable residents of the local *barrios* and were classified as *Los de abajos*, "the lowly ones."

A young Mexican-American scholar who is now teaching in a local university describes his boyhood problems as the child of crop-pickers—the wearing of corduroy trousers of a peculiar shade of green that marked them as "handouts" from the Bureau of Public Assistance; the jeering of schoolmates at his hands, stained by picking walnuts; and the many fights in which he had to participate to obtain status despite these handicaps.

Within the Mexican-American community a way of life was established that involved very little participation or interest in the larger, Anglo-dominated community. A stereotype grew up, a concept of the Mexican as an unskilled laborer, uninterested in education, political activity, or union membership.

Mexican-Americans developed attitudes of resignation and hopelessness. "Why should José go to high school? He's going to pick the fruit anyway." There was the feeling that the *gabachos* (an uncomplimentary term for Anglos) had all the money, all the power, all the jobs, plus control of the police force and the immigration service. English was considered the language of authority and power; Anglo schools prohibited Spanish, a despised medium for communication. Schools were legally segregated until 1948 and are still to a great extent segregated in fact by housing practices.

The extended history of the disenfranchisement of Mexican-Americans reached a climax during the depression of the thirties. Faced with a heavy relief load, Los Angeles officials sought to solve the problem by rounding up hundreds of thousands of Mexican-Americans—men, women, and children, many of them native-born—with their dogs, cats, and goats, their half-open suitcases and rolls of bedding, and shipping them back in wholesale lots to Mexico. Vivid reports of this period are given in McWilliams' *North From Mexico*[5] and Guzman's *Roots Without Rights*.[6]

Long-standing bitterness that had smoldered since the Treaty of Guadelupe-Hidalgo broke out nearly a hundred years later in Los Angeles with the "Zoot-Suit" riots in June 1943. Spearheaded by service men and further incited by the local press, Los Angeles citizens indulged in a week-long orgy of which the participants even today are ashamed. In brutality and unleashed hatred against Mexicans—especially teenagers— it rivaled anything that has ever been done to Negroes in the deep South.

On June 11, 1943, a formal inquiry was begun by the Department of State at the request of the Mexican ambassador in Washington. Shortly thereafter the Naval Department declared downtown Los Angeles "out of bounds." These official acts by federal authorities brought the local press and city officials to a realization of the disastrous international effects of the riots and the consequences of their own actions.

The residue of the hatred that boiled up in Anglos and Mexican-Americans at that time is felt today. An embittered respondent who was interviewed during a recent study attributes his inability to get jobs or to be accepted in the community to the fact that he acquired a police record during the riots. As he tells it, he was an innocent victim who, 20 years later, "is still paying for the crime of being of Mexican descent. . . ."

The Turning Point

For the Mexican-American in uniform, however, the World War II years brought experiences very different from those of his younger brother at home. The practice was for all military units, especially in the Army, to be composed of men from diverse backgrounds and from all parts of the country. The soldier with a Spanish surname met with none of the prejudice against which he had had to contend in his home neighborhood. Congressional Medals of Honor and other awards for valor were presented to proportionately more Mexican-Americans than to members of any other ethnic group.

The returning postwar veteran was a new type of citizen for East Los Angeles. He tended to be self-confident and interested in community activities. Thousands of these veterans took advantage of the various educational bills to complete their high school and college educations. They bought homes; they started independent businesses; they entered the professions. They placed a high value on education for themselves, their younger brothers, and for their children. It is hard to estimate—perhaps harder to overestimate—their influence in the changing picture of East Los Angeles since World War II, especially during the past decade.

In summary, Mexican-Americans in Los Angeles represented the first arrivals, the most numerous minority, and the largest urban concentration with Mexican antecedents outside of Mexico. Yet in 1956 less than 2 per cent of professional workers in the county were persons with Spanish surnames. In the late forties and early fifties Mexican-Americans were the largest and least assimilated group of people migrating into the area.

From about 1952 the attitudes of young Angelenos of Mexican descent changed rapidly. A few leaders began to voice concern about the educational problems of young people in the community; their children should be encouraged to take college preparatory courses instead of upholstery or cosmetology. Scholarship committees were formed to assist high school and college students.

East Los Angeles today is dominated by active, educated Americans of Mexican extraction; Spanish surnames are appearing increasingly in community and metropolitan newspapers as members of the professions of law, medicine, engineering, architecture, optometry, social work, and teaching. A Mexican-American Angeleno whose family were originally from New Mexico was elected first to the city council and then to Congress. There are an increasing number of political appointments.

Many of the older residents of Boyle Heights and East Los Angeles have retained their traditional ways of life with a minimum of community participation; the younger and young middle-aged people, however, have begun to get out of the ghetto; they have moved away in all directions. Some went west to suburban areas in the San Fernando Valley, Santa Monica, or West Los Angeles. Most took shorter steps to neighboring suburban communities. A number of business and professional men have retained offices in East Los Angeles but are moving their families out of the area.

East Los Angeles Today

The study on which this report is based was centered in East Los Angeles, although it included respondents from the mobile groups described above.

The area is a loosely defined series of neighborhoods, including both city and unincorporated county districts, extending from the Los Angeles River east to the ring of incorporated suburbs. Its population of several hundred thousand residents is approximately 70 per cent Mexican-American. Hollenbeck Heights, Boyle Heights, and other of the subcommunities contain many large older homes, which have been converted to apartments, rooming houses, or nonresidential uses. Local neighborhoods include Lincoln Heights, Boyle Heights, Hollenbeck, Wabash, City Terrace, Happy Valley, and several areas referred to by newspapers as hollows. These residential areas known to local residents as *El Hoyo*—the holes—are built in dry ravines, under bridges or major street or highway overpasses. Five city and county projects provide public low-cost housing for low-income families.

The houses are mostly small, four-or-five-room frame or stucco single dwellings, often two or three on tiny (30x50) lots. A few multiple dwellings and one-story duplexes are being built. This is not a slum area in the eastern-city sense, but it is defined as one of the two most extreme poverty areas and is considered among the least desirable sections of Los Angeles in which to live. Many of the houses built before 1910 have had bathrooms added since World War II, usually constructed of wood and added to the outer wall of the original house. There are few trees; side streets are in poor repair. The area is separated from the central business section of the city by the dry basin of the Los Angeles river and the railroad yards.

As the more mobile Mexican-Americans move out of East Los Angeles, other ethnic groups (principally Orientals and Negroes) are moving in, in small numbers. Store front signs illustrate the mixed history and character of the neighborhoods. There are "Mexicatessens" featuring "Kosher Burritos," and Oriental restaurants offering *Menudo* for Sunday morning headaches.

Subjects

The subjects of the Laboratory in Urban Culture's study of Los Angeles Mexican-Americans were two samples totaling 300 respondents selected from two contrasting groups. The first or area aggregate consisted of a statistically random sample of residents in a typical census tract in East Los Angeles, mostly working-class Mexican-Americans. The second sample, primarily from the middle or upper-middle class, was chosen from the lists of active members of the leading local Mexican-American organizations.

A summary of the history, present status, and goals of the principal organizations from whose membership lists most of the second sample respondents were drawn may be helpful for a fuller appreciation of the succeeding discussion.

Organizations

Respondents from the area or working-class sample tended to belong to no voluntary organizations or, at most, only one. Only 13.7 per cent belonged to any formally organized group other than a nominal membership in church groups and labor unions.

By definition, the organization respondents belonged to and participated actively in at least one major ethnic organization. Significantly, though, these second sample respondents tended to belong not to just one but to many different groups, so that the problem of multiple memberships complicated the sampling procedures. What developed was the picture of a relatively small number of persons who swelled the membership lists of many organizations.

One criterion for measuring the extent to which one of the emerging middle-class Mexican-Americans had become acculturated into the dominant Anglo-urban society was his affiliation with ethnic organizations—the type of organization and the nature of his active participation.

An unknown number have merged so completely with the dominant society that they have, to all intents and purposes, lost their identity as Mexican-Americans. Like the traditional immigrant to the cities on the eastern seaboard, they have followed the pattern of "moving up and out in three generations." We were concerned solely with the unique individuals who, retaining their ethnic ties and admitting or even boasting of their Spanish-Mexican heritage, have developed the skills and techniques to achieve socioeconomic superiority and to exert unusual influence on their peers and frequently on the life of the broader community—in other words, the actual or potential leaders.

There are in Los Angeles scores of organizations whose membership and/or purposes are solely or primarily Mexican-American. In 1961 the local Spanish-language newspaper, *La*

Opinion, recorded 85; the published directory of the Health and Welfare Planning Council listed 47; and the Council of Mexican American Affairs claimed 44 member organizations. An informed observer guessed that there were "hundreds—as of this week; next week there will be hundreds, but they will have different names and a different set of officers—and they'll still be broke."

There are casual social organizations that give a dance or two a year, perhaps for the benefit of an orphanage in Mexico, or sickness and burial societies that may collect dues as the need arises (fifty cents from each member when a death occurs). There is a Mexican American Chamber of Commerce with a monthly publication, *Commercio.* Several local chapters of national civic clubs are considered ethnic because they meet in the areas of heavy Mexican-American concentration, but the membership may be mixed, frequently less than half Mexican-American,—the Belvedere Rotary Club and the Mexican American Optimists' Club, for example. One group meets weekly in a downtown hotel, alternating its name from *La Mesa de L'Amisted* (Table of Friendship) to the Latin American Club, depending on the week. Another club whose membership list includes most of the wealthy Angelenos of Mexican descent is *Los Hambriados* (The Hungry Ones).

There are ephemeral clubs that organize, elect officers, plan a program and fund-raising campaign, often for scholarships, and somehow fail to survive the first year. There are increasing numbers of organizations raising funds for scholarships. One of the oldest, the Armando Castro Scholarship Fund, was organized at East Los Angeles College with some faculty leadership. It was started as a memorial to a popular student who was killed trying to stop a street fight between two local gangs.

Very few organizations have an office and a telephone. Only one Mexican-American organization, the Youth Opportunities Foundation, has a full-time staff member promoting the welfare of this ethnic group. Leaders and club members express deep concern that there are no effective organizations comparable with those financed and staffed by such other ethnic groups as Jews, Japanese, and Negroes. There is no one organization that can speak authoritatively for the whole Mexican community. This became apparent in 1963, when the issue of cooperating with Oriental and Negro groups caused a public split among Mexican-American leaders. A similar rift developed in 1965 over cooperating with other ethnic groups, primarily Negroes, to assure local representatives in the umbrella organization to administer funds under the Economic Opportunity Act.

The larger and more stable organizations tend to be those formed since World War II, with a high proportion of veterans and their wives. It is difficult to select representative groups, but the following accounts may give a picture of some of the current organizations. Because of the shifting and evanescent nature of some of the memberships, we are not concerned with the history and origins of each but with its influence and activity at the time of the study.

The Council of Mexican American Affairs. The Council of Mexican American Affairs was founded in 1953 to represent a cross-section of the Mexican-American community. As originally established, its governing board consisted of 13 members-at-large and 12 representatives of the House of Delegates, which listed 44 member organizations. Some of these organizations are social, some are made up of veterans, some have community service programs. All have predominantly Spanish-surname membership or orientation.

CMAA defines itself as a "non-partisan, non-sectarian and non-profit citizens' organization dedicated to the development of leadership among Americans of Mexican descent and to the promotion of coordination of effort among all the various organizations and groups concerned with the betterment of the Mexican American in the Los Angeles region."

The members are described as "interested individuals who are desirous of improving the social, economic, educational and cultural status of all persons of Mexican descent . . . and who want to contribute towards this goal their time, efforts and resources." They have included business, professional, and labor leaders.

In meetings and public pronouncements there has been constant emphasis on the need for cooperation, unity, and a better way of life. The organization had planned to offer information and counseling services to the Mexican-American community. Conferences were held on youth problems and delinquency, on narcotics, on education, and on job opportunities and training.

During the period of this study the organization maintained an office, a full-time executive director, and a secretary. A fund-raising campaign with a goal of $50,000 ($20,000 for educational scholarships) was under way. The campaign fell short of its quota, and the Council went heavily into debt.

Other problems had contributed to the crisis. At meetings of the Board it was apparent that member organizations were not paying their dues and that the CMAA could not raise a quorum of qualified delegates to elect officers or transact business. At one meeting attended by 25 or so people, only three of the 44 organizations they represented had paid the $25 membership fee necessary before their delegate could be allowed to vote.

There was considerable bitterness and discouragement. One officer said that "too many Mexican American organizations are dedicated to the destruction of each other." During this period there was a high turnover of board members and officers. Disagreements about the plan of organization, lack of funds, and personal problems resulted in the subsequent closing of the office and dismissal of the staff.

In 1963 there was a rebirth of interest under the leadership of new board members and officers, and committees on scholarships, job opportunities, and housing were formed. At this writing, however, the Council does not claim to have a mass base. Several of its former leaders became prominent in other organizations such as the newly organized (1962) Educational Opportunities Foundation, whose interests include raising money for scholarships and fighting job discrimination. Some became absorbed in political campaigns and in running for office.

This super-organization was supposed to coordinate all of the other existing organizations. Some of those who are or were active in CMAA have expressed the feeling that ". . . the community was not ready for this type of centralizing organization. It was too grandiose a scheme to be accepted."

Community Service Organization. Since 1947 the Community Service Organization has carried on an active campaign chiefly for and among Mexican-Americans in California. Its national and local headquarters were housed in the same building in East Los Angeles, but for some time there were not sufficient funds for even one paid staff member. Technically nonpolitical and nonpartisan, it has promoted voter registration of thousands of citizens of Mexican background, with a goal of 416,000 registrants with Spanish surnames. The local office claims a membership of 2000, but the members are only sporadically active. Close ties are maintained with labor organizations.

CSO has always been known as a grass roots organization and as a fighting organization. The intent is to unite the "sleeping giant" of California politics with other concerned groups to promote social action programs, including a minimum wage, medical service, and other benefits for migrant workers, investigation of incidents of police brutality, and the unionization of migrant workers. The CSO considers the passage of the law making noncitizens eligible for Old Age Assistance one of its most significant triumphs. They have received support from labor organizations, churches, and several foundations, including the Industrial Areas Foundation, and usually have been able to keep a team of workers in the field, full or part time, since the founding of the organization.

The stated philosophy is to get all Americans of Mexican background to register and to use their potential voting power to secure the passage of specific measures that will benefit all minority groups.

Its current and long-time local leader has developed and received approval and funding for an anti-poverty program of consumer education for low-income Mexican-American families in East Los Angeles. This was a major accomplishment that has given CSO a new lease on life. The organization will become the second to have an office as well as several full-time staff members. The achievement is doubly significant as it is the only proposal from the East Los Angeles community to be accepted and funded by both the local and national anti-poverty organizations.

The American G. I. Forum. The American G. I. Forum is a national service organization of Mexican-American veterans of World War II and the Korean conflict. It held its first California State Convention in Los Angeles in 1958. There are active chapters in most of the Mexican-American communities in and around Los Angeles.

This family organization has stated purposes that include "gaining first class citizenship through education" and the elimination of discrimination in all fields. Raising money for scholarships and working for fair employment practices have been major objectives. Under the motto "Education is our Freedom and Freedom should be Everybody's Business," activities have sometimes been diffuse. The membership includes some of the men and women who are most active in other Mexican-American ethnic organizations in and near East Los Angeles.

Although there is active participation by wives, the G. I. Forum is facing the problem of declining attendance. Its financial emergency is so acute that action has been restricted largely to writing letters.

Mexican American Political Association. The Mexican American Political Association was organized on a statewide basis in April 1960, when 150 volunteer delegates gathered at Fresno, California. In a year of Democratic landslide (1958), the defeat of Edward Roybal for county supervisor and Henry Lopez for California Secretary of State probably was keenly felt and led to the belief that a new organization and a new method were necessary to work for mutual betterment: "A non-partisan, statewide association that would be frankly political, and frankly Mexican-American." With the slogan, "Opportunity for All Through MAPA," the following objectives were set forth:

> To seek the social, economic, cultural and civic betterment of Mexican-Americans and other persons sympathetic to our aims,
> To take stands on political issues and present and endorse candidates for public office,
> To launch voter registration drives throughout California,
> To encourage increased activity within the political parties.

MAPA has opened offices during each major political campaign. The organization is statewide, but recent leadership has tended to come from northern California. In practice, the activities have been mostly support of the election and appointment of Mexican-Americans to public office.

(The formation in Texas of a national group known as PASSO, Political Association of Spanish Speaking Organizations, caused considerable controversy and confusion, since it included Puerto Ricans, Cubans, and people of South American background. The 1961 MAPA state convention officially went on record as favoring affiliation with the national group.)

It is difficult to assess the effectiveness of MAPA, but it has been active in all the campaigns for Mexican-American candidates—Leopoldo Sanchez for municipal judge, Edward Roybal for United States Congressman, Philip Soto and Antonio Bueno for state assemblymen. The success of a Mexican-American slate in taking over the government of Crystal City, Texas, was considered an encouraging omen for the MAPA type of program.

The backing of political candidates solely or primarily because they are Mexican-Americans is the policy in fact, regardless of policy statements. For example, in a district where the candidate was liberal, popular, and had no policy differences with MAPA, the organization still entered a Mexican-American in the campaign, admitting that he had some shortcomings but saying that "... you can't tell how good a man is until you get him elected." MAPA's Mexican-American candidate was defeated and the organization lost face as well as considerable support. A number of leaders in the San Francisco area disagree strongly with this policy, which is contrary to the Democratic tradition.

MAPA has not yet come to grips fully with the possibility of whole-hearted cooperation with Negroes as a means of influencing public policies.

At the time of the study (1961–1963) the list of major local groups did not include LULAC (League of United Latin American Citizens), one of the oldest of such organizations in the Southwest. Perhaps this was because it was founded and has had its major successes in Texas. Since the beginning of the study several LULAC chapters have been established in Los Angeles County and have developed increasing support, particularly in suburban towns.

Implications

The total picture presented by Mexican-American organizations in the Los Angeles area suggests that the number of active leaders is small compared with that of other ethnic groups. In our interview sample of men considered active in the community, 89 per cent were members of at least three organizations.

In the reports of meetings in the local press, the same names seem to appear regardless of the organization (CSO is an exception). The consensus of a leadership conference held under the auspices of the County Commission on Human Relations in the fall of 1963 was that "We are not yet ready for an over-all coordinating council." This situation presents a confusing image to the larger community. People of good will on the Los Angeles School Board, for example, feel frustrated in their attempts to plan programs for the Mexican-American districts. When an ad hoc committee was appointed to advise the Board, it was immediately attacked by *The Eagles*, a publication of one of the leaders of the Equal Opportunities Foundation, as unrepresentative and weak. When representatives of the National Urban League wanted to discuss cooperative programs, it was not possible to hold a public meeting with Mexican-American leaders.

A new and promising organization, Educators of Mexican Ancestry, is being fragmented by a power conflict between two rival slates of officers and their supporters. One can only speculate on the reasons. Teachers and educators in general represent the values of the white Anglo-Saxon Protestant, middle-class dominant society, but even here the traditional Mexican inability to work toward a common goal threatens to destroy an organization that would seem most likely to be based on Anglo patterns.

In November 1963, when a conference with Vice President Johnson and Secretary of Health, Education and Welfare Celebrezze was held in Los Angeles, a large number among the nominal Mexican-American leadership boycotted the meetings and made plans for a separate meeting in 1964, partly because they felt that too much attention was being paid to other minority groups.

The same 50-100 names appear at memorial dinners, meetings of boards, political promotion dinners. Certain people refuse to work or be on the same committees with certain others. Many successful Mexican-Americans do not choose to be identified with any ethnic organization. Some are considering forming new, more conservative groups to improve the Mexican-American image.

The existence of anglo-type Mexican-American young men and women dedicated to the advancement of Mexican-Americans is a phenomenon of recent years. It represents a breaking of the traditional working-class pattern of limited and informal relationships outside the extended family. Perhaps the phenomenon of an emerging middle class may be related also to acculturation, to a growing awareness of the methods needed to be effectual in urban Anglo society.

As mentioned, Beals[7] and others have pointed out that in the Mexican culture loyalty to persons tends to outweigh loyalty to ideas. The *machismo* concept, defined by Beals as "a purely masculine set of values which might, somewhat misleadingly, be translated as 'manliness,'" heightens the tendency toward individualism. The recurring strong man, the *caudillo*, in Latin American politics often is admired as being *muy macho*.

Middle-class Anglo-urban people, on the other hand, are conscious of the necessity for organization into committees and pressure groups in order to get things done. The pattern of Mexican-American organizations demonstrated by the research findings, a pattern of instability and flux, indicates that the acculturative process is incomplete at this time. The multiplicity of organizations demonstrated the awareness of many Mexican-Americans that these are necessary if recognition is to be achieved, if their ideas are to be heard by those in power, and if they are to take their place in the decision-making process. The ability to compromise, however, to give a little here and a little there to achieve a united front has not yet been demonstrated.

In 1961 a strong movement to incorporate East Los Angeles failed by a narrow margin. The reason most frequently given for the defeat was that certain powerful pressure groups from outside the community opposed the incorporation. A contributing cause may have been that some candidates for office in the proposed municipal government were so busily engaged campaigning for their personal election that they neglected to work for the total movement.

Organizations of other ethnic groups have their differences, but they seem to be able to work together more effectively than do Mexican-Americans. Reportedly there is little mutual affection between the American Jewish Congress and the Anti-Defamation League and yet they are able to present a strong front in working for the betterment of the Jewish people. The same willingness and ability to unite for the common good is being displayed by the NAACP, CORE, and other Negro organizations which, in spite of radical internal differences, are working together at local, state, and national levels.

This type of cooperation has not been demonstrated by organizations representing Mexican-Americans either in working for the common welfare of their own group or in working with other minority groups. A recent president of the Council of Mexican Affairs, commenting in the Los Angeles *Times* on a $100,000 foundation grant to the Japanese community for community redevelopment, pointed out that the Japanese had themselves first raised an equal amount; a campaign for scholarship funds conducted by the CMAA had yielded the "grand total of $25."

Efforts are being made to organize a regional conference of members of all minority groups to work for common goals related to education, employment, and administration of justice. It is encouraging that the initiative for the latest such effort was taken by Mexican-Americans.[8] On the other hand, there are increasingly frequent statements by prominent Mexican-Americans that Negroes are receiving a disproportionate share of anti-poverty funds in the Los Angeles area and that Mexican-Americans are hostile toward Negroes because they are displacing Mexican-Americans in the local job market.

In summary, there exist a few seemingly viable organizations whose members tend to shift their loyalties from one group to another, but no organization or group of organizations has yet demonstrated the ability to speak for any sizeable proportion of the Mexican-American population.

The Emerging Middle-Class Mexican-American in the Metropolis

The following discussion is based on a series of interviews conducted in 1961–62 with 89 Mexican-American men in the Los Angeles area. All were active in leading ethnic organizations and in community affairs. We are presenting here the way of life of the typical modal man within this group. When the pattern is not clear or strongly dominant, reference is made to other members of the aggregate. Occasionally the responses of a Mexican-American from a working-class district are used to indicate possible class differences.

Patterns of self-concept, ways of life, daily living practices, and other variables among the urban working-class sample were not significantly different from those described by a number of other scholars (Saunders, Samora, Simmons, and Madsen) from their studies in rural areas or small towns in Texas, New Mexico, and Southern Colorado.

We are concentrating on the other end of the continuum. The composite described here not only is urbanized but also has chosen a set of values different from those traditionally associated with working-class Mexican-Americans and also different from those described urban-Americans who live in the ghetto.

Our modal man has moved out, physically and symbolically; education is first in his list of goals. Our modal man is called Carlos, although he may prefer to be called Charles or even Charley or Chuck by his close friends.

Family

Carlos' father was born in Mexico (75 per cent of the sample). He was most likely to have been born in Chihuahua. The fathers of a few of his friends (17 per cent) were born in the southwestern United States, most of them in Texas. His mother also was born in Mexico (75 per cent). (The three states from which most of the mothers came were Chihuahua, Jalisco, Zacatecas.) Of his friends' mothers born in the United States (24 per cent), most were from Texas or New Mexico. A substantial majority of the parents immigrated to the United States and are living here or were before their death (fathers, 86 per cent; mothers, 92 per cent). In other words, they were permanent migrants.

Carlos was born in the United States (82 per cent), in Southern California. A few of his friends were born in Texas or Arizona. He is between 40 and 50 years old. He has spent nearly all of his life in the United States and completed his schooling here (92 per cent; 60 per cent in California). Carlos met his wife in the United States (94 per cent), probably in Los Angeles (74 per cent).

His wife also was born in the United States (79 per cent, but their birthplaces were more scattered than their spouses'. Forty-four per cent were born in Southern California; 33 per cent in other southwestern states.). She was educated in the United States, probably in California (67 per cent; 49 per cent in Southern California. Only five of the wives were from Mexico.).

Members of Carlos' group attended elementary and high school. If the family moved, it was to a southwestern city, not necessarily Los Angeles. A major characteristic of respondents in this sample was the high value placed on education. Nearly all were in the Army during World War II or the Korean conflict. After discharge from the Army, the typical members returned to finish high school if necessary and went on to college—often to graduate school.

He and his peers are happily married (88 per cent are or have been married; only 6 per cent divorced or separated); they probably married while still in school. His wife is not as well educated as he (average, four years less), but she is a high school graduate and has five more years of schooling than the typical Mexican-American working-class housewife (7.2 years).

Her husband expects his sons to complete college. His daughters will finish high school and perhaps will go on to college.

Carlos was one of seven children. He considers his childhood a happy one, and if he were to live his life over, he would choose the same size family in which to be reared. It was a hard-working family. Carlos is proud of that fact and also of the fact that at some time during his childhood he picked crops. He feels that the discipline in his home was just right and that he would like to bring up his children in the way he was brought up. Anglo homes, says Carlos, are much less strict and are weaker than the home in which he grew up. His father made all of the decisions. However, he expects major decisions in his own home to be made by himself and his wife.

Despite his age, Carlos is not a grandfather. He and his wife have three children, none of whom is married, although his oldest child is twenty. (In the working class group, 12 per cent of the parents had married children.)

In discussing possible marriage partners for his children, Carlos said that he would like to have the wives of his sons be "nice, easy to get along with, clean, with no bad habits." He does not care whether his children's spouses are of Mexican descent. (Only 26 per cent mentioned this preference in contrast to 46 per cent in the area sample.) However, he tends to feel (50 per cent) that it is important for the spouse to have the same religious affiliation.

When the question was asked in a different way—in terms of importance—Mexican descent was considered as not important by 76 per cent of the sample. In further discussion the qualifications for a good husband were that he have high status or be from the same social level. By comparison, the area sample specifications included being "a good provider" and "a good manager." In general, the discussion of preferred spouses yielded a wide variety of answers, particularly as compared with the working-class group. Most of the qualifications had to do with attitude and qualities of character.

Ties with Mexico

In general, Carlos' ties with Mexico are weaker than those of the area sample, and the visiting tends to be one way. His friends and relatives in Mexico tend to come to the United States to visit. (By contrast, in the working-class area sample, 59 per cent were born in Mexico, 39 per cent had lived most of their lives there, and 43 per cent were still Mexican citizens. Only 3 per cent of the organization sample were Mexican citizens.)

He does have relatives and friends (60 per cent relatives; 62 per cent friends) in Mexico, and three-fourths of them have visited the United States. Carlos, our typical man, has not been to Mexico for two years. Twenty per cent of his friends visit relatives in Mexico, but most of the visits are from Mexico to the United States.

The overall picture is that of a one-way pull; members of this group do not encourage their friends and relatives to come here to live. One unexpected finding was that 23 per cent would like to live in Mexico after retirement, for its atmosphere and its comfort—especially psychological comfort—or if they were rich. The majority did not want to live there because first, they like it here; second, there's more money here; third, the United States is "better for kids." A frequent comment was, "There's too much poverty in Mexico." By comparison, the working-class sample had pleasant memories of their life in Mexico and had primary family ties there.

Residence

Our subject participated in the general trend toward home ownership. Ninety per cent live in single family dwellings. Seventy-nine per cent own their own homes. Carlos bought his home five years ago for about $15,000; it is now worth about $20,000. He lives in a predominantly Anglo neighborhood with less than 25 per cent Mexican-American population. Before moving here he lived for about six years in a similar neighborhood. In other words, he is *two* steps from the ghetto.

Carlos does not refer to his neighbors spontaneously in terms of ethnicity. He likes the location of his house, and he likes his neighbors. He feels that the neighborhood is a good place to bring up children and has no complaints about the library, streets, or police department. He is aware of segregated areas but is not personally concerned. He would like more land and no close neighbors. For neighbors he would prefer people who are not troublemakers and who do not have ethnic preferences.

It is interesting to compare his neighborhood with that of a typical middle-social rank Anglo district such as Eagle Rock, the community in which Occidental College is located. In general, by objective socioeconomic standards, they are markedly similar in home ownership, family size, social rank, and urbanization.[10]

Self-image

In considering the self-perception of our respondents we were concerned primarily with their identification of themselves as persons of Mexican descent. Two main questions were raised: To what extent was the respondents' Mexican background important to their concept of themselves, to their self-image? To what extent did it determine their choices in various areas of personal and social concern?

In some instances the approach was direct; the interviewer would ask, "Do you think it would be important that your son marry a girl of Mexican descent?" At other times the approach was indirect; the interviewer would ask about the kind of neighborhood in which the respondent would like to live.

All through the interview, the term Mexican-American was used to refer to persons who, like the respondents, were of Mexican descent. At the very end of the interview the respondents were asked by what term they preferred to be called (1) by people who were also of Mexican descent, and (2) by people who were not of Mexican descent.

The findings of confusion and lack of agreement on terminology replicated those of other investigators.

Q.: "Do you mind telling me by what term you prefer to be called by people who are also of Mexican descent?"	
Total	99.9%
Mexican, Mexicano	18.0
Mexican-American	39.3
American	11.2
Other	31.4
N = 89	

Q.: "By what term do you like to be called by people who are not of Mexican descent?"	
Total	99.8%
Mexican, Mexicano	11.2
Mexican-American	33.7
American	28.1
Other (Spanish, Latin, etc.)	26.8
N = 89	

Ethnic terms used by the respondents during the interview	
Total	100.0%
Mexican, Mexicano	14.6
Mexican-American	55.0
Other (Spanish, Latin, etc.)	30.4
N = 89	

Language Preferences

At home, Carlos prefers to have the family speak English; however, he wants his children to bilingual. Only 37 per cent of his friends maintain a bilingual home; 7 per cent prefer to speak Spanish at home. The working class sample showed that 21 per cent spoke only Spanish at home; half spoke English at home. Carlos' children probably will learn less and less Spanish as time goes on.

Carlos and his wife prefer movies, television, and radio programs in English but listen to an occasional Spanish program. During the interview with the investigator he spoke in English, breaking into an occasional sentence in Spanish to clarify obscure points. (The interviewers were bilingual.) A number of his friends were happy to be interviewed in both languages, and 6 per cent preferred Spanish alone. When queried about the last shows they had seen, Carlos and all of his friends reported them as being in English.

Carlos and his wife do not try to select stores where Spanish is spoken but go to the most appropriate stores according to price and quality. Twenty per cent of the working-class sample preferred stores in which Spanish was spoken.

Community Relations

When asked what he would do in such personal crises as trouble with immigration or citizenship, Carlos said he would turn first to his lawyer. As second and third choices he mentioned social agencies and friends, but said that he would not go directly to the Immigration Service. (People in the area sample would have gone directly to the immigration authorities.)

In case of unemployment he might go to the employment office maintained by the state or federal government or possibly to the Social Security office. (The self-employed respondents found this question amusing.) If there were trouble with his youngsters at school, Carlos would go directly to the school authorities.

When asked whether he worried and, if so, what he worried about, Carlos joined most of his friends in saying that he had no worries and worried about nothing in particular. Some of his friends (12 per cent) mentioned financial worries; other worries seemed to be of low intensity and scattered, in comparison with the people in the working-class district, who did worry about money, job, and health. (Or perhaps, being less sophisticated, answered the question frankly and directly.)

Carlos described the sort of people with whom he would like to work as "pleasant," "easy to get along with." Only 5 per cent of his friends mentioned an ethnic preference, such as Mexican-American (28 per cent of the working-class sample preferred Mexican-Americans, and, on probing, 6 per cent specified "no Negroes"). In actuality, Carlos worked in an organization where there were few or no Mexican-Americans (63 per cent). The fellow workers of nearly one-fourth of his friends were "mostly Mexican-American." (In contrast, the fellow workers of 42 per cent of the area or blue-collar sample were *all* Mexican-Americans.)

Carlos' health is good, as is that of his family. He goes to a private doctor for medical care. Occasionally he uses public health clinics for shots or pregnancy advice for his wife. He is satisfied with the medical treatment he receives from either place. He learned of the clinic that he uses through neighbors, relatives, or advice from other public agencies—not from the mass media. He carries health insurance through his office.

He attends the local Roman Catholic church (15 per cent of his friends are Protestants) but is not active in its men's organizations.

Carlos lives in a suburb in the foothills. He is well satisfied with his community's public services: fire department, water, sewage disposal, transportation; he said that these services are either "satisfactory" or "very satisfactory." He tends not to take action to improve any of these facilities despite the poor paving on some streets.

When he and his friends were asked about community problems that concern large numbers of people, they mentioned delinquency, low educational standards, dropouts, drugs, traffic problems, inadequate police protection, and inadequate recreation, but the scatter was wide. No one problem predominated.

When asked about social classes, Carlos said that he considers himself in the middle class, but many of his friends consider themselves as working class. Members of the area sample considered themselves members of the working class (79 per cent).

	Per cent
Middle class	45
Working class	41
Upper class	2.2
Middle and working	8
Upper and middle	5
N = 89	101.2

Socioeconomic Status

Carlos is the only wage-earner in the family; his income is $12,500 a year. His friends make between $8,000 and $14,000. Sources of income other than his salary are negligible. He likes his job and refers to his co-workers as "fair," "decent," and "friendly and pleasant."

The sample of which Carlos is the typical man included several outstanding exceptions—men of wealth and economic power. These were slightly older than the other respondents and tended to have a "patron" attitude toward the Mexican-American community, although their generosity was limited and tended to benefit the givers more than the recipients.

Carlos and his wife have two cars in the medium price range, approximately two years old. They have a television set, telephone, and three radios. In comparison, 25 per cent of the working-class homes were without telephones. Television was almost universal.

Informal Social Relations

Carlos has friends all over Los Angeles. Ninety per cent of them do not live in his immediate neighborhood. People in the working-class sample tended to have social contacts only within their extended family or in the neighborhood. One-fourth of the working class said that they had no friends; another one-fourth never visited their friends. Carlos visits his friends often. Eighty-two per cent of the other members of his sample said that they have friends who are both Mexican and Anglo. A few of them have only Anglo friends. Eighteen per cent reported having only friends of Mexican descent.

Compadrazgo

Carlos, like most of his friends, is *compadre* with at least three other families. In the working-class sample, most of the *compadre* relationships were within the extended family. Ninety per cent of the relationships were formed at baptisms; the others were from confirmation or marriage. Nearly all (98 per cent) of the people with whom he is *compadre* are in the United States. Only 19 per cent live in areas that have heavy concentrations of Spanish-surname residents. Again in comparison, responses from the area sample showed that over half of the *compadres* lived in Spanish-surname census tracts.

Political Attitudes

Carlos normally votes a straight Democratic ticket. He says that he talks with and is influenced by friends in organizations, by relatives, and by co-workers. Among the various mass media, he thinks he is most influenced by television and radio, rather than magazines or local papers.

In national elections he feels he has been influenced by mass media more than by people. In local elections he is much more influenced by people (64 per cent).

In regard to national choices, he feels that issues are more important than party or personalities (percentages, 55–18–15). In local elections, however, he feels that issues should account for 70 per cent and personalities 18 per cent.

Carlos feels that his local political representative should be a Mexican-American, but many of his friends disagree. Some say it doesn't matter (28 per cent); others say he should not be a Mexican-American (6 per cent).

Carlos has been active in political meetings and has tried to persuade other people to change their vote or to follow his vote. He and all but one of his friends believe that women should be allowed to vote. He also believes that women should hold political office (82 per cent), but nine of his friends disagree. Carlos voted in the last elections, both national and local.

Leadership

When asked to name community leaders or people who had helped the community, Carlos spoke first of Congressman Roybal, as do 39 per cent of his friends. No other single individual was mentioned by a significant number of respondents as playing a leadership role or as able to help the community or willing to help an individual who is in trouble. Each respondent named one or more persons, but they tended to be different in almost every instance. In other words, only one person prominent in the Mexican-American community is considered by his fellow Mexican-Americans as a leader. The Congressman's leadership role was agreed on by an even larger proportion of the working-class sample; in fact, he was almost the only name mentioned by this group.

A few respondents in Carlos' sample (but not the sole person mentioned by many others) laughingly named themselves as leaders. By definition, respondents in this sample were outstanding, but their concept of themselves as leaders had little support from other respondents.

Among his friends there is a strong and sometimes bitter feeling toward certain persons who have used positions of leadership or potential leadership in the Mexican community for their own personal advancement, especially those who move out of the Southwest, typically to take jobs in Washington. These people are described as opportunists who marry an Anglo girl and "become Spanish grandees," no longer defining themselves as of Mexican descent.

Each respondent was willing to give between two and four hours of his time without any visible benefit to him. The subjective impression of the interviewers was that in the active sample, the members were less conscious of ethnicity in making choices and were more amenable to cooperating with other ethnic groups than members of the working-class sample.

Any description of Carlos would have to include such factors as optimism, mobility, high regard for education, active participation in political organizations, and a high civic spirit. He, his family and friends are in the process of becoming middle-class Americans, while at the same time retaining much of the heritage of the parent culture. He still identifies himself as Mexican-American, is bilingual, has strong ties to Mexico, and many of his attitudes and values relating to the family, religion, compadrazgo, and politics have a strong ethnic flavor. Yet the neighborhood in which he lives, the house and its material comforts, the family's recreational patterns, the type of employment, the amount of money that he earns, and his high educational acheivement—all of these characteristics—are American and middle class. It is very likely that Carlos' children will complete the task of assimilation that was begun by Carlos' parents when they first decided to cross the border into the United States.

REFERENCES

1. *Summary of the Proceedings of the Twelfth Southwest Conference, Occidental College,* April, 1963, pp. 25–28.

2. Ida Serena Lovey, "Certain Mexican Social Values: A Comparative Inquiry Into Tradition and Change" (unpublished master's essay, Department of Social Science, Roosevelt University, Chicago, 1962).
3. Ralph Beals and Norman D. Humphrey, *No Frontier to Learning: The Mexican Student in the United States* (Minneapolis: University of Minnesota Press, 1957).
4. Gordon Hewes, "Mexicans in Search of 'The Mexican'," *American Journal of Economics and Sociology,* 18 (January, 1954), 209–23. See also the summary of literature relating to upper- and middle-class Mexicans, in Ida B. Lovey's thesis, pp. 10–17.
5. Carey McWilliams, *North From Mexico* (Philadelphia: J. R. Lippincott Co., 1947).
6. Ralph Guzman, *Roots Without Rights* (Los Angeles, 1957. Mimeographed E.L.A. Chapter, ACLU).
7. Ralph Beals and Norman Humphrey, *No Frontier to Learning,* p. 17ff.
8. *Report of the Southwest Conference in Interstate Inter-Group Relations,* Phoenix, Arizona, April 10–12, 1964.
9. *Report of the Twelfth Annual Southwest Conference,* April 6, 1963, Occidental College, p. 26. (Write to: Laboratory in Urban Culture, Occidental College, Los Angeles 90041.)
10. For additional data on this middle-rank predominantly Anglo community, see Scott Greer and Ella Kube, *Urban Worlds.* Los Angeles, 1954. A report of a study of four Anglo census tracts in the Los Angeles area of middle social rank, the major variable being degree of urbanism. Reproduced in manuscript form by Occidental College under the sponsorship of the John Randolph Haynes and Dora Haynes Foundation.

vii : Demographic Characteristics

DONALD N. BARRETT

History and, more specifically, history books have generally not been kind to the Spanish tradition in the United States. Preference is given to glorifying contributions of Anglo courage, stamina, and power in subduing the hostile forces of the Southwest. Even in such accounts of historical events seldom is wisdom credited to Anglo forms of the civilizing process. A curious part of the Anglo character appears to be that it cannot afford much praise to a loser. Because of this peoples of early Spanish or more recent Mexican traditions in the United States have been largely ignored or unfavorably stereotyped and their contributions to the American success story overlooked. If a parallel may be drawn from the history of the Negro in the last one hundred years, there is a ray of hope for Americans of Spanish-Mexican background. The American public historically recognizes injustices and in time effectively desires to right past wrongs.

The Spanish-speaking make up only about 2.3 per cent of the United States population, but they are 12 per cent of the population of the southwestern states (compared with 7.6 per cent Negro, 0.9 per cent Japanese, and 0.6 per cent Indian). The following presentation through demographic analysis will attempt a general description of the characteristics of this population, pointing out problems and suggesting directions for the future.

General Distribution and Growth

Between 1950 and 1960 the most important change in distribution was the great increase in the proportion of Spanish-speaking in the state of California. Although this group's population increased in all the states in the Southwest during the ten-year period, proportionately Texas lost 4 per cent of the total Spanish-speaking in the five states, New Mexico 3 per cent, and Colorado 1 per cent. California increased its share by 8 per cent (see Table 1B). Not only did California increase its share of Spanish-speaking among the five southwestern states, but the group increased its proportion of the total California population. Today about one out of every 11

Table 1A

SPANISH-SPEAKING POPULATION IN THE SOUTHWEST, 1960

	Texas	New Mexico	Colorado	California	Arizona	Total
Total Spanish population	1,417,810	269,122	157,173	1,426,538	194,356	3,464,999

Table 1B

PERCENTAGE OF TOTAL SOUTHWESTERN SPANISH-SPEAKING POPULATION IN EACH STATE, 1950 AND 1960

	Texas	New Mexico	Colorado	California	Arizona	Total
% of total Spanish 1950	45.0	10.9	5.2	33.2	5.6	99.9
% of total Spanish 1960	40.9	7.8	4.5	41.2	5.6	100.0

California citizens is Spanish-speaking. Spanish-speaking also increased their percentage of the total Texas population so that about one out of every seven Texans is Spanish-speaking. Their proportions of state populations have declined in Arizona and New Mexico, but these are still substantial—one out of every seven in Arizona and one out of every three and five-tenths in New Mexico (see Table 1C).

Growth of the Spanish-speaking population has been quite

Table 1C

DISTRIBUTION OF SPANISH-SPEAKING, ANGLO,
AND NONWHITE IN THE SOUTHWEST, 1950 AND 1960

| Population | Texas | | New Mexico | | Colorado | |
	1950	1960	1950	1960	1950	1960
% Spanish	13.4	14.8	36.5	28.3	8.9	9.0
% Anglo	73.8	72.6	56.0	63.8	88.9	88.0
% Nonwhite	12.8	12.6	7.5	7.9	2.1	3.1
Total	100.0	100.0	100.0	100.0	99.9	100.1

| Population | California | | Arizona | | Total | |
	1950	1960	1950	1960	1950	1960
% Spanish	7.2	9.1	17.1	14.9	10.9	11.8
% Anglo	86.5	82.9	70.2	74.9	80.4	78.9
% Nonwhite	6.3	8.0	12.7	10.2	8.7	9.3
Total	100.0	100.0	100.0	100.0	100.0	100.0

rapid in each of the states except New Mexico. The high
growth rates of nonwhites (Indians and Negroes) in Colorado
involves comparatively few people, but the high growth of
both Spanish-speaking and nonwhites in California includes
substantial numbers (see Table 1D). The sharp increase in
Anglos in Arizona is worth noting since it is far greater than
that for Spanish-speaking or nonwhites. But the low growth
rate of New Mexico's Spanish-speaking demands some attempt
at explanation.

Table 1D

GROWTH OF SPANISH-SPEAKING, ANGLO, AND NONWHITE
POPULATIONS, 1950 TO 1960

Population	Texas	New Mexico	Colorado	California	Arizona	Total
% Spanish	37.1	8.1	33.0	87.6	51.5	51.3
% Anglo	22.2	59.1	30.9	42.4	85.3	36.5
% Nonwhite	22.4	47.6	88.8	88.0	39.4	49.0

The growth rate of 8.1 per cent (1950–1960) is a net increase of only about 20,000 persons. There are only four possible explanations for such a low growth rate: high mortality, low fertility, high net out-migration, or some combination of these. First, there are no mortality figures available, specifically for Spanish-speaking, but there are two indications of the facts. (1) As shown in Table 7A, the Spanish are a comparatively young population in New Mexico and so low death rates should be expected; (2) there are no public health records or other evidence showing rising or significantly high death rates for New Mexico's Spanish-speaking. Although death rates may be somewhat higher in lower socioeconomic groups, there is evidence of general decline of infant, maternal, and other mortality in New Mexico. Second, Table 9A shows that fertility ratios for Spanish-speaking (child-woman ratios) are quite high and indicates an increase in fertility between 1950 and 1960. Also, if the number of Spanish-speaking children under ten years of age (82,697) is taken as some evidence of fertility and calculated over the 1955 estimated Spanish-speaking population, the crude birth rate is about 32 per thousand total population, a level considerably higher than the Anglo rate.

Third, from Table 3A it can be calculated that out-migration of Spanish-speaking from New Mexico would have to exceed substantially the 26,946 who moved into the state between 1950 and 1960 (procedure: summing "different state," "abroad," and one-half of the "moved not reported" for "residence, 1955" and doubling this figure to estimate the 1950–1960 in-migration). If the growth of the Spanish-speaking in the decade (20,000) were attributable exclusively to natural increase (excess of births over deaths), the out-migration from the state would have to match the in-migration and also be 27,000. But on the assumption that growth is due to natural increase alone and that the number of children under ten years of age in 1960 (82,000) is some approximation of total births, there would have to have been 62,000 deaths or a death rate of about 24 per thousand, a patent unreality.

On the other hand, assuming a high death rate of 15 per thousand (high in view of the young age of the Spanish population) and a birth rate of 30 per thousand would yield an estimated natural increase of 39,000 over the decade. Adding the in-migration of 27,000, would bring total growth to 66,000.

Since the increase of Spanish-speaking in the state was reported at only 20,000, an out-migration of 46,000 from the state is required, about 18 per cent of the mid-decade population and over 170 per cent more than the in-migration. Although this may be closer to the reality, such a heavy movement out over a 10-year period would be remarkable, particularly in a state where in the past the Spanish-speaking have been considered relatively stable. The fact that the heavy out-migration has not been commented on elsewhere suggests that this possible change in mobility is not as strong as the reported figures imply.

A suggested explanation is that many thousands of Spanish-speaking have names that are not included in the 1960 list of Spanish surnames. Intermarriage with Anglos may be the major route for achieving this, since there is no evidence of massive recourse to the courts to change Spanish names in New Mexico. Another possibility, of course, is census under-enumeration of Spanish-speaking. In either instance the problem of undercount, as noted from the 1930 Mexican "race" data, may continue to be a substantial one in New Mexico. Saunders' gives evidence (*The Spanish-speaking Population of Texas*) that instead of only 62,000 Spanish-speaking in the state, one-half of the total population should have been so counted, that is, over 200,000.

Rural-Urban Residence

Table 2 shows that the Spanish-speaking have moved to urban centers by the hundreds of thousands in the short period from 1950 to 1960. In 1950 66.4 per cent were in urban centers, whereas in 1960 about 79.1 per cent were city people. Thus they have become as urban as Anglos in the five southwestern states and are considerably more so than non-whites. The fact that 6 per cent or less live in rural farm areas in the densely Mexican-American states of Texas and California indicates the source of the movement. Other data suggest that many are recent in-migrants.

Mobility

More specific data on migration are found in Table 3A. But first, we note that in 1960 about two-thirds of the Spanish-

Table 2

RESIDENCE OF SPANISH-SPEAKING, ANGLO, AND NONWHITE
POPULATIONS, 1950 AND 1960

Residence	Texas 1950	Texas 1960	New Mexico 1950	New Mexico 1960	Colorado 1950	Colorado 1960
Nonwhite:						
Urban	62.6	75.1	23.3	32.5	82.5	86.4
Rural nonfarm		19.8		55.7		10.6
Rural farm		5.0		11.7		3.0
Spanish:						
Urban	68.1	78.6	41.0	57.6	49.7	68.7
Rural nonfarm		15.0		36.7		25.2
Rural farm		6.5		5.7		6.1
Anglo:						
Urban	61.8	74.3	59.8	73.4	63.6	73.4
Rural nonfarm		17.9		20.9		18.6
Rural farm		7.8		5.6		7.5

Residence	California 1950	California 1960	Arizona 1950	Arizona 1960
Nonwhite:				
Urban	85.6	91.4	22.7	36.2
Rural nonfarm		7.0		50.9
Rural farm		1.6		12.9
Spanish:				
Urban	75.8	85.4	61.3	74.9
Rural nonfarm		10.8		19.0
Rural farm		3.8		6.1
Anglo:				
Urban	80.7	86.0	60.0	79.7
Rural nonfarm		12.0		18.2
Rural farm		2.0		2.1

speaking lived in the 34 Standard Metropolitan Statistical
Areas (SMSA's) of the five southwestern states. Generalizing,
we can say that about one-third live in four SMSA's (Los
Angeles, San Antonio, San Francisco, and El Paso), another
one-third in the remaining 30 SMSA's, and the final one-third
elsewhere.

Table 3A compares the current (1960) urban, rural nonfarm,

Table 3A

MOBILITY OF SPANISH-SPEAKING MALES
BETWEEN 1955 AND 1960

Residence 1955	Texas	New Mexico	Colorado	California	Arizona	Total
Urban	449,660	63,526	45,576	519,471	60,398	1,138,631
Same house, U.S.	48.1	52.5	39.4	36.6	47.5	42.8
Other house	47.8	45.5	57.2	54.0	46.6	50.9
Other county	9.3	15.4	19.1	14.0	12.1	12.3
Other state	2.4	6.6	6.9	6.0	7.2	5.1
Abroad	2.6	1.1	6.8	6.8	3.2	4.4
Mexico	2.0	0.4	0.2	5.1	2.7	3.3
Moved, not reported	1.4	0.9	2.3	2.6	2.7	2.0
Rural nonfarm	91,524	42,616	17,204	74,308	16,950	242,602
Same house, U.S.	51.8	65.4	49.6	29.7	39.3	46.4
Other house	41.9	30.8	48.2	54.8	47.2	44.7
Other county	13.6	8.6	17.1	25.1	18.5	16.8
Other state	2.2	4.5	7.2	10.7	11.0	6.2
Abroad	3.6	1.8	0.9	10.7	10.4	5.7
Mexico	3.0	1.5	0.1	9.3	9.7	4.9
Moved, not reported	2.7	2.0	1.2	4.8	3.1	3.2
Rural farm	41,776	7,320	4,278	30,729	7,894	91,999
Same house, U.S.	45.3	68.8	46.2	32.0	12.8	40.0
Other house	44.5	22.4	51.3	30.0	24.0	36.5
Other county	17.5	7.7	20.2	11.8	9.2	14.2
Other state	1.2	3.7	10.5	5.0	7.0	3.6
Abroad	8.0	7.2	0.7	25.1	52.8	17.1
Mexico	7.9	7.0	0.5	24.0	52.5	16.7
Moved, not reported	2.2	1.6	1.8	12.9	10.5	6.4

and rural farm residence of males with reported residence in 1955. The fact that about 50 per cent lived in another house in 1955 indicates that about one out of every ten Spanish-speaking move their place of residence each year. Of course, much of this movement occurs within the original county of residence, but except for a lower rate in Texas, over 20 per cent of the total population in the five states over five years of age in 1960 had moved across county lines in the preceding five years. Further, it appears that New Mexico does not receive many urban migrants from abroad (Mexico), whereas Texas, Arizona, and especially California receive many thousands in their urban areas. In fact, quantitatively more migrants move into urban areas than into the rural nonfarm or rural farm areas.

It is quite true, then, that large proportions of the Arizona and California rural farm populations are Spanish-speaking (53 and 24 per cent, respectively), but by far, most who move across county or state lines or from abroad move to urban centers. This is substantiated by the fact that California and Arizona rural nonfarm and rural farm populations have been considerably more migratory than their urban counterparts. In contrast the New Mexico, Texas, and Colorado Spanish-speaking in rural nonfarm and rural farm areas have been appreciably less migratory. This pattern suggests that in these three states movement has been strong but has involved less crossing of state and international boundaries compared with Arizona and California. The major movement can be characterized as westward and also northward. Unquestionably, however, the strongest movement has been to urban centers. Table 3B shows that about 24 per cent of the total Spanish-speaking population in the five states moved across county, state, or international boundaries. Of those who moved across county lines but remained within the state 72 per cent moved to urban areas; 76 per cent of those who moved across state lines within the United States moved to urban areas; 63 per cent of those who moved to some part of the southwestern states from abroad moved to urban areas. But this general pattern does not hold for those moving into Arizona and New Mexico from abroad (predominantly Mexico). The elevated percentage of Mexican immigrants to Texas, California, and Arizona also suggests that these are possibly braceros, viseros, and the like.

Nativity and Parentage

It is important to compare the distribution of native to foreign-born and the native-born of native-born parents with the native-born who have one or both parents born in a foreign country. Thus Table 4 shows three different categories of Spanish-speaking who have had different lengths of exposure to different influences. The proportion who are native-born increased between 1950 and 1960, and there was a corresponding decline in the proportion of foreign-born (although gross numbers of foreign-born rose). About 85 out of 100 Spanish-speaking in the five southwestern states are native-born. In New Mexico and Colorado, however, about 96 per cent are native-born in contrast to about 80 per cent in California and Arizona.

Table 3B

MOBILITY OF SPANISH-SPEAKING MALES
BETWEEN 1955 AND 1960

Residence 1955	Texas	New Mexico	Colorado	California	Arizona	Total
Males 5 yrs. & over, total 1960	582,960	113,462	67,058	624,508	85,242	1,473,230
Different county	10.6	12.3	18.6	15.2	13.1	13.2
Urban	68.0	69.7	69.5	76.5	65.5	72.2
Rural nonfarm	20.1	26.2	23.6	19.6	28.0	21.0
Rural farm	11.9	4.0	6.9	3.9	6.5	6.7
Different state	2.2	5.7	7.2	7.2	8.0	5.2
Urban	81.0	65.7	65.1	79.0	64.3	76.0
Rural nonfarm	15.2	30.1	25.6	17.5	27.6	19.6
Rural farm	3.8	4.2	9.3	3.5	8.1	4.4
Abroad	3.2	1.8	1.0	8.2	9.3	5.4
Urban	64.1	34.8	70.6	69.4	24.9	62.9
Rural nonfarm	17.9	39.0	24.8	15.6	22.4	17.4
Rural farm	18.0	26.2	4.6	15.0	52.8	19.7
Mexico	2.6	1.3	0.2	6.5	8.7	4.4
Urban	60.2	19.4	69.6	65.1	21.8	58.0
Rural nonfarm	18.2	45.1	16.9	16.9	22.2	18.4
Rural farm	21.6	35.5	13.5	18.0	56.0	23.6

Further, over 50 per cent of all Spanish-speaking are native-born of native-born parents, that is, at least second-generation citizens of the United States. There has been a net decline in the proportion who are native-born of foreign-born parents, a decline that is appreciable in California, Arizona, and to a lesser extent Texas. In 1960 about one-third of the Spanish-speaking in these three states were native-born of foreign-born parents (predominantly Mexican). Therefore, it would be a gross inaccuracy to denominate Spanish-speaking in New Mex-

Table 4

NATIVITY AND PARENTAGE OF SPANISH-SPEAKING
1950 AND 1960

Nativity and Parentage	Texas		New Mexico		Colorado	
	1950	1960	1950	1960	1950	1960
Native-born	81.8	86.0	95.7	96.1	95.8	96.5
Of native parents	46.5	54.8	87.2	87.4	83.2	86.1
Of foreign or mixed	35.3	31.2	8.5	8.6	12.6	10.4
Of Mexican parents		30.2		8.0		8.5
Other, not reported		1.0		0.6		1.9
Foreign-born	18.2	14.0	4.2	3.9	4.2	3.5
Born in Mexico	17.9	13.6	3.6	3.8	3.7	2.9
Other, not reported	0.3	0.4	0.6	0.1	0.5	0.6

Nativity and Parentage	California		Arizona	
	1950	1960	1950	1960
Native-born	78.0	80.0	81.9	82.4
Of native parents	35.2	46.0	41.5	49.3
Of foreign or mixed	42.8	34.0	40.4	33.1
Of Mexican parents		27.6		31.6
Other, not reported		6.4		1.5
Foreign-born	22.0	20.0	18.1	17.6
Born in Mexico	19.1	16.0	17.3	17.1
Other, not reported	2.9	4.0	0.8	0.5

ico and Colorado as Mexican in any real and general sense;
also Mexican can only very loosely be applied to Spanish-
speaking in the other three states, since less than one-third of
the native-born are of Mexican parents and only about 15 per
cent were themselves born in Mexico. The proportions born
in Mexico have appreciably declined in Texas and California,
whereas they have remained relatively stable in Arizona (17
per cent), New Mexico (3.8 per cent), and Colorado (2.9 per
cent). It is of interest that 6.4 per cent of foreign or mixed
parentage in California are not of Mexican parentage.

Sex Ratios Among Spanish-Speaking

In what may be demographically considered a "normal"
population there is usually a ratio of 100 to 105 males for every

100 females. In the United States as a whole, however, the ratio has declined to less than 98 males per 100 females. In Table 5 sex ratios of Spanish-speaking in each state are broken down into urban, rural nonfarm, and rural farm, as well as native-born of native-born parents and those of Mexican birth. The differences are striking. The *rural farm* groups for the *native of native-born* in California and Arizona show particularly high proportions of males per 100 females, 143 and 133, respectively. The Texas *urban* segment manifests a particularly low ratio of 95 males per 100 females. In contrast there are wide differences in sex ratios for the Mexican-born. Very low ratios are found among Spanish-speaking in *urban* Texas and Arizona, but the Colorado urban group shows a high excess of males. Among Mexican-born in *rural nonfarm* and *rural farm* populations, however, the sex ratios are particularly high showing 200, 300, and 500 or more males per 100 females in the rural farm areas of each of the five states.

Table 5

NUMBER OF MALES PER 100 FEMALES BY NATIVITY
AND RESIDENCE, 1960

	Texas	New Mexico	Colorado	California	Arizona	Total
Native-born of Native Parentage						
Total	97.0	99.8	100.4	96.0	101.4	97.5
Urban	95.1	97.5	98.1	92.8	98.6	94.8
Rural nonfarm	103.3	102.2	105.1	172.8	108.4	105.3
Rural farm	103.8	109.8	109.6	143.3	132.7	113.2
Mexican-born						
Total	99.5	135.4	157.9	133.8	145.2	118.6
Urban	87.6	97.0	151.8	116.3	94.1	102.0
Rural nonfarm	135.9	143.6	167.1	212.9	184.0	170.0
Rural farm	237.6	311.3	195.6	500.0	1164.7	358.4

One may well ask whether people can live fairly normal lives in communities where there are three, five, or more males for every female. Undoubtedly the migratory agricultural workers account to some extent for the unbalanced sex ratios, in terms of labor demand and supply, but the sociocultural questions of community life remain.

Age Composition of Spanish Surname

In the discussion of mobility of the Spanish-speaking, we stated that these are predominantly a young people. If a "median" measure is used, that is, the age at which 50 per cent of the Spanish-speaking fall below and above 50 per cent, the relative youth of this population is clear, as in Table 6a. The median age is somewhat over 19 years, compared with over 28 years for the total white population in the five states. If the Spanish-speaking group were withdrawn from the total white category, the Anglo median ages would be higher than that given for total white. Differences of 8 years (New Mexico) to 11 years (Texas) would be characteristic. Overall, Spanish-speaking are considerably younger than nonwhites also.

Table 6A

MEDIAN AGES OF TOTAL WHITE, SPANISH-SPEAKING AND
NONWHITE POPULATIONS, 1950 AND 1960

	Texas		New Mexico		Colorado		California		Arizona	
	1950	1960	1950	1960	1950	1960	1950	1960	1950	1960
Total white	28.1	27.4	24.4	23.4	29.6	28.0	32.3	30.4	27.8	26.7
Spanish	19.6	18.0	19.2	18.3	18.2	18.1	22.7	22.1	19.8	19.3
Nonwhite	26.7	24.1	19.3	17.6	28.8	24.8	29.0	25.9	20.3	18.5

During the period 1950 to 1960 fertility in the United States remained relatively high until the end of the decade, and since fertility is the major explanation for age changes (rather than mortality), median ages for all three categories were lowered. But the instructive factor is that the Spanish median age, already quite low (thus reflecting high fertility) in 1950, could go still lower. The median age for the Spanish-speaking in

California is somewhat high compared with that in the other four states. We may assume that the same forces are operative here as in mobility changes. Table 6B shows important age differences within the Spanish-speaking group. The Mexican-born show median ages

Table 6B

MEDIAN AGES OF SPANISH-SPEAKING BY NATIVITY, PARENTAGE, AND RESIDENCE, 1960

	Texas	New Mexico	Colorado	California	Arizona	Totals
All classes	18.0	18.3	18.1	22.1	19.3	19.6
Native parentage						
Urban	12.0	16.7	16.4	12.5	11.8	12.8
Rural nonfarm	13.2	17.3	16.2	13.6	12.5	14.4
Rural farm	13.0	18.0	15.4	14.9	11.9	14.0
Mexican parentage						
Urban	23.5	25.2	25.0	24.2	23.3	23.9
Rural nonfarm	21.0	20.9	21.5	18.8	21.6	20.1
Rural farm	20.9	16.7	18.2	15.5	16.4	18.8
Mexican-born						
Urban	46.5	46.8	54.5	42.7	45.3	44.8
Rural nonfarm	44.3	38.0	57.2	38.3	38.4	40.3
Rural farm	37.2	33.8	44.2	33.7	29.7	34.4

more than double the median ages of the native-born of native-born parents (43.0 compared with 13.1). Native-born of Mexican parentage show intermediary median ages, although considerably lower than the median ages of the Mexican-born. This "fits" the sex ratio data and the urban movement explanations. The lower median ages for rural farm and rural nonfarm, both of Mexican parentage and Mexican birth, suggest that older workers are moving to the urban centers, leaving younger people behind. Mexican-born migrants who move regularly with families would also be expected to exhibit lower fertility and thus higher median ages. The most striking feature of this set of data, however, is the low median age level of the native-born of native-born parents (predominantly median ages of 12 and 13 years). There are few important differences between urban and rural groups. Since most Spanish-speaking are native-born of native-born parentage, one would expect to find high fertility and large families among them; this should be evident in urban as well as rural areas. In addition, such low median ages imply very high dependency ratios, that is, the number of dependents (under 15 years and over 65 years) compared with the number eligible for economic production and income (15 years to 64).

Marriage and Family

Compared with Anglo or nonwhite males, considerably fewer Spanish 14 years of age and over have been married. In Texas, for example, about 76 per cent of the total white and 73 per cent of the nonwhite have been married, compared with 68.5 per cent for the Spanish-speaking. Quite possibly the high sex ratios are responsible to some degree for the thousands of never-married Spanish males in the five states. Since this analysis interprets the data within a cultural matrix, the problem of absent spouses can be outlined. A married person with "spouse present," as indicated in Table 7A, is defined as "a man or woman whose spouse was enumerated as a member of the same household even though he or she may have been temporarily absent on business or vacation, visiting, in a hospital, etc. at the time of enumeration." Further, "spouse absent," which is implied here, includes persons separated, widowed,

Table 7A

MARITAL STATUS OF SPANISH-SPEAKING MALES, 1960

Marital status (14 years and over)	Texas	N. Mexico	Colorado	California	Arizona
Single	31.5	32.0	31.2	30.3	33.8
Ever married	68.5	68.0	68.8	69.7	66.2
Spouse present	59.2	58.8	58.7	56.8	51.7
Urban	61.1	63.0	59.1	60.0	58.8
Nonfarm	54.1	54.8	57.4	45.5	47.5
Farm	50.4	47.1	59.8	43.0	16.2

or divorced. Thus, a large proportion of these families are structurally incomplete, with 40 to 50 per cent in the implied category of "spouse absent." In addition, the proportion that is structurally complete ("spouse present") declines from urban to rural nonfarm to rural farm families. Farm families, then, are more likely to be structurally incomplete; in Arizona, for example, only 16.2 per cent of the rural farm families have "spouse present." Only one-fourth of all Spanish-speaking rural farm families in the five states have "spouse present"; only 64 per cent of urban families have "spouse present"; 57 per cent of all Spanish-speaking families in the five states are structurally complete, having "spouse present."

Table 7B presents the proportion of nonwhite, Spanish, and Anglo families according to the number of their own children under 18 years of age. Three to four times the number of

Table 7B

PERCENTAGE OF NONWHITE, SPANISH-SPEAKING, AND
ANGLO FAMILIES WITH CHILDREN UNDER
18 YEARS OF AGE, 1960

	Texas	New Mexico	Colorado	California	Arizona
Total families	2,392,568	221,951	438,815	3,991,500	312,036
Nonwhite	264,833	13,393	11,606	276,467	24,200
None	46.8%	28.7	38.4	39.2	31.6
1	15.4	16.8	17.6	18.5	15.6
2	11.5	15.0	17.4	16.5	13.2
3	9.0	12.3	11.9	11.2	12.5
4 or more	17.2	27.2	14.6	14.6	27.1
Spanish	270,438	54,300	31,765	304,830	9,380
None	26.5%	26.4	25.1	29.9	25.6
1	16.0	16.7	17.1	18.1	15.5
2	15.8	16.4	17.2	19.2	16.7
3	13.5	13.8	14.0	14.4	14.7
4 or more	28.2	26.7	26.5	18.4	27.4
Anglo	1,857,297	154,258	395,444	3,410,203	251,142
None	42.7%	35.4	41.4	43.8	40.4
1	10.8	19.8	18.1	18.9	19.1
2	19.4	21.1	19.4	19.4	19.2
3	11.0	13.5	12.1	10.9	12.0
4 or more	7.1	10.2	8.9	6.9	9.3

Spanish-speaking families have four or more such children compared with Anglo families. By percentage there are more Spanish-speaking families with four or more children than nonwhite families, except in New Mexico and Arizona, where Indians make up most of the nonwhite category. Correlatively far fewer Spanish-speaking have no children compared with Anglo or nonwhite families, with the exception of New Mexico and Arizona.

The number of adults in families may vary greatly, especially insofar as many Spanish-speaking have "spouse absent," yet other adult relatives or friends may be incorporated in the family matrix. Table 7C shows that five to eight times the proportion of Spanish-speaking families have seven or more persons compared with nonwhite, but except for the Indian states the differences are in the same direction. Far fewer Spanish-

Table 7C

FAMILY SIZE OF SPANISH-SPEAKING, NONWHITE, AND
ANGLO POPULATIONS, 1960

Size of Family	Texas	N. Mexico	Colorado	California	Arizona
Spanish					
2 persons	14.9%	17.0%	17.1%	21.1%	15.4%
3 persons	16.3	17.8	16.8	18.6	16.2
4 persons	16.8	17.5	18.4	20.0	17.4
5 persons	14.8	15.1	15.4	16.1	15.9
6 persons	12.3	12.1	12.2	10.6	13.2
7+ persons	24.8	20.5	20.1	13.5	21.8
Nonwhite					
2 persons	32.1	19.2	30.7	29.7	21.2
3 persons	19.4	16.0	20.6	21.0	16.3
4 persons	14.4	15.4	18.2	17.8	14.1
5 persons	10.9	13.5	13.1	12.9	13.1
6 persons	8.2	12.0	7.6	8.3	10.4
7+ persons	15.1	24.0	9.8	10.3	24.8
Anglo					
2 persons	34.8	30.0	34.8	37.2	30.6
3 persons	22.5	21.2	20.4	21.3	20.6
4 persons	20.9	21.7	20.6	20.5	20.2
5 persons	12.5	14.7	13.3	12.2	12.9
6 persons	5.6	7.3	6.7	5.5	6.8
7+ persons	3.7	5.1	4.3	3.2	4.9

speaking families are two-person or three-person groups than Anglo families.

Spanish-speaking families in California exhibit interesting differences from those in other states. More California families report no children and fewer show four or more under 18 years of age. Correspondingly fewer of these families have seven or more persons and more have two, three, or four persons. These differences may be part of the selective factors in migration, but also, and perhaps more important, they may suggest nascent adaptation to the dominant American family system. The higher median age and urban concentration of Spanish-speaking in California are certainly part of this complex of factors.

Fertility

From the preceding discussions of family and age factors it may be surmised that fertility among the Spanish-speaking is quite high. This is unquestionably true. Table 8A makes a

Table 8A

CHILD-WOMAN RATIOS* OF SPANISH-SPEAKING, ANGLO
AND NONWHITE POPULATIONS, 1950 AND 1960

Population	Texas 1950	1960	N. Mexico 1950	1960	Colorado 1950	1960	California 1950	1960	Arizona 1950	1960
Spanish	772	819	781	836	824	812	628	721	720	824
Anglo	461	530	516	615	475	563	440	513	476	554
Nonwhite	413	711	720	866	465	683	464	636	723	934
% gain 1950–1960										
Spanish	6.1		7.0		–1.5		14.8		14.4	
Anglo	15.0		19.2		18.5		16.6		16.4	
Nonwhite	72.2		20.3		46.9		37.1		29.2	

* Child-woman ratio is the number of children under 5 years per 1000 women 15–44 years of age.

comparison of fertility rates for 1950 and 1960 among Spanish, Anglo, and nonwhite groups in each of the five states. It is unfortunate that there are no direct fertility data for the Spanish-speaking , but with the information available it is possible to compute a fertility ratio, or what has been called the child-woman ratio. This designates the number of children under five years of age per 1000 women aged 15 to 44. This measure does not take into account such factors as mortality of children under five years, but like the crude birth rate it offers a useful index for some gross comparisons.

The ratios for the Spanish-speaking are about 50 per cent higher than the ratios for Anglos and also those for nonwhites, except for the 1960 ratios of nonwhites (predominantly Indian) in New Mexico and Arizona. California Spanish-speaking show lower ratios than those in the other four states. Nonwhites show the sharpest gains in fertility between 1950 and 1960, and the Spanish-speaking show the smallest gains. It would be helpful to know whether the rise in nonwhite fertility ratios is due to an appreciable decline in infant and maternal mortality or to simple increases in births; the sharp jump in fertility among nonwhites in Texas and Colorado implies more than simple increase in births as an explanation.

The proportion of Spanish females 15 to 44 years of age to total white females of the same ages in each of the five states compares rather closely with the proportion of total Spanish-speaking to the total white population of each state (Table 8b). But the proportion of Spanish-speaking under five years of age to total white children under five years is appreciably higher in each state. In Texas, for example, Spanish-speaking make up 14.8 per cent of the total population, but Spanish-speaking children under five years make up about 24 per cent of all white children under five. Also the fact that the numbers of children under five years increased at such different rates in each state suggests that most probably fertility differences combine with differences in mobility rates and to a lesser degree with differences in mortality rates. Thus these young children under five years increased by almost 100 per cent in California between the 1950 and 1960 census years, by about 54 per cent in Arizona, 25 per cent in Colorado, and an unlikely 8 per cent in New Mexico (recall the discussion of New Mexico's Spanish-speaking population in the section on mobility).

Table 8C gives SMSA fertility ratios in order to show the persistence of patterns at local levels. Fertility ratios for Spanish-speaking average about 250 more children per 1000 women 15 to 44 years of age than comparable Anglo women—that is, 50 per cent highter fertility. However, there is a suggestion

Table 8B

SPANISH-SPEAKING PERCENTAGE OF TOTAL WHITE
POPULATION IN CERTAIN AGE CATEGORIES,
1950 AND 1960

	Texas 1950 1960	*N. Mexico* 1950 1960	*Colorado* 1950 1960
Spanish percentage of total white under 5 years	22.3 23.9	46.5 35.7	14.2 12.5

		California 1950 1960	*Arizona* 1950 1960
Spanish percentage of total white under 5 years		10.7 13.8	26.1 22.2

	Texas 1950 1960	*N. Mexico* 1950 1960	*Colorado* 1950 1960
Percentage Spanish females of total white 15–44 years	14.7 16.9	36.5 29.0	8.7 9.0

		California 1950 1960	*Arizona* 1950 1960
Percentage Spanish females of total white 15–44 years		7.8 10.3	18.9 16.1

that the larger Spanish-speaking concentrations tend to have somewhat lower fertility rates. Also the SMSA's located in predominantly rural areas tend to higher fertility rates in spite of being metropolitan cities, Fresno, for example. Where the proportion of Spanish-speaking in the total community is lower, higher fertility rates tend to appear. And in confirmation of a previous point, where the proportion of Mexican-born is very

Table 8C

CHILD-WOMAN RATIO FOR SPANISH-SPEAKING, OTHER
WHITE, AND NONWHITE POPULATIONS, 1960

	Spanish Surname Ratio	Other White Ratio	Nonwhite Ratio
Arizona			
Phoenix	896	547	850
Tucson	776	525	762
California			
Bakersfield	846	557	797
Fresno	814	511	720
Los Angeles-Long Beach	717	493	605
Sacramento	702	570	691
San Bernardino-Riverside-Ontario	786	569	787
San Diego	705	554	755
San Francisco-Oakland	605	476	613
San Jose	778	563	590
Santa Barbara	715	527	703
Stockton	719	490	729
Colorado			
Colorado Springs	839	575	725
Denver	798	554	664
Pueblo	837	569	614
New Mexico			
Albuquerque	826	592	720
Texas			
Abilene	933	527	695
Austin	899	456	593
Beaumont-Port Arthur	622	553	678
Corpus Christi	864	543	609
Dallas	771	510	722

low the fertility rate tends to be quite high. In all except seven SMSA's (out of 31), the Spanish fertility ratios are higher than those of nonwhites. By reason of such tendencies very low fertility ratios for Spanish-speaking are found in San Francisco (605), Los Angeles (717), and El Paso (728), whereas high ratios are found in Lubbock (1201), Odessa (1042), and Abilene (939). This may be further evidence of the selectivity of Spanish-speaking urban migration and their gradual adoption of urban fertility patterns.

School Attainment and Enrollment

Education is one of the chief means for upward social mobility in the United States, and high proportions of Spanish have been and are age-eligible for schooling. The Mexican-born who have come more recently to the United States have been at a disadvantage insofar as they received little schooling in Mexico. Further, the predominantly rural residence of all Spanish-speaking until the past generation, in addition to the pressures to put their children to work at early ages (and at

Table 9A

MEDIAN SCHOOL YEARS COMPLETED BY SPANISH-SPEAKING, TOTAL WHITE, AND NONWHITE POPULATIONS, 1950 AND 1960*

	Texas		New Mexico		Colorado	
	1950	1960	1950	1960	1950	1960
Spanish	3.6	6.1	7.4	8.4	6.4	8.6
Total White	9.7	10.8	9.5	11.5	10.9	12.1
Nonwhite	7.0	8.1	5.8	7.1	9.8	11.2

	California		Arizona	
	1950	1960	1950	1960
Spanish	7.6	9.0	6.1	7.9
Total White	11.8	12.1	10.6	11.7
Nonwhite	8.9	10.5	5.5	7.0

* For both sexes, 14 years and over.

low wages) to provide for their large families, has reduced the school attainment of Spanish-speaking in the southwestern states. Table 9A shows that the median years of school attained by Spanish 14 years of age and over are considerably less than the median years attained by Anglos in every state in 1950 and in 1960. In Texas the Spanish-speaking in 1950 had about one-third the years of schooling (3.6 years) of the Anglo (9.7 for total white); by 1960 the comparison was a little better for the Spanish, but attainment still has not reached a functional level (6.1 compared with 10.8 for total white). In each of the other four states the Spanish-speaking in 1960 averaged three to four years less schooling than all whites. In Texas and Arizona the Spanish-speaking attained a median schooling of less than elementary school, but the Anglos had attained a median of almost 12 years of schooling. In New Mexico the total white population rose in median school attainment a full two years, whereas the median for the Spanish-speaking rose one year.

Nonwhites, except in New Mexico and Arizona, increased in school attainment from levels notably above that of Spanish-speaking to levels more comparable with those of the total white. Arizona and New Mexico show lower attainment for nonwhites generally than for Spanish-speaking, but in states where the major minority is Negro there has been a greater rise in median school attainment than for Spanish-speaking. Their attainment in 1960 in Texas, Colorado, and California hardly reached the 1950 levels for nonwhites (predominantly Negro).

In 1960 about 118,000 Spanish-speaking had absolutely no formal schooling and about 75 per cent of these lived in urban areas where school systems are said to be more effective. Over 49 per cent of Spanish-speaking in the southwestern states had less than eight grades of schooling. Four grades or less of schooling is said to result in "functional illiteracy," insufficient grasp of basic skills to operate effectively in our society. This measure reveals 28.6 per cent of Spanish-speaking males in 1960 as functional illiterates. Among the individual states there is much variation: Arizona 30 per cent, California 21 per cent, Colorado 17.6 per cent, New Mexico 22 per cent, and Texas about 40 per cent. Although the picture is a grim one, the data in Table 9B indicate that the situation has improved notably in the period between 1950 and 1960. The proportions of Spanish-speaking who have completed high school or even gone on to college and beyond increased in the decade almost 75 per cent. Unquestionably California has been more successful in the education of Spanish-speaking than the other four states. These gains should not obscure the fact that most Spanish-speaking attain comparatively little schooling.

A most interesting feature of school attainment of Spanish-speaking is to be found in median years attained according to

Table 9B

SCHOOL YEARS COMPLETED BY SPANISH-SPEAKING, 1950 AND 1960*

| | Texas | | New Mexico | | Colorado | |
	1950	1960	1950	1960	1950	1960
No school years	19.9%	16.0%	8.6%	6.6%	6.9%	5.3%
1–4 years	33.0	23.5	22.1	15.3	19.5	12.3
5–7 years	23.2	25.3	26.4	22.5	27.8	22.3
8 years	6.0	9.5	14.0	15.1	17.1	19.2
High school						
1–3 years	8.4	13.6	14.2	21.6	15.1	22.9
4 years	4.0	7.4	7.3	11.8	6.4	11.8
College or more	2.2	4.6	4.1	7.1	2.7	6.1

| | California | | Arizona | |
	1950	1960	1950	1960
No school years	8.4%	8.3%	9.7%	11.5%
1–4 years	15.4	12.8	20.7	18.6
5–7 years	20.2	16.2	26.5	21.5
8 years	14.7	14.2	15.5	16.1
High school				
1–3 years	21.2	24.8	13.8	17.5
4 years	11.7	14.9	6.5	9.7
College or more	4.6	8.8	3.2	4.8

* For males 14 years and over.

their nativity and parentage. Table 9C shows these medians for males 14 years of age and over. If it is possible to assume that the three categories (native-born of native-born parents, native-born of foreign or Mexican parents, and foreign-born) represent different stages of acculturation to general norms, then there is some hope for educational improvement for the Spanish-speaking. It has been shown that the population of native-born of native-born parents rose sharply, while the native-born of foreign-born declined and the proportion of foreign-born declined somewhat during the period 1950 to 1960. The present data show that the native of native-born have achieved the highest median years of schooling; the native of foreign parentage achieved an intermediary amount, and the foreign-born achieved the least. This pattern was true in 1950 and in 1960. But in the decade the native-born of native-born raised their median school attainment level much more than the native of mixed parentage and considerably more than the foreign-born.

Table 9C

MEDIAN SCHOOL YEARS COMPLETED BY SPANISH-SPEAKING
BY NATIVITY AND PARENTAGE, 1950 AND 1960

		Texas	New Mexico	Colorado	California	Arizona	Total
Total 1960	males	6.2	8.4	8.5	8.9	7.8	8.1
	females	6.1	8.5	8.7	9.2	8.2	8.2
Native of native	males	7.2	8.5	8.6	10.1	8.6	8.6
Native of Mexican	males	6.6	8.2	8.6	9.6	8.4	8.4
Mexican-born	males	3.2	3.9	3.7	4.9	3.6	4.1
Total 1950	males	4.4	7.0	7.3	8.3	7.0	
	females	4.5	7.3	7.6	8.5	7.1	
Native of native	males	5.3	7.3	7.4	9.3	8.0	
Native of foreign	males	5.3	6.8	8.1	8.9	7.8	
Foreign-born	males	2.5	3.4	3.8	4.9	3.9	

It is difficult to imagine that 50 per cent of the foreign-born Spanish-speaking achieved four grades of schooling or less in 1960. California Spanish-speaking who were native-born of native-born attained the highest median of all categories and states (10.1 years), but the school median of California foreign-born remained the same in 1960 as in 1950 (4.9 years).

Attainment by persons 14 years of age and over suffers as a measure of educational competence in that it says nothing about the near future. In Table 9D a rough measure of current enrollment is given for Spanish-speaking in each state according to their nativity and parentage and according to their urban and rural residence. The measure is rough insofar as the table includes the percentages enrolled of all persons in each category for ages five through 34 years. The top row in each panel of the table (enrollment percentages for all nativity and parentage categories) shows that enrollment rates decline perceptibly in rural compared with urban areas in Texas, California, and especially Arizona; no such declines are found in New Mexico and Colorado.

Seldom do human data fall into a really clear pattern, but the data in Table 9D show that nativity and parentage make a consistent and major difference in enrollment rates, whereas

Table 9D

PERCENTAGE OF SPANISH-SPEAKING ENROLLED IN
SCHOOL BY NATIVITY, PARENTAGE, AND RESIDENCE, 1960

5–34 Years	Total	Urban	Nonfarm	Rural farm
		Texas		
All classes	49.5	50.1	47.9	46.6
Native of native	56.5	57.3	53.6	53.9
Native of Mexican-born	41.3	41.2	41.7	41.8
Born in Mexico	33.1	36.7	21.5	17.1
		New Mexico		
All classes	56.2	55.1	57.8	56.8
Native of native	57.9	56.6	59.3	63.0
Native of Mexican-born	45.7	44.2	46.5	51.8
Born in Mexico	39.1	40.1	47.9	20.0
		Colorado		
All classes	55.9	55.3	57.4	56.1
Native of native	58.1	57.7	59.0	59.0
Native of Mexican-born	41.9	39.7	46.7	46.0
Born in Mexico	35.2	36.7	—	—
		California		
All classes	51.4	52.2	48.4	43.9
Native of native	63.2	63.8	58.6	62.1
Native of Mexican-born	43.0	42.3	46.0	50.8
Born in Mexico	29.4	32.4	22.4	11.9
		Arizona		
All classes	50.9	53.4	49.8	26.1
Native of native	61.0	62.0	58.4	52.7
Native of Mexican-born	45.3	45.1	47.2	41.3
Born in Mexico	23.1	33.9	18.2	5.9

rural-urban residence is only partly patterned. Always the native-born of native-born show higher enrollment rates than native-born of Mexican parents; and in all but one of the 20 comparisons the native-born of Mexican parents show higher enrollment rates than those born in Mexico. Often for native of native parents and occasionally for native of Mexican parents, rural residence means higher enrollment rates than urban residence. But for the Mexican-born the combination of foreign birth and rural residence always results in very low enrollment rates: 5.9 per cent in Arizona, 11.9 per cent in California, 17.1 per cent in Texas. Fortunately the numbers in this category are much smaller than those in urban and native-born groups.

Table 9E makes a comparison between Spanish-speaking and the total state populations for ages 5 and 6, 7 to 13, 14 and 15, 16 and 17, 18 and 19. At ages 5 and 6 the Spanish have appreciably lower enrollment rates (a difference of 5 per cent) in Texas and Colorado. For ages 7 through 13 inclusive the enrollment rates are high (94 to 98 per cent), and there is little difference between Spanish-speaking and the total state.

Table 9E

PERCENTAGE OF ELIGIBLE SPANISH-SPEAKING AND STATE
POPULATIONS ENROLLED IN SCHOOL, 1960

	Texas		New Mexico		Colorado	
	Spanish	State	Spanish	State	Spanish	State
5 and 6 years	34.5	39.0	49.6	50.9	63.9	69.3
7 – 13 years	94.5	96.9	96.4	96.8	97.4	98.1
14 – 15 years	82.7	91.6	93.3	93.4	89.4	95.2
16 – 17 years	58.6	76.3	76.3	81.5	68.7	83.5
18 – 19 years	31.1	41.9	41.7	41.6	34.0	48.0

	California		Arizona	
	Spanish	State	Spanish	State
5 and 6 years	79.9	82.8	55.0	57.5
7 – 13 years	97.6	98.2	96.2	96.9
14 – 15 years	92.9	96.3	90.2	92.9
16 – 17 years	73.7	83.3	68.3	79.1
18 – 19 years	33.1	40.8	36.6	45.4

But at ages 14 and 15 significantly lower enrollment rates for Spanish-speaking appear in Texas and Colorado again. The difference between Spanish and total enrollment rates widens greatly at ages 16 and 17 in Texas and Colorado, but by these ages significant differences appear in Arizona, California, and New Mexico also (18 per cent lower for Spanish-speaking in Texas, 15 per cent in Colorado, 11 per cent in Arizona, 10 per cent in California, and 5 per cent in New Mexico). The differences narrow somewhat at ages 18 and 19, largely the result of the sharper drop in the enrollment rate for the total state groups, but the differences are persistently significant (ranging from 8 to 14 per cent lower for Spanish-speaking compared with total state) except for New Mexico.

From these data the greater dropout rates for Spanish-speaking are readily visible. But the very fact that 59 per cent of the Texas 16-and 17-year-olds are still enrolled (76 per cent in New Mexico, 69 per cent in Colorado, 74 per cent in California, and 68 per cent in Arizona) suggests that the median school attainment levels for Spanish-speaking in 1970 should be appreciably higher than in 1960. Whether such predicted rises will match the continued rise of Anglo and nonwhite school attainment remains to be seen. It will certainly take a major effort of Spanish youth (as well as adults) for the entire Spanish-speaking population to reach the same levels of educational attainment as the Anglo and Negro in the five southwestern states.

Part of the explanation for lower school attainment for Spanish-speaking may be found in the relatively low level achieved by family heads. Table 9F shows that in 1960, whereas 40 per cent of Texas Spanish-speaking males 14 years and over had achieved only four years of school or less, 50 per cent of Texas family heads had received less than five years; 28 per cent of New Mexico Spanish-speaking family heads were "functional illiterates," compared with 22 per cent of all males 14 years and over. Colorado shows a similar lower school attainment for family heads than for total Spanish, but in California and Arizona the school attainment level of family heads is almost the same as for total Spanish-speaking in the state.

Housing, Labor Force, Occupation and Income

Housing is not just physical facilities; it measures the social and cultural conditions under which people must live their daily lives. Living quarters do influence personal and family dispositions, values, and behavior.

Table 9F

SCHOOL YEARS COMPLETED BY SPANISH-SPEAKING
HEADS OF FAMILIES, 1960

Education of Family Head	Texas	New Mexico	Colorado	California	Arizona
Less than 5 years	49.8%	27.7%	22.2%	20.5%	30.1%
5–7 years	21.4	22.5	22.8	17.3	22.2
8 years	7.0	14.5	18.1	14.3	16.3
9–11 years	9.4	15.7	18.0	21.8	14.6
12 years	7.5	12.0	12.3	16.3	11.2
13+ years	4.8	7.6	6.6	9.7	5.6

Table 10A gives a comparison of Spanish-speaking Anglo, and nonwhite housing in each of 31 SMSA's grouped according to state. Compared with Anglo homes Spanish homes are two to three times as frequently deteriorated. In Texas from 25 to 30 per cent of Spanish homes are deteriorated compared with about 12 per cent for Anglo homes. The extreme is found in Stockton, where homes of Spanish-speaking are deteriorated almost seven times as Anglo homes. None of the SMSA's show as much as 21 per cent deterioration for Anglos, whereas 15 of the 31 SMSA's have over 25 per cent deteriorated for Spanish-speaking. Also there is at least twice the percentage of dilapidation for Spanish-occupied homes compared with those of Anglos in all 31 cities. San Antonio Spanish-speaking, for example, have two and one-half times the deterioration of Anglos and almost four times the dilapidation. Lubbock shows almost four times the deterioration and about six times the dilapidation for the Spanish as for the Anglo. A large proportion of Spanish-occupied homes are rented and thus dilapidation of homes with absent owners becomes an important economic and social issue.

Table 10A

QUALITY OF HOUSING OCCUPIED BY SPANISH-SPEAKING, ANGLO, AND NONWHITE POPULATIONS, 1960

Area	Spanish surname Deteriorated	Spanish surname Dilapidated	Anglo Deteriorated	Anglo Dilapidated	Nonwhite Deteriorated	Nonwhite Dilapidated
Arizona						
Phoenix	27.10%	15.6%	14.4%	5.5%	26.7%	23.7%
Tucson	19.9	11.7	7.1	2.2	23.5	28.3
California						
Bakersfield	25.3	14.0	14.2	5.6	24.9	12.1
Fresno	27.4	19.8	12.4	5.2	24.9	18.2
Los Angeles & Long Beach	15.3	5.1	5.2	1.0	12.8	2.6
Sacramento	11.2	4.8	8.3	2.0	21.2	7.8
San Bernardino	19.6	7.7	11.3	2.9	19.9	13.0
San Diego	15.2	5.6	6.5	1.5	19.3	6.0
San Francisco	10.1	3.8	6.3	1.4	16.4	5.1
San Jose	14.8	8.5	4.8	1.7	13.9	5.9
Santa Barbara	21.7	8.8	11.7	4.7	23.9	13.8
Stockton	35.5	10.3	5.3	2.2	18.3	11.3
Colorado						
Colorado Springs	21.4	6.5	10.2	2.3	30.3	9.4
Denver	26.0	5.7	8.4	1.4	26.4	3.5
Pueblo	26.9	11.0	16.5	2.0	18.2	13.6
New Mexico						
Albuquerque	18.1	30.0	13.6	5.4	31.0	34.1
Texas						
Abilene	26.4	11.0	16.5	2.0	18.2	13.6
Austin	24.6	18.1	9.9	3.8	26.1	21.8
Beaumont	20.3	6.6	13.6	3.8	30.0	16.1
Corpus Christi	28.1	12.1	10.8	5.9	30.0	11.0
Dallas	26.6	7.5	10.1	3.0	30.8	14.6
El Paso	22.4	14.5	8.4	2.1	16.5	6.7
Fort Worth	19.5	8.5	11.3	3.5	24.9	13.4
Galveston	26.3	12.8	12.7	4.8	28.7	18.9
Houston	23.8	6.1	9.1	2.1	24.6	6.6
Laredo	31.2	22.7	21.0	15.1	—	—
Lubbock	38.5	18.0	10.9	2.9	28.7	27.0
Odessa	30.6	14.0	12.6	6.1	32.4	—
San Angelo	32.4	12.6	13.4	3.4	—	—
San Antonio	24.9	12.6	10.3	3.3	23.5	9.5
Waco	32.5	13.6	12.7	5.5	28.6	28.8

Texas and California Spanish-speaking are in the labor force in practically the same proportion as all males in the states. The New Mexico Spanish-speaking labor force participation rate (69.3 per cent) is suspiciously lower than that for the state (77.5), but a question has already been raised about the completeness of the Spanish-speaking count in New Mexico. Colorado has the lowest rate of participation. The changes in unemployment rates from 1950 to 1960 for Spanish-speaking though uniformly downward, are not consistent in degree. In almost all of the states the Spanish-speaking rate of unemployment would be defined as a serious economic crisis if it were characteristic of a total community. Thus the decline from 11.0 per cent to 10.3 per cent unemployed in New Mexico leaves unemployment still a critical economic factor. The same may be said for Colorado (15.6 to 9.5 per cent unemployed), Texas (9.5 to 8.2), and California (13.0 to 7.7). With such high unemployment rates it is understandable why some do not participate in the labor force (the minimum definition for inclusion in labor force is that the person must be "looking for work"). The percentage of unemployed males for the total white population of Texas is just about one-half the Spanish rate. However, the group's unemployment in California and Arizona is appreciably less than that for nonwhites (Table 10B).

Spanish females are entering the labor force in far greater numbers than ever before; 22 per cent were in the labor force in 1950 and 29 per cent in 1960. Whereas females 14 years and over rose from 1950 to 1960 by 47 per cent, labor force participation rose by 93 per cent. This is a major change for the Spanish, but Spanish-speaking females still do not enter the labor force as commonly as all females in these states (30 to 33 per cent); their participation is considerably below that of nonwhites (about 40 per cent of all nonwhite females in California and Texas). Unemployment of female Spanish-speaking is higher in Texas than for all females, but lower than the rate for nonwhites; in California Spanish-speaking females (versus all females) show higher rates of unemployment and even higher than for nonwhite females. This may reflect the difficulties for new entrants to the labor force, especially those who have moved recently to cities in California.

Explanation for the unemployment rates of Spanish-speaking is to be found not only in lower educational achievement levels, but especially in occupational distribution, as is shown in Table 10C. If the three groups of Spanish can be visualized as three different generations, the differences become meaningful. A definite shift upward is perceived from the Mexican-born

Table 10B

PERCENTAGE OF SPANISH-SPEAKING IN THE
LABOR FORCE, 1960

	Texas		New Mexico		Colorado	
	1950	1960	1950	1960	1950	1960
Males 14 and over						
% in labor force	77.4	76.9	69.7	69.3	69.9	70.9
Civilian labor force	99.1	98.1	99.2	98.5	98.7	97.6
Employed	90.5	89.0	89.7	84.4	90.5	90.5
Unemployed	9.5	8.2	11.0	10.3	15.6	9.5
Not in labor force	22.6	23.1	30.3	30.7	30.1	29.1
Enrolled in school		45.7		43.2		37.9
% Growth labor force						
1950–1960		24.7		3.4		32.2
% Growth males 14+		25.6		4.1		30.5
% Females in lbr. force	20.4	27.0	16.0	23.9	16.6	25.5
% Unemployed	7.8	8.2	6.6	8.6	12.7	8.9
% Growth female l. f.		79.2		56.0		104.2
% Growth females 14+		34.3		4.6		33.1

	California		Arizona		Totals	
	1950	1960	1950	1960	1950	1960
Males 14 and over						
% in labor force	78.1	79.9	75.2	78.8	76.4	77.5
Civilian labor force	98.2	97.3	99.2	98.7	98.7	97.8
Employed	87.0	92.3	86.5	93.8	88.6	91.9
Unemployed	13.0	7.7	13.4	6.2	11.4	8.0
Not in labor force	21.8	20.1	24.8	21.2	23.6	22.4
Enrolled in school		42.7		44.5		43.7
% Growth labor force						
1950–1960		80.3		61.2		45.5
% Growth males 14+		76.4		53.9		43.4
% Females in lbr. force	26.9	32.2	18.8	24.9	21.9	28.8
% Unemployed	15.9	11.2	12.4	8.1	11.5	9.7
% Growth female l. f.		113.5		88.1		93.3
% Growth females 14+		78.6		40.9		46.7

up to the native-born of Mexican parents, to the native-born of native-born. Over 50 per cent of the Mexican-born in California are farm or other laborers, but only 25 per cent of the native-born of Mexican parents are such laborers; and less than 17 per

Table 10C

SELECTED OCCUPATIONS OF SPANISH-SPEAKING MALES
BY NATIVITY AND PARENTAGE, 1960

	California	Arizona	New Mexico	Texas
Native of native				
Professional	5.8%	3.3%	6.5%	3.1%
Clerical	5.7	3.0	6.9	4.6
Craftsmen	16.7	15.0	17.0	14.8
Operatives	23.3	25.0	20.2	22.3
Service	6.0	25.0	11.6	7.4
Farm laborers	5.8	12.2	5.4	14.3
Other laborers	10.6	15.5	15.7	14.7
Native of Mexican				
Professional	4.1	2.6	5.8	3.1
Clerical	5.7	3.8	4.2	5.7
Craftsmen	19.6	17.8	16.9	17.1
Operatives	31.5	29.4	24.9	24.4
Service	5.7	6.5	10.5	7.6
Farm laborers	9.3	13.9	11.2	12.9
Other laborers	15.4	15.9	13.8	16.4
Mexican-born				
Professional	1.6	0.9	1.9	2.1
Clerical	2.1	0.9	1.5	2.2
Craftsmen	10.8	7.4	11.4	15.5
Operatives	19.0	12.1	12.7	17.2
Service	6.4	3.3	6.3	7.2
Farm laborers	37.4	59.5	43.8	25.4
Other laborers	15.0	10.1	11.1	17.3

cent of the native-born of native-born parents are farm and other kinds of laborers. The same pattern is true of Texas, New Mexico, and Arizona.

The reverse pattern is found for the service occupations in Arizona and New Mexico (service occupation percentages increase from Mexican-born to native of native-born), but the service percentages remain about the same in California and Texas. The occupations classified as "operatives," however, show an interesting change in percentages; these tend to be smaller (fewer persons in such jobs) for Mexican-born; they are largest for the native of Mexican parents and they decline for native of native-born, in which case Spanish-speaking males have pushed upward in the scale toward crafts and other positions. The upward pattern for craft occupations is generally similar to that of operatives, but the net gain for the native born of native-born (over the Mexican-born) is proportionately much greater for craftsmen than for operatives. Similarly clerical occupations tend to move upward as the progression is toward the native-born of native-born. Finally, the category of professional, technical and kindred shows a uniform upward change without any regression in the percentages. The entrance of women into the labor force may help explain the rise in clerical and professional (teachers) categories. This outlines an important shift upward by generations in occupational status for the Spanish-speaking.

But the question arises at what speed upward shifts are occurring. Table 10D attempts to grapple with this central question, although unfortunately only a ten-year change can be observed (data prior to 1950 are not comparable for the Spanish). In the previous analysis the important assumption was made that the three nativity-parentage statuses could be viewed as three generations. In this table we can observe time changes directly.

For males the percentage decline in farm laborers and other laborers between 1950 and 1960 has been considerable (from about 43 to 31 per cent of all employed). The declines in farm laborers alone among Spanish-speaking in New Mexico and Colorado has been almost 50 per cent, and it has been considerable in Texas and California; but the proportion in farm labor has actually increased in Arizona. Service occupations have slightly higher percentages in 1960 than in 1950, but in New Mexico the rise is comparatively great. The increase in operatives was greater than for service occupations (from 18.8 to 22.9 per cent), largely because of the great increase in Texas (and in spite of the decline in operatives in Arizona). Craftsmen have grown by about 3 per cent throughout most of the states and clerical workers about 2 per cent (in spite of the decline in the latter category in Arizona). Managers and officials are found in the same proportion in 1960 as in 1950, but farmers and farm managers have declined by over one-half.

Table 10D

SELECTED OCCUPATIONS OF SPANISH-SPEAKING MALES,
1950 AND 1960

Occupation	Texas		New Mexico		Colorado	
	1950	1960	1950	1960	1950	1960
Professional & technical	1.7	3.1	3.0	6.0	1.9	4.2
Farmers & f. manager	5.2	2.6	13.1	3.5	7.6	2.8
Managers, officials	4.4	4.6	4.4	5.2	3.0	3.2
Clerical, kindred	6.6	4.5	6.5	6.3	4.4	4.2
Sales		3.7		3.7		2.7
Craftsmen, foremen	12.4	15.9	13.0	16.06	9.1	12.7
Operatives, *et al*	16.4	21.8	14.8	20.0	22.2	26.1
Service, exc., prvt. house	6.5	7.4	6.9	11.0	5.4	8.5
Farm laborers, foremen	26.8	16.2	16.9	9.0	22.7	11.0
Other laborers	18.8	15.8	19.0	15.0	22.2	20.3

Occupation	California		Arizona		Totals	
	1950	1960	1950	1960	1950	1960
Professional & technical	2.6	4.5	1.6	2.6	2.1	3.9
Farmers & f. manager	2.8	1.9	1.8	0.7	5.0	2.2
Managers, officials	4.6	4.1	3.7	3.8	4.4	4.3
Clerical, kindred	6.4	4.7	6.1	2.6	6.4	4.6
Sales		3.2		2.7		3.4
Craftsmen, foremen	14.0	16.3	13.1	13.5	12.9	15.8
Operatives, *et al*	21.6	24.0	25.4	22.0	18.8	22.9
Service, exc., prvt. house	5.6	6.4	5.4	6.0	6.1	7.2
Farm laborers, foremen	23.6	15.6	24.3	28.0	24.4	16.0
Other laborers	17.8	12.8	17.2	13.7	18.5	14.5

Finally, there has been a percentage doubling of professional, technical, and kindred workers, but the proportion of Spanish-speaking males in this category is still low (about 4.0 per cent) compared with the total white group (about 8 per cent). The conclusion is clear that there is a perceptible change toward the more skilled, white collar, nonfarm, nonlaborer occupations. Overall, New Mexico Spanish-speaking show the most regular and persistent movement upward, and the high density states of California and Texas show slower movement. In some respects Arizona may be manifesting a slight downward movement.

Table 10E compares median incomes for 1950 and 1960. The first thing that strikes one is the very low incomes both in 1950 and 1960. The urban California figures for the Spanish-speaking must be compared with medians of $3697 and $2323 for total whites in 1960 and 1950, respectively and also with medians of $2736 and $1713 for nonwhites in 1960 and 1950. Thus Spanish median incomes are somewhat above those of nonwhites and appreciably below those of total whites. The urban medians for Spanish-speaking in the other densely populated state, Texas, must be compared with $2901 and $2018 for total whites in 1960 and 1950 and with medians of $1349 and $971 for nonwhites in the same years. Again, incomes of Spanish-speaking are a bit higher than those for nonwhites but considerably below the incomes for total whites. This pattern is general, except that nonwhites in New Mexico and Arizona (large concentrations of Indians) show median incomes considerably below those of Spanish and total white.

One of the more interesting features of Table 10E consists in the comparison of 1949 and 1959 money incomes of the three nativity-parentage groups. First, *urban comparisons* indicate that in 1950 the Spanish foreign-born had incomes almost equal to those of native-born of native-born. In Colorado the foreign-born had appreciably higher incomes, and in Arizona they had lower incomes. But by 1960 the incomes of the foreign-born were considerably lower than incomes of native of native-born except in Colorado. The rural farm Spanish-speaking populations in Texas and California indicate that the foreign-born received far greater income increases than native of native-born. There was little change in median income for Arizona Spanish foreign-born and the California rural farm who are native-born of native-born.

A problem is found in the general pattern in each of the five states: the urban native-born of foreign parentage by 1960 were receiving higher incomes than either the native of native or the foreign-born. Further, their increases in median income between 1950 and 1960 are truly remarkable, actually greater than any of the other categories. It is impossible at this stage to supply an explanation.

Finally, the urban-rural comparisons are in order. In general the income differences between urban and rural farm Spanish-speaking widened appreciably from 1950 to 1960. This greater

Table 10E

MEDIAN INCOME OF SPANISH-SPEAKING BY NATIVITY AND RESIDENCE, 1950 AND 1960

	Texas		New Mexico		Colorado	
	1950	1960	1950	1960	1950	1960
Native of native						
Urban	$1187	1664	1411	2260	1252	2071
Rural nonfarm	824	1111	1022	1525	882	1553
Rural farm	856	1012	872	1540	864	1605
Native of foreign						
Urban	1089	1859	1189	2573	1512	2757
Rural non farm	782	1111	1209	1787	842	1781
Rural farm	672	1075	1031	1758	898	1994
Foreign-born						
Urban	1142	1434	1348	1782	1664	2021
Rural nonfarm	733	1000−	1418	1464	1243	1541
Rural farm	704	1239	985	1387	−	1667

	California		Arizona	
	1950	1960	1950	1960
Native of native				
Urban	$1907	2954	1553	2125
Rural nonfarm	1280	1810	1460	1809
Rural farm	1294	1287	1198	1322
Native of foreign				
Urban	1683	3560	1399	2671
Rural nonfarm	1130	2021	1063	2174
Rural farm	1130	2365	1038	2159
Foreign-born				
Urban	1825	2563	1284	1668
Rural nonfarm	1361	1648	1476	1448
Rural farm	1165	1559	1262	1197

differential in income helps explain the movement to the cities. The differentials between incomes of urban and rural farm Spanish-speaking are greater for native of native-born than for foreign-born, and even greater for the native of foreign parentage than for native of native or foreign-born. Reasoning from this limited single economic indicator, one might predict that more Spanish, especially foreign-born, will move to the urban areas in the near future, unless the income differentials are narrowed.

Income levels have been used to define a generalized poverty level in the United States. Thus certain poverty programs now being implemented in various parts of the United States are designed to aid persons or families with less than $3000 income per annum. Table 10F shows that according to this criterion over one-third (34.8 per cent) of the Spanish-speaking qualify at the poverty level. One in every five Spanish families in California may be considered officially poor; in Arizona and Colorado about one in every three so qualify; 41 per cent meet the criterion in New Mexico; and over 50 per cent of Spanish families in Texas are at this low income level.

Table 10F

INCOME LEVELS OF SPANISH-SPEAKING FAMILIES, 1960

	Texas	N. Mexico	Colorado	California	Arizona
Less than $3000	51.6%	41.5%	35.0%	19.1%	30.8%
$10,000 and over	2.7	4.5	4.8	10.8	4.6

Summary and Interpretations

The Spanish-speaking population in the five southwestern states has remained a socially and economically underprivileged group during the 117 years since the treaty of Guadalupe-Hidalgo. In this treaty the United States made solemn promises to accord the Spanish-speaking all the rights and privileges of citizenship. The influx of Mexicans after World War I did not bring forth any effort to provide adequate schooling, housing, or employment, but eventuated in grim poverty-stricken clusters of persons eking out a pitiable existence. The shortage of labor during World War II resulted in demands for Mexican farm labor, but the massive influx of Mexican workers did not occur until after the war, when Anglo farmers demanded the continuing supply of cheap labor. By 1950 the census of Spanish-surname people revealed that over 83 per cent were American citizens, yet there was little evidence of their obtaining the schooling, income, and housing which characterized the Anglo in the same areas.

The 1960 census data show that the Spanish-speaking population had grown rapidly in the previous ten years, an increase of 51.3 per cent in the five states, yet 85 per cent of Spanish-speaking were born in the United States. Most of the total growth has been due to natural increase (excess of births over deaths). Spanish fertility is considerably higher (60 per cent or more) than that of Anglo and higher also than nonwhite fertility. As a low socioeconomic group their mortality and morbidity rates are also higher than that of Anglos. In addition, the Spanish have been moving to urban centers far more rapidly than Anglo and nonwhite, so that they are now as urban as Anglos and considerably more urban than nonwhite. The movement is also relatively heavy westward, so that the increase in Spanish-speaking in California in the ten years from 1950 to 1960 was 87.6 per cent.

Since over four out of every five Spanish-speaking live in either California or Texas, the urban problems attendant with this recent movement are many and serious. The overwhelming majority of Spanish-surname people are white, and Spanish is still the basic family language. However, the percentage who are native-born of native-born United States parents (third generation in United States) has increased rapidly to over 50 per cent of the total, and the native-born of foreign or mixed parentage has declined to less than one-third of the total. The proportion of foreign-born has also declined. Language differences, as barriers to educational and economic opportunities, are in decline. This is very important for such a young population, whose average age is less than twenty years, compared with twenty-eight years for all white persons in the five states. The high fertility not only results in the dominance of youth for the Spanish but is also correlated with large families.

help of government and school programs, to bring this group into some approximation of equal opportunities with the Anglos and nonwhites.

Housing for the Spanish-speaking is at a very low level compared with Anglo housing. Deterioration and dilapidation rates are considerably higher. Crowding is far more characteristic of the homes of Spanish-speaking. But regardless of economic values, the social implications of this situation for healthy and constructive development of human dignity cannot be ignored by government, urban affairs, and planning programs.

Unemployment rates are consistently higher for Spanish-speaking than for Anglo and Negro. The entry of Spanish females into the labor force is one of the most important contemporary trends in the economic picture of Spanish-speaking.

Persons without skills of some sort are rarely needed in a highly technical and industrial society. About 30 per cent of Spanish males are in the categories of "farm laborers," "foremen," and "other laborers." But a noticeable shift out of such occupations has occurred. This 30 per cent in 1960 is a considerable decline from 1950, when 42 per cent of Spanish-speaking males were laborers. An increase in the proportion of "service" and "operatives" workers is clear. Small but important increases are found in the craftsmen, clerical and professional-technician categories. Spanish females are still mostly operatives and service workers, but there are signs of increase for them in clerical and professional-technical occupations. A definite move upward in the occupational structure is apparent, although at the 1950 to 1960 rate it would probably take many decades for the Spanish-speaking to approximate Anglo distributions.

A second way of looking at occupational change is to understand the differences among native-born of native-born parents, native-born of foreign-born, and foreign-born. The data show that the three statuses have markedly different occupational structures. For example, in California over 50 per cent of the Mexican-born Spanish-speaking are laborers, but only 25 per cent of the native-born of Mexican parents are laborers, and only 17 per cent of the native-born of native-born are laborers. More of the native-born of native-born have moved into craftsmen or higher occupations. The increase from foreign-born to native of native-born in professional-technical workers is clear and uniform, although the percentage of Spanish-speaking in this category is still quite low, even among native of native-born. Thus the Spanish are manifesting a distinct move upward in the occupational structure. The New Mexico Spanish show greater movement; the large populations in California and Texas show slower change.

Incomes of all whites in California are much higher than incomes in Texas, and incomes of Spanish are higher in the former than the latter state. Incomes of Spanish-speaking are much closer to those of Negroes than to total white incomes. All incomes rose from 1950 to 1960, but Spanish native of native-born incomes rose faster than those of foreign-born in the urban centers. In the rural areas the foreign-born received greater income increases than native of native-born. It is a puzzle that native-born of foreign or mixed parentage received higher incomes than foreign-born or native-born (regardless of whether the residence was rural or urban). Since income is such a sensitive measure of a host of economic and cultural factors, much more research is needed.

The relatively low incomes in Texas is some explanation of the outward migration, and the higher incomes in urban centers explain the urban movement. Finally, the poverty-level of income (under $3000) was characteristic of about 243,000 families, or more than an estimated 1,206,000 Spanish-speaking persons. Fifty per cent of Spanish families in Texas are at poverty levels. The Spanish-speaking population has a long way to go before achieving any approximation of the standard of living characteristic of most other citizens of the United States.

And thus the struggle continues. The direction and pace may have changed, but the problems remain. There is good evidence of some improvement, but the rapid change by nonwhites and Anglos makes it most difficult for the Spanish-speaking to catch up. This population must be given aid to improve their educational attainment, to escape the circle of poverty, to preserve their values and customs as they wish.

Conclusion

When these papers were completed and submitted to the editor, an editorial conference was held for their critical discussion. Mr. Herman Gallegos, Mr. Lyle Saunders, and Mr. Julian Samora were appointed to summarize the relevant issues for action programs, broad policy decisions, and research needs. This discussion depends in part on the presentation in previous chapters and in part on the San Francisco conference.

Action Programs

It is encouraging that Spanish-speaking organizations and individuals are demonstrating a growing sophistication and ability to cooperate and work toward common goals in action programs, ranging from conferences and meetings to power-producing community organization efforts, nonpartisan voter registration, get-out-the-vote campaigns, partisan political activity, and, more recently, picketing and social protest efforts.

Usually these action programs have focused on such specific problems as narcotics, unemployment, health, education, housing, farm labor, and civil rights. In most instances they have been focused on local areas, rather than on a state or region. Lacking strong organizations and the ability to finance broad programs, the Spanish-speaking leadership has been unable to attack the problems on a regional or national basis. The fact that there is a growing awareness of common goals among the existing leadership leads one to believe that in the future it will not be as difficult to implement action programs for this ethnic minority as it has been in the past.

The important problem may be how to discover and finance the most effective and workable machinery that can, for the largest ethnic group in the Southwest, lead to the resolution of the problems that beset it. A number of practical attempts to establish relationships between the Spanish-speaking and Anglo communities suggest increased possibilities for general support in the dominant community for the implementation of action programs. To finance their operations most Spanish-speaking organizations have concentrated in the past on raising money within the ethnic group, thus ensuring their independence and, hopefully, gaining greater effectiveness in relationships with existing institutions. The Spanish-speaking organizations have not attracted the interest of public and private agencies and have not received their support.

Several of the older and larger Spanish-speaking organizations have been able to maintain operations over a period of years without outside financial support. The American GI Forum, Community Service Organization, League of Latin-American Citizens, National Farm Workers Association, Mexican-American Political Association, Political Association of Spanish-Speaking Organizations, and others have capably stated the demands of the Spanish-speaking and have implemented limited programs for the advancement of the group. There is endless speculation on how much might have been accomplished if sufficient outside support had been forthcoming.

The organizing talents of Fred Ross and Saul Alinsky, plus contributions from the Industrial Areas Foundation, helped create the CSO in California during the 1950's. This example illustrates how the aspirations of a group can be effectively aided with outside support. Similarly, the massive voter registration of the CSO and the "spontaneous" "Viva Kennedy" movement in 1960 helped move the Spanish-speaking people into the spotlight of American politics.

In establishing priority for the expansion of action programs, the first need might be a broad structure that could effect the acquisition of funds from large public and private agencies. This would assist existing organizations to set up and maintain effective services for rural and urban neighborhoods.

The need for funds and other assistance from the dominant community implies that the Spanish-speaking must consider the type of relationship to be developed with those who are willing to work with them.

Some problems can best be solved by the Spanish-speaking who continue to work or live in their communities. The situation of the agricultural workers is one instance. Although the Spanish-speaking must continue to provide leadership, this does not mean that others should not be encouraged to make political, financial, and other contributions, and this should not preclude the Spanish-speaking from raising funds within their own group before seeking support from others.

Far too many of the Spanish-speaking are born and reared in an atmosphere of public assistance, public housing, public health, public education, and to some degree public employment, without experiencing the significant influence of private enterprise.

The role that foundations will play in financing is not known at this time. The foundations must extend their aid to the struggling minorities as they have never done to increase their opportunities for maximum participation in our society.

Foundations should also give financial assistance to action programs that cannot be advanced through federal funding. They should provide technical advice for program proposals that are meaningful to the minorities. Too often those groups that are proficient in writing proposals and display sophisticated grantsmanship are the ones that secure funds rather than the more disadvantaged and less sophisticated groups.

Even though financing is available, there is another problem. The few leaders of the more disadvantaged groups are siphoned off into the broader programs. Thus the training of the resident poor for responsible roles in these programs is neglected. One result of the antipoverty program has been the recruiting of leaders into federal staffs, with loss of time, interest, and energy to the local Spanish-speaking communities. Those leaders previously active in the resolution of the problems of the Spanish-speaking must now deal with the collective poor, because in a given community the Anglo poor or the Negro poor might constitute a significantly larger proportion of the impoverished. There is also the possibility that leaders at all levels might be converted from social-protest actionists to persons providing only social service.

The most effective way for encouraging the Spanish-speaking to program initiation, planning, and administration appears to be aggressive programs of community organization and political action. Such efforts are not likely to secure financing easily, particularly when they are related to social-protest movements or challenge existing political leadership for a redistribution of power and a share in control of benefit systems.

Financial assistance is the key to resolution of the problems of this minority. The potential for leadership and organization already exists, and existing leadership can administer meaningful programs for this population.

Policy Decisions

During the two days of the conference, discussion ranged over many issues and problems. A dominant theme was the disadvantaged position of the Spanish-speaking—socially, politically, economically—relative to that of the English-speaking majority; a recurring question was how to develop programs that could rapidly and surely reduce or eliminate the inequalities documented in the papers.

Some of the factors that have helped to perpetuate the unfavorable status of the Spanish-speaking derive from the Anglo majority—for example, overt discrimination, a lack of understanding of the impediments the Spanish-speaking have to overcome, and a tendency to be little concerned about what happens to minority groups. Some factors come from the history and cultural characteristics of the Spanish-speaking themselves—their concentration in areas of the Southwest, the persistence of cultural forms inimical to rapid assimilation, the diversity of background and condition of residence in this country. Still others arise from various institutional defects that limit opportunities for the Spanish-speaking to improve their position in the larger society.

There is a growing concern about the disadvantaged position of the Spanish-speaking, both within the group and among informed Anglos, and this concern is finding expression in a wide range of organized activity directed at one or another of the many facets of this complex problem. During the conference there was mention of the objectives, the programs, the accomplishments—and the failures—of various government agencies, philanthropic foundations, political parties, civic action groups, educational organizations and institutions, religious organizations, and both special and general welfare groups. It was apparent that much of the activity has been piecemeal, sporadic, and uncoordinated and that the total present effort is not commensurate with the size and complexity of the problem.

Although never explicitly stated, the major question seemed to be how to create an organism that would be capable of: (1) clarifying and articulating the aspirations of the Spanish-speaking population and subgroups within it; (2) building a national leadership structure that can speak for the group and stimulate and guide a common direction; and (3) mobilizing resources needed to improve the social, economic, and educational status of the group and implementing plans for bringing about substantial improvement.

Although no formal action was taken, the trend of the discussion seemed to point toward exploring how such a mechanism could be developed, and there was a suggestion that sufficient resources might become available to permit some steps to be taken in the near future.

Should the question of an appropriate structure be resolved, a great many other policy questions would immediately become relevant. The following illustrate the wide range of questions on which policy decisions may have to be made.

In any national effort how can the differing views of large subgroups within the Spanish-speaking population be reconciled and given expression?

Would it be best to work toward a single national organization, several independent organizations, a federation of relatively autonomous organizations, or some other structure?

What program priorities are needed? Should the effort be focused on one or two areas such as employment or education, or should it emphasize a more general across-the-board approach?

What stance should the leadership take in developing its program—militant, cooperative, pressing for quick results, aiming at long-term progress, aiming at local problem areas or wider regional or national ones?

How much political involvement is desirable? At what levels should it occur—national, state, local?

Should the effort be under professional or nonprofessional direction?

How can the momentum generated by existing organizations and programs be maintained and used to best advantage?

The Spanish-speaking people of this country have never yet been able to mount a sustained, concerted national drive for an improvement of their status. There are those who think they never will. But in recent years there have been many changes in the group, and the conditions that would permit such a drive may now be at hand. Certainly this conference was characterized by a seriousness, a solidarity, a singleness of purpose, and a sophistication that would not have been possible ten years ago. Perhaps it is evidence that the collective consensus needed for a national movement may have been achieved. If so, the policy questions discussed are likely to arise in more specific contexts as the Spanish-speaking group moves toward formulation of a national program to further its collective aims.

Research

Not many scholars have concerned themselves with the Spanish-speaking people. During the last twenty-five years only a few books have been written on them, and most of these have been on specialized topics. The population has been the subject of several graduate theses, but these also have been focused on relatively narrow topics. The textbooks that deal with minority groups have not treated this ethnic group with the same thoroughness devoted to other groups. This is understandable because of the scarcity of materials, most of which are to be found in journal articles, specialized reports, and proceedings of conferences. It is no surprise that the professionals in private and public agencies have a limited knowledge and understanding of these people whom they would serve.

The Spanish-speaking minority has been "discovered" in this decade, and public and private agencies (including federal agencies, state departments of public health, city social welfare departments, private foundations, and even local school districts) are requesting basic data about this group. Although sometimes difficult to obtain, this is available, but there are more important questions. These relate to the degree of acculturation of certain populations, the value orientation of specific subcultural groups, the attitudes, values, and belief systems underlying certain modes of behavior, the family structure, the effectiveness of ethnic organizations, the extent of political participation, the development of indigenous leadership, the geographical migration patterns, and the projection of the size of the population in the future. We propose that an extensive research program be launched for advancing knowledge and assisting those professionals and agencies involved in service programs.

The following research topics are suggested.

History—1850 to the Present

Central to an appreciation and understanding of any population or ethnic group is their history. Valuable works have been written about the early periods of exploration, conquest, and colonization in the Southwest, giving us important information about this population from the 1500's up to 1850. However, it is most difficult to find materials for the period 1850 to 1900, and from 1900, when the big migrations from Mexico began, to the present time there is little material available. During the period from 1850 to the present, Spanish-speaking in the southwestern United States increased from an estimated one hundred thousand persons to approximately four million.

Census Data

In recent years the Census Bureau has tabulated separate material on the Spanish-surname population in the five southwestern states. These data describe the housing, age and sex structures, fertility ratios, marital status, income, employment and educational levels, and movements of this population. The enumeration of the Spanish-surname population should be expanded to include the rest of the United States also.

Immigration and Migration

Relatively little is known of the past and present population movements from Mexico into the United States. More information is needed about the sources of immigration, the characteristics of the population, the places to which these people move, and the numbers who enter both legally and illegally in any given year. Nor do we know much about whether these are permanent or temporary immigrants. There appears to be an enormous movement of people back and forth across the border. We can only guess at the implications for the two countries concerned. Related to this is the commuter situation; thousands of Mexicans cross the border every day to work in the United States, returning to their homes in Mexico at the end of the day's work. We can only guess at the effect that this has on the employment structures in the cities in the United States and on the economy of the Mexican border cities, to say nothing of the cultural contact among the people involved.

Organizations—Leadership

The establishment and effectiveness of voluntary organizations within the Spanish-speaking group has not been adequately researched. Hundreds of organizations have come into being in the last thirty years, two or three of which have achieved national prominence. There is need for research concerning the proliferation of organizations, their history, influence, and objectives. There are also questions about the types of people to whom these organizations appeal, the kinds of problems with which they are concerned, and the areas in which they are effective. We need to know what techniques of organization have been most successful.

There has been little research on the question of leadership. How does it come into being? How can leaders function effectively given the condition that a subordinate group has to resolve its problems within the structure of a dominant society? A further problem exists in that the dominant society tends to siphon off those persons who have the characteristics for potential leadership. There is the problem of the alienation between the subordinate group and its would-be leaders. Related to this is social mobility and "cultural passing" and their effect on the development of effective organizations for the group.

Minority Status—Self-Identification

From the viewpoint of class, culture, race, education, and nativity, this is one of the most heterogeneous groups under one label, be it Mexican-American, Latin-American, Spanish-surname, Spanish-speaking, or Spanish-American. There is no consensus among Spanish-speaking people in the United States as to their self-image. There is no consensus about what they would like to be called. Certainly there is little knowledge of the image that Anglos have of this ethnic group and the image that the ethnic group has of the Anglos. These are questions for research with many implications for internal and external group relationships.

Education

In American society the educational system has served as the means for upward social mobility for most ethnic groups. To the extent that the Spanish-speaking take advantage of the public school system it has been a vehicle of mobility for them. For a variety of reasons, however, the educational system has not been as effective with this group as it has with others. Some research suggests the problems of cultural differences, language handicaps, high dropout rates, lack of motivation, discrimination, and segregation. But we have no systematic research addressed to the question of how the minority perceives the educational system. What has the school system done or not done to encourage or discourage school participation? How do teacher-training institutions prepare teachers and administrators who are to work with minority groups? What adjustments in the curriculum are necessary to keep children of ethnic minorities in school? How do teachers perceive their work with the ethnic groups? In what way does the educational structure and the community climate influence the motivation of the ethnic group? Are special programs necessary for this heterogeneous group, and is there equality of opportunity in the schools?

Migrant Agricultural Labor

Although there have been many studies of migrant agricultural labor, one phenomenon that has not been studied is the process whereby migrants leave the migrant stream to form small communities of their own or attach themselves to the fringes of the cities in various parts of the country. We do not know what motivates these people, the problems they encounter, how they resolve them. We can only suggest that the tremendous increase of the Spanish-speaking population in the Middle West and in the North Central area has been the result of this process. Knowledge of what is involved in the process might give us clues for the resolution of urbanization problems in other parts of the United States.

Family

The existing literature provides some general description of traditional family structure. We know that the Spanish-speaking population is relatively a young one, is predominantly Catholic, and has the highest fertility rate in the United States. We know also that the structure of the family has undergone considerable change, undoubtedly influenced by urbanization and the culture of the dominant society. We do not have any details of the extent of the change or the consequences to the people. There are any number of questions concerning role perceptions, role relationships, value orientations, and family disorganization.

Political Participation

Political participation of this ethnic group ranges from complete control of the power structure in certain counties and cities of northern New Mexico and southern Colorado to complete disinterest in registration and voting in other regions. Obviously there are a number of related factors, among them the history of the ethnic group in a particular area, the recency of migration, the relative sizes of the subordinate and dominant groups, the political party systems in the area, the effectiveness of voluntary organizations, and the general status of the ethnic population.

Spanish-Language Radio and Newspapers

We do not know how effective the Spanish-language press and radio are among the population, but we do know that there are many Spanish-language organs in the United States. We have no idea of their audience or how it perceives them. We do not know whether these could be used effectively in programs of acculturation, in dissemination of information, in political activity, or in education. They might be obstacles to the acculturation of the population, or they might be useful in bringing it about more rapidly.

Public Agencies

Attention should be given to the relationships of the ethnic population to such public agencies as social welfare, public health, hospitals, police, the court system, and other local governmental agencies. How do these help or hinder the optimum participation of the minority group in the life of the society? It is clear that there is an interrelationship among all of the problems that have been raised, and it is also clear that not all possibilities for research have been mentioned. However, most of these questions are worthy of study to gain more adequate understanding of one of the largest ethnic groups in the United States.

The Spanish-speaking population has reached a stage in its development where its influence is being felt in local, regional, and national matters. Private and public agencies at all levels are ready to listen to the ideas and even the demands that the group is ready to express. The national recognition of this population, although very late in coming, is moving at such a rapid rate that at this writing plans are being made for a White House conference on the problems faced by this group. Action programs involving the group are being established in many areas. Continued research is imperative in the immediate future to provide some basis for important policy decisions.

Index

A

Acculturation: diversity of Spanish language, 3; mixture of Indian culture in New Spain, 4, 5; Moors and Christians in Spain, 3; New Mexico undertakes reform measures toward, 8; stimulated by World War I, 7; threats to effective program of, 9

Action programs, 8; based on studies of different persons and groups, 60; financing to implement, 201–4; policy decisions and questions involved in, 204–6; role of foundations in, 203; specific problems confronting, 201; suggested research topics involving: history—1850 to present, census data, immigration and migration, organizations—leadership, minority status, education, migrant agricultural labor, family, political participation, Spanish-language radio and newspapers, public agencies, 207–11

Agricultural migrant (*also* seasonal farm laborer), xiv, 64; factors mitigating against improving economic conditions of, 65–6; fundamental needs of, 89; future prospects for, 88–9; pilot school for, 17; sources of, 1948–65 (table), 67; states visited by those from Texas, 30–1; states worked in by those from Texas in 1964 (table), 68; work pattern of, 74

Agricultural Workers Organizing Committee: action in Delano harvester strike, 85

American Board of Catholic Missions: unified and coordinated work among Spanish-speaking, 36

American Coordinating Council of Political Education (ACCPE) of Arizona, 51–55

Anderson, Mrs. Eleanor, vii

B

Bicultural (*also* biculturalism): Alamo its symbol, 14; problem increased by migration from Mexico, 9

Bilingualism, 2; as alleged handicap in education, 15–19; approaches to solving problem of, 19–23; implications of, 10; need to appreciate virtues and problems of, 21; preserved by Mexican-Americans, 10

As predominantly a new group of in-migrant families to the cities (most have been living in the cities for one generation or *less*), the adjustment to urban housing, schooling, occupation, and so forth is far from complete. Such insecurity encourages the Spanish-speaking to locate in clusters in urban centers. Since their purchasing power is relatively low, it is more likely that the concentrated settlement will be in slums or poor areas. The net result of this pattern is that the Spanish become more visible to Anglos as poor, different, and "foreign," and thus the many kinds of subtle and not so subtle prejudice, discrimination, and stereotyping occur.

One of the most important routes by which the Spanish may reach some measure of equal opportunity with other American citizens is schooling. A look at school data for one year, 1950 or 1960, for example, the Spanish situation compares very unfavorably with both Anglo and nonwhite. In Texas, the Spanish in 1950 achieved only one-third the years of schooling of Anglos, and the situation was not much better in 1960. Spanish attainment in 1960 in California, Colorado, and Texas did not even reach the 1950 attainment levels of nonwhites (predominantly Negro). About 118,000 Spanish-speaking had absolutely no schooling and 75 per cent of these lived in urban areas where school systems are said to be generally more effective in youth and adult education. In 1960 about 50 per cent of all Spanish had less than eight grades of schooling, and about 40 per cent in Texas were functional illiterates. Dropout rates for Spanish are notably higher from ages fourteen to seventeen, compared with total state groups. One reason for this is the low school attainment by heads of families, the primary motivators for children to continue and attain education (in Texas over 50 per cent of Spanish family heads are functional illiterates).

But the picture is not all bleak. The native-born of native-born are increasing their percentage of the total Spanish population, and their school attainment is far higher than that of native of foreign-born; the latter have far higher attainment than the foreign-born. Spanish are rapidly moving out of rural areas where attainment levels are lower; the foreign-born, whose attainment is lowest of all, are declining as a proportion of the total Spanish. Native of native-born are persisting in their schooling far longer than foreign-born. These are hopeful signs, but it will take a major effort of the Spanish, with the